Translating Culture Specific References on Television
The Case of Dubbing

Irene Ranzato

NEW YORK AND LONDON

First published 2016
by Routledge
711 Third Avenue, New York, NY 10017

and by Routledge
2 Park Square, Milton Park, Abingdon, Oxon OX14 4RN

First issued in paperback 2017

Routledge is an imprint of the Taylor & Francis Group, an informa business

© 2016 Taylor & Francis

The right of Irene Ranzato to be identified as author of this work has been asserted by her in accordance with sections 77 and 78 of the Copyright, Designs and Patents Act 1988.

All rights reserved. No part of this book may be reprinted or reproduced or utilised in any form or by any electronic, mechanical, or other means, now known or hereafter invented, including photocopying and recording, or in any information storage or retrieval system, without permission in writing from the publishers.

Trademark Notice: Product or corporate names may be trademarks or registered trademarks, and are used only for identification and explanation without intent to infringe.

Library of Congress Cataloging-in-Publication Data

Ranzato, Irene.
 Translating culture specific references on television : the case of dubbing / Irene Ranzato.
     pages cm. — (Routledge Advances in Translation Studies; #11)
 Includes bibliographical references and index.
 1. Translating and interpreting—Multimedia translating. 2. Dubbing of television programs. 3. Closed captioning. 4. Language and culture. I. Title.
 P306.93.R36 2015
 418'.020285—dc23
 2015017175

ISBN 13: 978-1-138-49913-3 (pbk)
ISBN 13: 978-1-138-92940-1 (hbk)

Typeset in Sabon
by Apex CoVantage, LLC

Contents

List of Figures and Tables   vii
Abbreviations   ix
Acknowledgements   xi
Preface by Jorge Díaz Cintas   xiii

1. Introduction   1
2. Theoretical Framework   12
3. Censorship and the Film Industry: A Historical Overview of Dubbing in Italy   28
4. Culture Specific References   53
5. "The Lesser-Known *I Don't Have a Dream* Speech": Cultural Humour in *Friends*   104
6. "Follow the Yellow Brick Road": Cultural Time and Place in *Life on Mars*   150
7. Coffee Bars in Slumber Rooms: Culture Specific Death in *Six Feet Under*   187
8. Conclusions   221

Appendix: Sample Pages From the Corpus   231
Name Index   237
General Index   243

Figures and Tables

Figures
5.1	Distribution of CSRs in the analysed seasons of *Friends*	118
5.2	Translation strategies in *Friends*	119
5.3	Translation strategies in *Friends* Season 1	120
5.4	Translation strategies in *Friends* Season 2	120
5.5	Translation strategies in *Friends* Season 3	121
5.6	Translation strategies in *Friends* Season 5	121
5.7	Translation strategies in *Friends* Season 8	122
5.8	Translation strategies in *Friends* Season 10	122
6.1	Distribution of CSRs in the two seasons of *Life on Mars*	154
6.2	Translation strategies used in *Life on Mars*	172
6.3	Translation strategies used in *Life on Mars* Season 1	182
6.4	Translation strategies used in *Life on Mars* Season 2	183
7.1	Distribution of CSRs in the analysed seasons of *Six Feet Under*	190
7.2	Translation strategies used in *Six Feet Under*	191
7.3	Translation strategies used in *Six Feet Under* Season 1	192
7.4	Translation strategies used in *Six Feet Under* Season 3	193
8.1	Distribution per category through the three series	222
8.2	Translation strategies: comparative overview of the three series	225

Tables
4.1	Classification of CSRs	64
5.1	*Friends's* viewers	106
5.2	'Respectful' vs. 'manipulative' strategies	141
5.3	Types of references in *Friends*	143
6.1	Types of references in *Life on Mars*	155
6.2	Deleted excerpts in *Life on Mars* Season 1	166
6.3	Deleted excerpts in *Life on Mars* Season 2	166
7.1	*Six Feet Under's* viewership	189

Abbreviations

AVT	audiovisual translation
CS	culture specific
CSR	culture specific reference
SA	source audience
SC	source culture
SL	source language
ST	source text
TA	target audience
TC	target culture
TL	target language
TT	target text

Acknowledgements

The acknowledgements page is always a great opportunity: remembering those who helped and especially those who did not help shape the course of one's research is tempting. However, not wishing to write a book within the book, which would necessarily take me back to my first endeavours, when encouraged by my mother's passions, I translated the first chapters of Alcott's *Little Women* from Italian into English (sic), I will content myself with thanking those who helped me specifically to write this volume.

I would like to thank Professor Jorge Díaz Cintas for being at the right place (and the right place is always London) at the right time and for crucially broadening my horizons, both intellectually and professionally. More to the point, this book is the result of extended discussions, advice, encouragement, and clarifications that Jorge copiously bestowed on me. I thank him especially for helping me define the concepts of asynchronous references, for showing me the infinite benefits of a method and, last but not least, for conceiving this book's preface on the Nile, something very few scholars can boast of, I think.

My deepest thanks to Professor Frederic Chaume for his charming, unassuming way of being a scholar of the highest level and for his precious advice. He knows how to show you the other side of the coin, lighting up some unexpected corners. This book, in this form, I owe to him, too.

I would like to thank my mentor and friend (more friend than mentor), Professor Donatella Montini, for helping me steer the wheel decidedly in the right direction, for her invaluable support in these extraordinary but difficult years, and for being a great scholar and a great human being.

My thanks to Professor Maria Pavesi for her advice and support. Her work on film dialogue has always been an inspiration, thus her appreciation is invaluable.

Thank you to Rocío Baños Piñero, a great expert on dubbing translation, for her intelligent insights and for her generosity.

I dedicate this book to the artist Bruno Lisi, by whose side it was written.

Preface

A lot has been written about audiovisual translation in recent years, propelling the field from the peripheral margins to centre stage in translation studies and gaining it the accolade of being the fastest-growing strand in our academic discipline. This well-deserved visibility has been mainly due to the proliferation and distribution of audiovisual materials in our society, the burgeoning of dedicated events and conferences, the publication of numerous articles and special volumes, as well as the development of undergraduate and postgraduate modules. Audiovisual translation has finally and decisively come of age in academia.

Encompassing a vast array of professional practices, such as dubbing, subtitling, voice-over, narration, subtitling for the deaf and the hard of hearing, and audio description for the blind and the visually impaired amongst others, audiovisual translation has been around for nearly as long as cinema itself. Of these, dubbing and subtitling are credited to have been the first to make appearances in the industry following the invention of the talkies in the late 1920s. And yet, despite this long tradition, research into dubbing has been modest to say the least. Even now that the output of articles and books is most healthy, interest in dubbing remains stubbornly low, particularly when compared with its sibling subtitling, which has known an unprecedented and exponential growth in the last couple of decades, or with the newer accessibility modes, which have also blossomed in scholarly exchanges.

This exciting volume has the potential of reversing this trend by raising the visibility of dubbing and promoting its study from a variegated perspective. Focussing on the world's perhaps most popular and watched genre, TV series, this monograph constitutes one of the first sustained, rigorous treatments of the dubbing of culture specific references; a subject that has widely been recognised by scholars as being one of the most problematic in translation studies, not only in the case of dubbing but also in other areas such as literary and drama translation. The analysis is conducted on a corpus of popular television fiction shows—*Friends*, *Life on Mars* and *Six Feet Under*—which is not only sufficiently large to draw meaningful conclusions but also diverse in terms of genre, content, language usage and expected target audiences.

In addition to providing a much-needed model for the investigation of the challenges encountered by translators when dealing with the translation of culture specific references, the book also offers, and successfully exploits, a most fruitful taxonomy of translational strategies that proves instrumental in teasing out some of the recurrent tendencies prevalent in contemporary dubbing practices.

Far from being restricted to micro-level textual analysis, it broadens its research scope by exploring the sociocultural, pragmatic, technical and ideological implications that typify the professional practice of dubbing for the small screen. Of special interest is the emphasis placed on the creative synergies established between the translators and the dubbing adaptors or dialogue writers. In an academic landscape in which descriptive studies have exerted such a strong grip on research conducted in translation studies, and especially on audiovisual translation, one of the most refreshing upsides of this book is the author's willingness to embark not only on a quantitative analysis of the data but also on a qualitative excursus to try and understand the translators' behaviour, given the cultural environment in which they operate, as well as the reasons behind the final choices heard on screen.

Written in an accessible and engaging prose, *Translating Culture Specific References on Television: The Case of Dubbing* does not only present the readers with a solid and systematic analysis into this vibrant professional and academic field, but it also offers invaluable guidance for those interested in further research. An informative and stimulating read for students, academics and professionals alike, whether they are already involved or simply keen to enter the dubbing world, this book promises to trigger a renewed interest in dubbing and contribute to its firm consolidation as a worthy academic endeavour. It's a must-have in any personal, departmental or company bookshelf.

Jorge Díaz Cintas
London, April 2015

1 Introduction

Dubbing has always been Italy's preferred form of audiovisual translation (AVT). Apart from a modestly growing share of cinemagoers and film experts who advocate the superiority of subtitling over dubbing, it is symptomatic that in Rome—the capital of the country and the city with the largest number of cinema theatres in Italy[1]—there is only one cinema which regularly shows films in the original version with Italian subtitles and five cinemas which show films in their subtitled versions on selected days and times. Very few film critics, in their reviews, occasionally recommend their readers to watch some films in the original version with subtitles.[2] As for dubbing, it is rarely commented on and ends up being mostly ignored as if it were not a part of the end product or too natural a part of it to need any comment. It is a fact that this vital component of the target film is somehow taken for granted by the general public and is seldom put into question by the experts in the field.

Statistical surveys report that, in 2014, 91.1% of people above 3 years of age in Italy watched television and, among these, 88.4% did so every day (Istat 2014: 253). This figure is consistent with the general European trend which stated 97.6 percent as the percentage of television viewers across Europe in 2002 (Spadaro 2002: 2), but a comparison with the data relative to book readers and newspaper readers in Italy[3] shows that the percentages are lower and sometimes much lower than the ones relative to many other European countries.[4] These data clearly show that television is the vehicle of information and entertainment most favoured by Italians.[5]

The percentage of foreign fictional programmes on Italian television is much higher than that of Italian productions. Autochthonous programmes are still a minority against the massive importation of foreign programmes, especially from the USA, that has been taking place since 1956 and, more steadily, since the 1970s.[6] Foreign fictional programmes on television have always been dubbed. Since the beginning of satellite television in 1994, cable television in 1997, and more recently, terrestrial digital television in 2003, Italian viewers have been given the option to watch most films and serials in the original version with subtitles, but the number of people who avail themselves of this possibility is small, and the large majority watches them dubbed in Italian. However, the increasing presence of audiovisual materials on the internet in the last few years and the spreading phenomenon of fansubbing among young people (Bruti and Zanotti 2013; Díaz Cintas and Muñoz Sánchez 2006; Massidda 2015; Pérez-González 2006) have started a process which will probably change, at least partially, people's relationship with subtitled programmes in Italy and, presumably, in other countries too.[7]

This substantial exposure to translated audiovisual texts has had an impact on the Italian language, which has been analysed both by AVT scholars (Baccolini *et al.* 1994; Bollettieri Bosinelli *et al.* 2000; Freddi and Pavesi 2009; Heiss *et al.* 1996; Pavesi 2006; Pavesi, Formentelli and Ghia 2014) and by researchers interested in the evolution of the Italian language (Banfi and Sobrero 1992; Cresti 1982; De Mauro 1991; Maraschio 1982; Mengaldo 1994; Pasolini 1972/1991; Raffaelli 1983, 1985, 1991, 1994, 1996, 2001; Rossi 1997, 1999, 2002, 2003, 2008; Setti 2003). Most of the analyses carried out to date clearly show that today's Italian language contains numerous calques, loan words, and translational routines directly derived from the translated dialogues of films and TV series, particularly from English. Even words which have not entered the everyday lexicon and are recognised as restricted to film dialogue—such as *strizzacervelli,* partly calqued on 'shrink'—are considered acceptable in some contexts, generally ironic or comedic.

Studies on dubbing in Italy, however, have not evidenced the differences, if any, between the adaptations for cinema and those made for television, either from a translational or technical (i.e., sound mixing, lip synchronisation, or acting) point of view. This is somehow surprising as the attitude of professionals and audiences towards the two media is very different in present-day Italy. Cinema has gradually come to be perceived as an art form as well as a form of entertainment, and the behaviour of the professionals involved in the creation of the dubbed versions and in the distribution of the films has changed accordingly over the decades. In addition, cinema is perceived by many as a source of culture and/or entertainment which is actively chosen by viewers. On the contrary, works of fiction primarily broadcast on television are considered in Italy purely as a form of entertainment and are, on the whole, more passively received. In this sense, television has traditionally been regarded as a popular medium suitable for mainstream productions and for less-demanding audiences. There is almost no discussion in Italy, if not in academic circles, on themes such as quality TV or auteur television, which have long been the object of television studies and of critics' reviews in other countries (Edgerton and Jones 2009; Jancovich and Lyons 2003; Leverette *et at.* 2008; McCabe and Akass 2007; Nelson 2007)[8]. It is impossible to overlook the gap which divides the often very high standard—in terms of script writing, acting, camera work, photography, art direction, costumes, and editing—of the original quality programmes imported from countries such as the USA and the UK from the often much lower standard of fiction shows produced by the Italian neotelevision.[9]

Nonetheless, both dubbing for cinema and for television share some common ground as it was Mussolini and his Fascist government (1922–1943) who created Italy's dubbing industry from scratch. As it happened in other European countries which experienced similar dictatorial governments, notably Spain and Germany (Danan 1991: 612; Díaz Cintas 2001: 64–66), dubbing in Italy served as one of the most useful tools of control on language and content, and it was actively used to this end. The origins and the evolution of early film dubbing in Italy still weigh heavily in the present day through overt and covert manipulating and censoring practices, on the translators' attitudes towards the audiovisual text, and on the translation strategies they implement.

The general aim of this book is to describe the strategies adopted by translators in their dubbing of television series from English into Italian. More specifically, I intend to detect the norms, if any, which govern the work of the translators in this field. To draw substantial conclusions, my analysis is conducted on a corpus of television fiction shows which is not only sufficiently large but also varied in terms of genre, content, language use, target audiences and audience reception.

The main focus of my analysis is the translation of culture specific references (CSRs). This subject, which is explored from a theoretical point of view in Chapter 4, has widely been recognised as one of the most problematic translation issues, not only in the field of audiovisuals (Pedersen 2005, 2007, 2011) but also in literary translation in general (Leppihalme 1994, 1997, 2011). Their transfer into other languages and cultures is particularly relevant in the case of fiction television texts as this kind of audiovisual programme usually contains a great number of cultural elements. Their role in the text can be varied, and the specific function they fulfil in the various series composing the corpus is analysed in the corresponding chapters. Generally speaking, such elements are used by authors to give colour and substance to their scripts and to provide the text with features which are often intimately embedded in the source culture (SC) and to which the audience, or parts of the audience, can relate. They stimulate mnemonic associations and at the same time appeal directly to people's emotions as they can evoke images and feelings that are familiar to the source audience (SA).

As mentioned, the social and historical contexts in which dubbing was originally created in Italy have had an impact on its subsequent evolution that can still be seen when dealing with issues of censorship and manipulation of content. As the specific lens through which I have decided to carry out my translational analysis is that of CSRs, the concept of manipulation seems to be, in this respect, more relevant than that of censorship, as discussed in Chapter 3. Potentially sensitive (and thus potentially more censurable) features such as bad language (swear words, taboo words, etc.) and contents related to political and sexual themes are, deliberately, not the object of this analysis, as they would have opened up new and compelling areas of research. However, as the concepts of censorship and manipulation are closely related, they will be relevant for some of the case studies, in particular *Six Feet Under*, discussed in Chapter 7.

The methodological foundation of my research is Toury's (1980, 1995) notion of norms in translation. Descriptive Translation Studies, of which Toury is one of the major representatives, see translation as the result of a socially contexted behavioural type of activity. Toury (1980: 51) defines norms as being central to the act and the event of translating as they are "the translation of general values or ideas shared by a certain community—as to what is right and wrong, adequate and inadequate—into specific performance-instructions appropriate for and applicable to specific situations".

My aim is to map out the strategies activated by translators in response to cultural constraints and detect the norms that are prevalent in the case of dubbing into Italian. What are the patterns that can be detected, if any? Do the professionals involved in the creation of the new target version (translators, adapters, and dubbing directors) consistently behave according to given patterns? As discussed by Even-Zohar (1990), when an external culture is central and considered an important reference model for the importing system, the texts from that culture tend to be translated preserving many elements typical of the original culture. Even if they are difficult for the receiving audience to understand, these elements are the object of great interest. The examples contained in the corpus are used to verify this assumption. What are, in other words, the translators' attitudes towards what Lefevere (1992) calls the universe of discourse (objects, customs and beliefs) expressed in the original text in relation to the universe of discourse of their own society?

The main criterion to have guided the selection of the material for this analysis was the need of compiling a sufficiently large corpus since it was deemed that norms, trends, tendencies or regularities in translation could not be detected with sufficient clarity by analysing only one television programme. Not only should the corpus be large, but it should also cover various genres, contain a substantial number of episodes, and possibly involve different adapters so that the findings could be considered representative. This is in line with the Tourian theories, as expounded in Chapter 2, which generally recommend studies on large and varied corpora. The longer series present in the corpus, especially *Friends*, would also allow for a diachronic analysis of the data, which is also in accord with a descriptive translation paradigm and its historical take on the problems of translation and unlike the essentially ahistoric prescriptive approach (Toury 1995: 61).

The series included in the corpus, whose plots, characters, and themes will be dealt with more thoroughly in the respective chapters on the case studies, are briefly introduced in the following paragraphs.

FRIENDS (DAVID CRANE AND MARTA KAUFFMAN, 1994–2004, USA)—SITCOM

Friends is an American sitcom which ran on the channel NBC in the United States from 22 September 1994 to 6 May 2004.

The main plot of the series is very simple, revolving around a group of New York City friends—Chandler, Joey, Monica, Phoebe, Rachel and Ross—and their way of coping with reality and growing up. They are in their 20s at the beginning of the series and early 30s at the end, which allows the authors to cover a wide range of issues and situations and portray the characters in their personal development and evolution. In spite of moments of romanticism and the occasional pensive treatment of a few sensitive issues, the key of the show, as it is the case with most sitcoms, is comedic. The jokes found in *Friends* can be quite sophisticated, but the programme's target audience is certainly mainstream, which in turn means that the contents of the dialogues are seldom disturbing.

Friends received positive reviews throughout most of its run and became one of the most popular sitcoms of all time, translated into numerous languages.

I analysed seasons 1, 2, 3, 5, 8 and 10 out of 10 seasons of *Friends* for a total of 145 episodes of about 22 minutes each. This adds up to a total of approximately 3,190 minutes of programme.

Friends was chosen for its global popularity, its long life span, and its rich array of CSRs.

LIFE ON MARS (MATTHEW GRAHAM, TONY JORDAN AND ASHLEY PHAROAH, 2006–2007, UK)—POLICE PROCEDURAL/SCIENCE FICTION DRAMA

Life on Mars is a British television series which inserts elements of science fiction into a traditional detective story. It was broadcast by BBC One in Britain between January 2006 and April 2007.

Life on Mars is set mainly in 1970s Manchester, and it depicts quite accurately the atmosphere and social mores of Britain at the time. It is the story of police Detective Inspector Sam Tyler who, after an accident with his car in 2006, wakes up inexplicably in 1973. Each episode of the series follows a typical police procedural plot interspersed by moments which have been defined as science fiction elements but have actually more to do with a psychological thriller. This complex storyline was well received in the UK, as the figures included in Chapter 6 show.

Each episode, of 60 minutes in the original version, was reduced by an average of seven to eight minutes in the Italian version. This substantial difference in length will be discussed in the relative chapter.

The analysis covers both Seasons 1 and 2 of *Life on Mars*, which is a total of 16 episodes of 60 minutes each and comes to 960 minutes of programme in total.

Life on Mars was chosen for the sophisticated quality of its writing and for its special set of CSRs, which are not only specific to a culture but linked to a specific moment of the past.

SIX FEET UNDER (ALAN BALL, 2001–2005, USA)—DRAMA

Six Feet Under is an American drama series written by well-known scriptwriter Alan Ball. Broadcast by HBO from June 2001 to August 2005, it is one of the highest examples of auteur television, and it has been the object of several academic film studies (Akass and McCabe 2005; Buonomo 2008; Bury 2008; Edgerton and Jones 2009; Fahy 2006; McCabe and Akass 2007; Petrunti 2011) and of unanimously praising reviews.

This dramatic series, full of moments of black humour and sophisticated jokes, deals with potentially disturbing content and centres on the life of a family of undertakers, the Fishers. Crucial to the plot is the relationship between Ruth, the mother, who in the very first episode becomes the widow of Nathaniel senior (still a recurrent character who appears to his relatives and makes comments on their lives), and her three complex, tormented children: the socially conservative and emotionally repressed David (in his early 30s), the well-meaning, only apparently carefree Nate (late 30s), and the rebellious, gifted Claire (late teens).

The analysis focuses on seasons 1 and 3 out of 5 of *Six Feet Under*, for a total of 26 episodes of 60 minutes each, that is, approximately 1,560 minutes of programme.

Six Feet Under was chosen for its unquestionable status as one of the best drama series ever produced and for the ideological implications that even a descriptive analysis on the translation of CSRs unambiguously reveals.

It is important to emphasise how the variety of the corpus—the differences of genres, of length, of themes, of nationality, of target audiences and of many other elements which will be illustrated in the respective chapters—calls for the careful evaluation of the various shows' distinctive features. *Friends*, for example, is a globally known, mainstream and now canonical sitcom, while the other two programmes appeal to more selected audiences. Although the main focus of my research is to evince norms and tendencies in the dubbing of CSRs, each case study has some other characteristics which make a uniform approach challenging, whilst opening new angles and perspectives to the researcher.

As for the methodological procedure followed, all the series have been watched in their Italian dubbed version using the original DVDs. I contrasted the Italian dialogue with the original dialogue transcripts available on various websites (Web 1, no longer available; Web 2; Web 3; Web 4; Web 5, no longer available; and *The Annotated Martian*, Web 6). The original dialogues found on the net were transcribed accurately by fans and corresponded perfectly to the actors' utterances. Once an element of interest was spotted in the Italian dubbed version, I switched the soundtrack to listen to the actual dialogue in the English original language so as to double-check the accuracy of the dialogue lists found on the web. The aim was to detect all the cultural elements present both in the original texts and in their translations and to assess the translation strategies implemented by the translators. The next step was to transcribe both the original (it was faster than copying and pasting from the transcripts, and the original-language subtitles helped in the process) and the dubbed dialogue excerpts in Italian. The latter were then provided with a back translation in English so that readers who have not mastered Italian can still appreciate the nuances of the translations and follow my argumentation.

The ultimate aim was to analyse the handling of CSRs on a specific medium (television) and through a specific form of AVT (dubbing), whilst keeping a close look at the strategies activated when dealing with the translation of sensitive content (racial, sexual and political) and of challenging linguistic features (such as slang, idioms and words in dialect), which helped me form a more detailed picture of the work carried out by the dubbing adapters, Italy's very own cinema and television authors.

NOTES

1. Sixty-three cinemas in the city of Rome, of which 40 are multiplex theatres, for a total of 242 screens (data collected from the official website of the *Ministero dei beni e delle attività culturali e del turismo—Direzione generale cinema*, www.cinema.beniculturali.it/ElencoSaleCinematografiche/74/elenco-nazionale-sale-cinematografiche/, last accessed 28 February 2015).
2. One of these critics is Fabio Ferzetti, who writes on the popular national newspaper *Il Messaggero*. In one of his reviews, he wrote, for example, "Today, in Italy, two films are premiered starring Sacha Baron Cohen, a wonderful English comedian [. . .]. They are both entitled *Borat* and recount the exploits of an unlikely Kazakh reporter wandering about the United States. But only one of the two films, hidden in one of the very few theatres which show the film in the original version [. . .], is the true, brilliant, outrageous, irresistible *Borat*, conceived and acted by its author-actor. The other one is a bad copy, mutilated by the Italian dubbing which flattens out, when it does not annihilate altogether, the two foundations of the film. That is to say, the truthfulness of the reactions stirred by Borat [. . .] and the unmasking of the most invisible and insidious racism, implied in the spontaneous reactions of many common

people, reactions which Baron Cohen obtained by working on his words as well as his looks. To cut a long story short: the dubbed *Borat* makes you laugh ten times less than the original one which is incredibly more eloquent thanks to the crazy 'grammelot' spoken by its protagonist (a Jewish-Polish-Armenian-Romanian mix, as it sounds) [. . .]" (Ferzetti 2007: 29, my translation).
3. In 2014, an average of 41.4 percent of Italian people above 6 years of age declared to have read at least one book in the preceding 12 months (Istat 2015: 1). In the same year, an average of 47.1 percent of Italian people above 6 years of age read the newspaper at least once a week (Istat 2014: 253).
4. In Northern European countries there is a higher tendency to read books than in other regions, mostly for leisure: 71.8 percent of people in Sweden, 66.2 percent in Finland, and 63.2 percent in the UK declared reading for other reasons than for work or study. The highest percentages of newspaper readers can also be found in Northern European countries (Spadaro 2002: 5).
5. However, statistical data show the consistent growth in the percentage of people who used the internet in the years 2011–2013 in Italy (http://dati.istat.it/Index.aspx?DataSetCode=DCCV_USOINTPC, last accessed 31 March 2015), and this information will clearly influence any analysis of this type in future years.
6. The first US series imported in Italy in 1956 was *The Adventures of Rin Tin Tin* (Robert G. Walker and William Beaudine, 1954–1959).
7. The fact that people's relationships with subtitles may, indeed, be changing is supported by early 2013 news on a historic overtake of dubbing by subtitling: in the Barberini cinema theatre in Rome, more people watched the box-office hit *Django Unchained* (Quentin Tarantino 2012) in the original version with subtitles than watched it dubbed (Montini 2013).
8. As with fansubbing, there are indications of a shift in the audience's appreciation and evaluation of TV series which are, however, more often enjoyed through different means (such as internet downloading and streaming) rather than regular television programming.
9. I use this term in the sense given to it by Eco (1985) to refer to the crucial change that occurred in Italian television in the early 1980s due to the arrival of commercial television as opposed to state, public television. A new language, new codes and new objectives, which have had a profound impact on the Italian society to this day, were introduced into what used to be an essentially pedagogic format. In the field of serialised drama fiction, in recent years, only three Italian products have been widely recognised as quality programmes and have enjoyed good international distribution: *Il commissario Montalbano* (Andrea Camilleri 1999-in production); *Romanzo criminale* (Stefano Sollima 2008–2010); *Gomorra—La serie* (Giovanni Bianconi et al. 2014-in production).

REFERENCES

Akass, Kim and Janet McCabe (eds.). 2005. *Six Feet Under TV To Die For*. London: I.B. Tauris & Co.
Baccolini, Raffaella, Rosa Maria Bollettieri Bosinelli and Laura Gavioli (eds.). 1994. *Il doppiaggio—trasposizioni linguistiche e culturali*. Bologna: Clueb.
Banfi, Emanuele and Alberto A. Sobrero (eds.). 1992. *Il linguaggio giovanile degli anni Novanta. Regole, invenzioni, gioco*. Bari: Laterza.

Bollettieri Bosinelli, Rosa Maria, Christine Heiss, Marcello Soffritti and Silvia Bernardini (eds.). 2000. *La traduzione multimediale. Quale traduzione per quale testo?* Bologna: Clueb.
Bruti, Silvia and Serenella Zanotti. 2013. "Frontiere della traduzione audiovisiva: il fenomeno del fansubbing e i suoi aspetti linguistici", in Cristina Bosisio and Stefania Cavagnoli (eds.) *Comunicare le discipline attraverso le lingue: prospettive traduttiva, didattica, socioculturale*, Atti del XII Congresso dell'Associazione Italiana di Linguistica Applicata, Macerata, 23–24 febbraio 2012, Perugia: Guerra Edizioni, 119–142.
Buonomo, Leonardo. 2008. "*Six Feet Under*. La morte è di casa". *Ácoma* 36: 110–121.
Bury, Rhiannon. 2008. "Setting David Fisher straight: homophobia and heterosexism in 'Six Feet Under' online fan culture". *Critical Studies in Television* 3(2): 59–79.
Cresti, Emanuela. 1982. "La lingua del cinema come fattore della trasformazione linguistica nazionale", in Centro di Studi di Grammatica Italiana (ed.) *La lingua italiana in movimento. Atti del Convegno* (Firenze, 26 February–4 June 1982). Firenze: Accademia della Crusca, 279–319.
Danan, Martine. 1991. "Dubbing as an expression of nationalism". *Meta* 36(4): 606–614.
De Mauro, Tullio. 1991. *Storia linguistica dell'Italia unita*. Bari: Laterza.
Díaz Cintas, Jorge. 2001. *La traducción audiovisual: el subtitulado*. Salamanca: Ediciones Almar.
Díaz Cintas, Jorge and Pablo Muñoz Sánchez. 2006. "Fansubs: Audiovisual Translation in an amateur environment". *The Journal of Specialised Translation* 6: 37–52.
Eco, Umberto. 1985. "TV: la trasparenza perduta", in Umberto Eco (ed.) *Sette anni di desiderio—Cronache 1977–1983*. Milano: Bompiani, 163–179.
Edgerton, Gary R. and Jeffrey P. Jones (eds.). 2009. *The Essential HBO Reader*. Lexington: The University Press of Kentucky.
Even-Zohar, Itamar. 1990. "Polysystem Studies". *Poetics Today* 11(1): 45–51.
Fahy, Thomas (ed.). 2006. *Considering Alan Ball: Essays on Sexuality, Death and America in the Television and Film Writings*. Jefferson: McFarland & Company.
Ferzetti, Fabio. 2007. "Un reporter al di sotto di ogni sospetto". *Il Messaggero*, 2nd March, 29.
Freddi, Maria and Maria Pavesi (eds.). 2009. *Analysing Audiovisual Dialogue. Linguistic and Translation Insights*. Bologna: Clueb.
Heiss, Christine and Rosa Maria Bollettieri Bosinelli (eds.). 1996. *Traduzione multimediale per il cinema, la televisione e la scena*. Bologna: Clueb.
Istat. 2014. Annuario Statistico Italiano 2014. 8. Cultura e tempo libero. http://www.istat.it/it/files/2014/11/C08.pdf: 247–282.
Istat. 2015. *La produzione e la lettura di libri in Italia. Anni 2013 e 2014*. http://www.istat.it/it/files/2015/01/lettura-libri.pdf?title=Produzione+e+lettura+di+libri+-+15%2Fgen%2F2015+-+Testo+integrale.pdf.
Jancovich, Mark and James Lyons (eds.). 2003. *Quality Popular Television: Cult TV, The Industry and Fans*. London: BFI Publishing.
Lefevere, André. 1992. *Translation, Rewriting and the Manipulation of Literary Fame*. London: Routledge.
Leppihalme, Ritva. 1994. *Culture Bumps: On the Translation of Allusions*. Helsinki: Helsinki University.
Leppihalme, Ritva. 1997. *Culture Bumps. An Empirical Approach to the Translation of Allusions*. Clevedon: Multilingual Matters.
Leppihalme, Ritva. 2011. "Realia", in Yves Gambier and Luc van Doorslaer (eds.) *Handbook of Translations Studies*. Amsterdam: John Benjamins, 126–130.

Leverette, Mark, Brian L. Ott and Cara Louise Buckley. 2008. *It's not TV. Watching HBO in the Post-Television Era*. New York: Routledge.
Maraschio, Nicoletta. 1982. "L'italiano del doppiaggio", in Centro di Studi di Grammatica Italiana (ed.) *La lingua italiana in movimento. Atti del Convegno* (Firenze, 26 February–4 June 1982). Firenze: Accademia della Crusca, 137–157.
Massidda, Serenella. 2015. *Audiovisual Translation in the Digital Age. The Italian Fansubbing Phenomenon*. London: Palgrave Macmillan.
McCabe, Janet and Kim Akass (eds.). 2007. *Quality TV. Contemporary American Television and Beyond*. London: I.B. Tauris.
Mengaldo, Pier Vincenzo. 1994. *Storia della lingua italiana. Il Novecento*. Bologna: Il Mulino.
Montini, Franco. 2013. "Senza doppiaggio il cinema piace di più". *La Repubblica. it*, 28th January, http://www.repubblica.it/spettacoli-e-cultura/2013/01/28/news/film_lingua_originale-51432963/?refresh_ce, last accessed 22nd June 2015.
Nelson, Robin. 2007. *State of Play. Contemporary "High-end" TV Drama*. Manchester: Manchester University Press.
Pasolini, Pier Paolo. 1972/1991. *Empirismo eretico*. Milano: Garzanti.
Pavesi, Maria. 2006. *La traduzione filmica. Aspetti del parlato doppiato dall'inglese all'italiano Disponibilità immediata*. Roma: Carocci.
Pavesi, Maria, Maicol Formentelli and Elisa Ghia (eds.). 2014. *The Languages of Dubbing*. Bern: Peter Lang.
Pedersen, Jan. 2005. "How is culture rendered in subtitles?". *MuTra 2005—Challenges of Multidimensional Translation: Conference Proceedings*, in www.euroconferences.info/proceedings/2005_Proceedings/2005_Pedersen_Jan.pdf, last accessed 27th March 2015.
Pedersen, Jan. 2007. *Scandinavian Subtitles. A Comparative Study of Subtitling Norms in Sweden and Denmark with a Focus on Extralinguistic Cultural References*. PhD thesis. Stockholm: Stockholm University.
Pedersen, Jan. 2011. *Subtitling Norms for Television*. Amsterdam: John Benjamins.
Pérez-González, Luis. 2006. "Fansubbing Anime: Insights into the 'Butterfly Effect' of Globalisation on Audiovisual Translation". *Perspectives: Studies in Translatology*, 14(4): 260–277.
Petrunti, Silvia. 2011. "Six Feet Under", in Barbara Maio (ed.) *HBO. Televisione, autorialità, estetica*. Roma: Bulzoni, 69–79.
Raffaelli, Sergio. 1983. "Il dialetto del cinema in Italia (1896–1983)". *Rivista italiana di dialettologia* 7: 13–96.
Raffaelli, Sergio. 1985. "Cinema e dialetto: lineamenti di storia e prospettive di studio". *Bollettino dell'Associazione italiana di cinematografia scientifica*, June: 7–13.
Raffaelli, Sergio. 1991. *La lingua filmata. Didascalie e dialoghi nel cinema italiano*. Firenze: Le Lettere.
Raffaelli, Sergio. 1994. "Il parlato cinematografico e televisivo", in Luca Serianni and Pietro Trifone (eds.) *Storia della lingua italiana, II, Scritto e parlato*. Torino: Einaudi: 271–290.
Raffaelli, Sergio. 1996. "Un italiano per tutte le stagioni", in Eleonora Di Fortunato and Mario Paolinelli (eds.) *Barriere linguistiche e circolazione delle opere audiovisiva: la questione del doppiaggio*. Roma: Aidac, 25–28.
Raffaelli, Sergio. 2001. "La parola e la lingua", in Gian Piero Brunetta (ed.) *Storia del cinema mondiale, vol. V. Teorie, strumenti, memorie*. Torino: Einaudi, 887–901.
Rossi, Fabio. 1997. "L'italiano doppiato". *Italiano e Oltre* 12(2): 116–124.
Rossi, Fabio. 1999. *Le parole dello schermo. Analisi linguistica del parlato di sei film dal 1948 al 1957*. Roma: Bulzoni.
Rossi, Fabio. 2002. "Il dialogo nel parlato filmico", in Carla Bazzanella (ed.) *Sul dialogo. Contesti e forme di interazione verbale*. Milano: Guerini, 161–175.

Rossi, Fabio. 2003. "Il parlato cinematografico: il codice del compromesso", in Nicoletta Maraschio and Teresa Poggi Salani (eds.) *Italia linguistica anno Mille Italia linguistica anno Duemila. Atti del XXXIV Congresso internazionale di studi della Società di linguistica italiana (SLI)*. Firenze, 19–21 October 2000. Roma: Bulzoni, 449–460.

Rossi, Fabio. 2008. *Lingua italiana e cinema*. Roma: Carocci.

Setti, Raffaella. 2003. "Prospettive evolutive della lingua del cinema italiano contemporaneo", in Nicoletta Maraschio and Teresa Poggi Salani (eds.) *Italia linguistica anno Mille Italia linguistica anno Duemila. Atti del XXXIV Congresso internazionale di studi della Società di linguistica italiana (SLI)*. Firenze, 19–21 October 2000. Roma: Bulzoni, 461–472.

Spadaro, Rosario. 2002. *Europeans' Participation in Cultural Activities. A Eurobarometer Survey Carried Out at the Request of the European Commission*, Eurostat. http://ec.europa.eu/culture/pdf/doc967_en.pdf.

Toury, Gideon. 1980. *In Search of a Theory of Translation*. Tel Aviv: The Porter Institute for Poetics and Semiotics, Tel Aviv University.

Toury, Gideon. 1995. *Descriptive Translation Studies and Beyond*. Amsterdam: John Benjamins.

Web 1: www.friendscafe.org, no longer available.
Web 2: www.friendstranscripts.tk, last accessed 28th February 2015.
Web 3: www.simplyscripts.com/tvrs.html, last accessed 28th February 2015.
Web 4: www.script-o-rama.com, last accessed 28th February 2015.
Web 5: www.twiztv.com, no longer available.
Web 6: The Annotated Martian: http://versaphile.com/lom, last accessed 28th February 2015.

Filmography

The Adventures of Rin Tin Tin (Le avventure di Rin Tin Tin), Robert G. Walker and William Beaudine, 1954–1959, USA.

Borat: Cultural Learnings of America for Make Benefit Glorious Nation of Kazakhstan (Borat), Larry Charles, 2006, USA/UK.

Il commissario Montalbano, Andrea Camilleri, 1999-in production, Italy.

Django Unchained, Quentin Tarantino, 2012, USA.

Friends, Marta Kauffman and David Crane, 1994–2004, USA.

Gomorra—La serie, Giovanni Bianconi, Stefano Bises, Leonardo Fasoli, Ludovica Rampoldi and Roberto Saviano, 2014-in production, Italy.

Life on Mars, Matthew Graham, Tony Jordan and Ashley Pharoah, 2006–2007, UK.

Romanzo criminale, Stefano Sollima, 2008–2010, Italy.

Six Feet Under, Alan Ball, 2001–2005, USA.

2 Theoretical Framework

INTRODUCTION

Ignoring regularities of behaviour makes it very easy to back one's claims with mere examples. Although this book is full of examples, the ultimate aim is to offer representativeness through a large selection of data analysed to find such regularities.

This chapter illustrates the theories in the field of Translation Studies in whose framework this research and analysis have been conducted. More precisely, it considers the relevant parts of these theories, which have a direct bearing on this study. The aim is not to give an exhaustive account of all concepts, contributions and points of view and their several implications but to use the same theories only insofar as they represent useful tools for this analysis. As this research has been carried out in the framework of Descriptive Translation Studies, whose main representative and theoretician is Gideon Toury, this chapter will give an account of his position especially in relation to his concept of translation norms.

The rest of the chapter discusses ideas and premises put forward by other scholars and which have also influenced, to a certain extent, the set-up of this research, namely the work of Even-Zohar, Lefevere, and Vermeer. Studies and theories relative to the conceptualisation and the translation of culture-bound terms, the main subject of this work, are dealt with separately in Chapter 4.

DESCRIPTIVE TRANSLATION STUDIES

At a time in which Translation Studies decidedly were marked by source-orientedness, the works of Gideon Toury in the 1980s and of Itamar Even-Zohar before him in the 1970s (see the following section) have contributed to deviate the course of this young discipline toward an attention and emphasis onto the target text. Indeed, translations are for Toury (1995: 29) "facts of target cultures; on occasion facts of a special status, sometimes even constituting identifiable (sub)systems of their own, but of the target culture in any event". This important premise means not only that a foreign text is appropriated and absorbed by the receiving cultures in ways that reflect a given culture's attitude—and, more specifically, the translators' and the patrons' attitudes—towards foreignness but also that the introduction of a text in a new context is likely to cause changes in the receiving system:

> The likelihood of causing changes in the receiving system beyond the mere introduction of the target text itself stems from the fact that, while translations are indeed intended to cater for the needs of a target culture, they also tend to *deviate* from its sanctioned patterns, on one level or another, not least because of the postulate of retaining invariant at least some features of the source text which seems to be part of any culture-internal notion of translation (ibid.: 28).

In other words, in Toury's opinion, it is not only the text which inevitably changes in the process of its introduction into the new cultural system, but this very receiving system also experiences minor or major changes. This is because translations, while catering for the needs of the TC, also "deviate from its sanctioned patterns" (ibid.) as they keep at least some features of the ST unaltered. Toury's reasoning proves to be particularly insightful if applied to the field of dubbing, as will be explained in the following subsection and, in more detail, in Chapter 3, centred on the influence of dubbing on the evolution of the Italian language.

For the discipline of Translation Studies to stand on more solid scientific grounds and to be able to study more thoroughly this reciprocal interplay of influences between ST (and culture) and TT (and culture), Toury advocates the need for methodology and research techniques which go beyond sets of isolated and randomly selected examples and pay attention to regularities of translational behaviour by analysing a substantial corpus of purposefully selected material. By the notion of 'regularities of behaviour', Toury (ibid.: 3) encourages the researcher to look for what he labels 'norms', a notion which is central to his entire position and makes reference to recurrent patterns of translation behaviour.

Toury's Concept of Norms

Borrowing the notion of norms from sociology and social psychology, Toury (ibid.: 55) understands norms as

> the translation of general values or ideas shared by a community—as to what is right and wrong, adequate and inadequate—into performance instructions appropriate for and applicable to particular situations, specifying what is prescribed and forbidden as well as what is tolerated and permitted in a certain behavioural dimension [...]. Norms are acquired by the individual during his/her socialization and always imply *sanctions*—actual or potential, negative as well as positive.

For Toury (ibid.: 54), norms occupy a middle position between two extremes: that of absolute rules on the one hand and of pure idiosyncrasies on the other:

> Between these two poles lies a vast middle-ground occupied by inter-subjective factors commonly designated norms. The norms themselves form a graded continuum along the scale: some are stronger, and hence more rule-like, others are weaker, and hence almost idiosyncratic. The borderlines between the various types of constraints are thus diffuse. Each of the concepts, including the grading itself, is relative too.

If this is true for norms in terms of their potency, Toury (ibid.) argues that the temporal axis is also to be taken into account as "mere whims may catch on and become more and more normative, and norms can gain so much validity that, for all practical purposes, they become as binding as rules; or the other way around, of course".

This concept, too, is to have a direct influence, as we will see, on this research, when the translation of some lexical elements is followed over the years—a diachronic analysis that is made possible if the studied programme covers a long period of time, as it is the case, in this corpus, with the sitcom *Friends* (M. Kauffman and D. Crane, 1994–2004), which expanded over 10 years.

Translation as a norm-governed activity, as it is conceived by Toury (ibid.: 55), allows for a certain amount of deviation from prevailing norms, although "there would normally be a price to pay for opting for any deviant kind of behaviour", in the sense that deviations may then jeopardise the success of the resulting translation.

Toury divides norms into preliminary norms—which influence behaviour before the start of the actual translation process, such as in the selection of the texts to be translated into the TL—and operational norms—which interest the act of translation itself. The latter are further divided into matricial norms, which may govern "the very *existence* of target-language material as a substitute for the corresponding source-language material (and hence the degree of *fullness* of translation), its location in the text (or the form of actual *distribution*), as well as the textual *segmentation*" (ibid.: 58–59), and into textual-linguistic norms, which describe translated material and translation operations, such as the ones analysed in this work. They are conceived as norms which "govern the selection of material to formulate the target text in, or replace the original textual and linguistic material with" (ibid.: 59). These latter norms can in turn be general or particular, applying in the first case to "translation qua translation" (ibid.) or, in the second case, to particular types and modes of translation only, that is, in our case, AVT. A norm in dubbing, for example, is that whenever an actor on screen is shot in a close-up, lip-synch considerations tend to prevail over semantic ones.

Toury's fundamental insight is that although some translational norms can be identical to norms governing the production of non-translational types of text, such an identity should not be taken for granted. In his opinion, this is "the methodological reason why no study of translation can, or should proceed from the assumption that the latter is representative of the target language, or of any overall textual tradition thereof" (ibid.). Some of the translational routines used in dubbing, which make the dubbed dialogue sound different, to some extent, from natural conversation and from other types of original texts (literary or theatrical), indicate that the production of dubbed texts follows norms that are not identical to those that govern the production of non-translational types of text.

Through the concept of norms, Toury (ibid.: 61) reintroduces in Translation Studies the notion of equivalence, "which various contemporary approaches (e.g., Hönig and Kussmaul 1982; Holz-Mänttäri 1984; Snell-Hornby 1988) have tried to do without". He goes on to argue that it is "norms that determine the (type and extent of) equivalence manifested by actual translations" (Toury ibid.: 61). By retaining the notion of equivalence, Toury (ibid.) supports, at the same time, the introduction of an essential change into it: "from an ahistorical, largely prescriptive concept to a historical one". Equivalence, then, should not be understood as an abstract *tertium comparationis* between ST and TT, that is, the benchmark which tells a good translation from a bad one, but as a historically bound, changing concept which reflects a particular relationship between a certain TT and ST in a particular time and space. Equivalence between two texts should be described according to the norms that govern translation in a given time and space.

Toury (ibid.: 65) further clarifies how the object of study for the researcher is not so much norms themselves as rather "norm-governed instances of behaviour" and, more frequently, the products of such behaviour. Norms are thus entities to be reconstructed, to account for translational behaviour, by using two major sources, textual and extratextual. The former are the texts themselves, which can be considered, in Toury's (ibid.) opinion, "*primary* products of norm-regulated behaviour", while the latter include prescriptive theories or statements made by translators and by all professionals involved in the translating process—editors, publishers, critics, distributors and broadcasters—and being partially biased and arbitrary, they should be handled and used only with extreme care. As Baker (2001: 164) argues, Toury's theoretical operation in introducing the concept of norms was to take the dualism that was common in linguistics, such as Noam Chomsky's competence and performance and Ferdinand de Saussure's *langue* and *parole*,

> and introduce an interlevel which allows him to investigate what is typical rather than simply what is or what can be. This interlevel of norms enables the analyst to make sense of both the raw data of performance and the idealized potential of competence.

16 Theoretical Framework

Toury's (ibid.: 163) advocacy of the descriptive approach generally associated to his name and, in particular, his notion of norms have had a huge influence on Translation Studies, supporting "the most active research programme" in this field to date.[1]

Implications and Influence of Toury's Theories on This Study

One of the implications of Toury's target-oriented approach is that the life of the new translated text in its socio-historical context assumes an importance that is unprecedented in the former, more source-oriented approaches to Translation Studies. One of the consequences is that this very socio-historical context becomes fundamental in understanding the behaviour of translators and their norm-oriented choices. Although this appears to be an important and natural outcome of Toury's studies, a socio-historical assessment of the TC context seldom accompanies analyses of the descriptive kind in AVT, with some exceptions, such as the work carried out by Gutiérrez Lanza (1999). In this book, however, this aspect is considered of foremost importance, and for this reason Chapter 3 is devoted to the historical evolution of dubbing in Italy, with a focus on its early background and its impact on the evolution of the Italian language. My assumption, derived from Toury's outlook, is that the socio-historical circumstances in which this type of translation was born in Italy can shed light on the translators' behaviour in general and on AVT as carried out in Italy in particular.

Toury's concept, by which the TC is bound to be influenced and in some way modified by the introduction of the translated texts, finds evidence in the ways the language spoken in Italy and even the culture of the importing country have been influenced, over the years, by the introduction and translation of foreign audiovisual programmes, especially Anglo-American. Chapter 3 focuses on this vast subject.

As seen, Toury emphasises the need to collect a representatively large corpus so that its analysis can have real validity. In this sense, many AVT studies with descriptive slants do not always follow this recommendation and tend to rely on limited corpora. This shortcoming has been taken into due account in this research, and consideration has been given not only to one or a few films but rather to a large amount of audiovisual programmes. Although the ensuing analysis is both quantitative and qualitative, the latter shedding further light on the data provided by the former, the possibility of drawing statistical conclusions thanks to the vast amount of information under scrutiny can be considered quintessentially Tourian in its quest for regularities of translational behaviour.

The role of preliminary norms, as they have been explained, may account for editorial choices such as cuts in a montage, which is observed in various occurrences in the case studies but especially in *Life on Mars* (M. Graham, T. Jordan and A. Pharoah, 2006–2007) (Chapter 6). The concept of preliminary norms can thus be useful not only to evaluate critically the process of selection of the texts to be distributed and broadcast but also to analyse editorial choices, such as cuts and scene suppressions, that have taken place before the actual translation and adaptation process.

Operational norms which govern the act of translation itself have a more direct bearing on the present research. The existence of matricial norms is addressed in this research every time the linguistic material at the disposal of the translator is questioned, as in the case of the analysis of the gayspeak lexicon in *Six Feet Under* (A. Ball, 2001–2005) (Chapter 7). The lack of a rich Italian vocabulary in this particular field questions, in Toury's (1995: 58) words, "the very *existence* of target-language material as a substitute for the corresponding source-language material". In general, matricial norms are the ones to be more often under discussion in the analysis of translated texts together with textual-linguistic norms, also included by Toury under the umbrella term of 'operational norms'. Textual-linguistic norms have an impact on the solutions chosen to replace the original material and on the strategies chosen to translate the texts, which in turn, are revelatory of any norm-governed behaviour, the main concern of this analysis.

Toury further subdivides textual-linguistic norms into those which apply to translation in general and those which apply to particular types of translation only. This distinction has been taken into account by considering a set of translation strategies as a taxonomy for the subsequent analysis of dubbed texts (see Chapter 4).

Finally, in line with Toury's recommendations, my analysis focuses on the primary products of norm-regulated behaviour, that is, the translated texts themselves, taking into account only with due care secondary products such as statements by the experts involved in the translating process. Dubbing adapters, dubbing directors, even dubbing actors, distributors and broadcasters are, in fact, professionals in the field who, over the years, have expressed in various ways their opinions about the translational and adapting processes they conduct or participate in.[2] Their extratextual statements have sometimes been taken into consideration in this study which is, however, mainly centred on the texts themselves, letting the translated words speak for themselves.

THE WORK OF EVEN-ZOHAR AND THE POLYSYSTEM THEORY

The work of Toury was developed in correlation with the research carried out by another Tel Aviv scholar, Itamar Even-Zohar, who before Toury, developed a target-oriented approach to translation which stresses the importance of the socio-historical context in understanding the translating process and the translated products in all their implications. Even-Zohar's work gave impetus and prepared the ground to an approach to translation which includes an explicit refusal to make a priori statements about what translation is, what it should be, or what kinds of relationship a translated text should have with its original; an insistence on examining all translation-related issues historically, in terms of the conditions which operate in the receiving culture at any point in time; and an interest in extending the context of research beyond the examination of translated texts, in particular to include examining the evaluative writing on translation, for example preface, reviews, reflective essays, and so on. (Baker 2001: 163)

Drawing from the writings of the Russian formalists (namely Jurij Tynjanov, Roman Jakobson and Boris Ejkhenbaum), Even-Zohar developed the polysystem theory, which is central to his thinking and one of the most stimulating and fruitful theories in Translation Studies. Although the terms 'system' and 'polysystem' are often used interchangeably by the author, the latter term stresses the more dynamic nature of the concept in contrast to the more static quality of the formalists' 'system' (Shuttleworth 2001: 177). The polysystem, as formulated by Even-Zohar (ibid.), is "conceived as a heterogeneous, hierarchized conglomerate (or system) of systems which interact to bring about an ongoing dynamic process of evolution within the polysystem as a whole". In this light

> the polysystem of a given national literature is viewed as one element making up the larger socio-cultural polysystem, which itself comprises other polysystems besides the literary, such as for example the artistic, the religious or the political. Furthermore, being placed in this way in a large sociocultural context, 'literature' comes to be viewed not just as a collection of texts, but more broadly as a set of factors governing the production, promotion and reception of these texts. (ibid.)

In Even-Zohar's (1990a: 28) own words, the "literary system" can be formulated to mean "the network of relations that is hypothesized to obtain between a number of activities called 'literary', and consequently these activities themselves observed via that network". Although Even-Zohar wrote his theory bearing literary texts in mind, his views can productively be applied to audiovisual texts. Lefevere (1992: 2–3), whose work can be considered a continuation and development of Even-Zohar's, explicitly states, quoting Hillis Miller (1987), that Western civilization has to witness the end of a period in which the book occupied a central position, a place occupied today by cinema, television and popular music. His argumentation indirectly acknowledges the existence of a different system—the 'audiovisual system'—that functions as the literary one.

As a consequence, this particular audiovisual system, which is composed of dubbed, subtitled or otherwise translated audiovisual texts, can be viewed in the broader picture of the factors which govern the production, promotion and reception of the texts themselves. This larger context, of which texts are probably the most important pieces but by no means the only ones, guides the present analysis in the sense that reference is made to the already-mentioned factors: considerations on the TA in terms of age, social status and the like; and considerations linked to the degree of success of the programme, among others. Special emphasis will be placed on the importance of reception, although this is not, and cannot be, a reception study, which would require a completely different approach.

Furthermore, it is useful to interrogate oneself on the role of dubbed texts in the larger polysystem of Italian culture as its relationship to literature may shed some light not only on the choices made when selecting the texts to be translated but also on the strategies used to translate them (Chapter 1 illustrates the role and importance of dubbing in Italy nowadays, while Chapter 3 looks at its development from a historical perspective).

Even-Zohar (1990b: 46) refuses to see translated literature as holding a peripheral position in the literary polysystem, even if it is sometimes treated as such in the study of literature. He, on the contrary, thinks that it is an active force in shaping the centre of the polysystem itself:

> Through the foreign works, features (both principles and elements) are introduced into the home literature which did not exist there before. These include possibly not only new models of reality to replace the old and established ones that are no longer effective, but a whole range of other features as well, such as a new (poetic) language, or compositional patterns and techniques. (ibid.)

As is described in Chapter 3, these words, which echo Toury's on the reshaping of the recipient culture, have a direct bearing on the very nature of the Italian that is used in dubbing, a language that has absorbed "a whole range of other features as well, such as a new (poetic) language, or compositional patterns and techniques", after its contact with the foreign, displaying its own special way of re-elaborating the foreign. Furthermore, Even-Zohar's words seem particularly suitable in a study on culture specific elements which, through foreign works, are introduced as new elements to the home literature.

The role of dubbing in Italy has certainly always held a central, far from peripheral, position in the audiovisual polysystem. Even-Zohar (ibid.: 47) discerns three major conditions which favour the centrality of translated texts within a culture:

> (a) when a polysystem has not yet been crystallized, that is to say, when a literature is "young", in the process of being established; (b) when a literature is either "peripheral" (within a large group of correlated literatures) or "weak", or both; and (c) when there are turning points, crises, or literary vacuums in literature.

As it will also become clearer from the account of the historical development of dubbing in Italy, the central role which dubbed texts have always held in the Italian audiovisual system might be explained by Italy's weak, peripheral position towards the powerful US culture, in particular in the field of film and television fiction programme production. The development of a language of dubbing in Italy, which is partly calqued on conversational routines and lexicon which belong to the 'stronger' Anglo-American culture (Pavesi 2006: 42–46), may be explained in Even-Zohar's terms: in 'weak' nations, developing nations or nations in crisis, the poetics of translation tends to favour the forms of the source texts.

In conclusion, Even-Zohar's polysystem theory does not influence the method of the analysis directly but generally shapes the perspective by which this research has been carried out.

LEFEVERE AND REWRITING: THE MANIPULATION SCHOOL

Although the name of 'Manipulation School' is derived from the title of a collection of essays edited by Hermans (1985), the translation scholar who has arguably contributed most significantly to investigate the concept of manipulation in translation is Lefevere (1985, 1992, with Bassnett 1990, 1998). His studies, conducted in the field of literary translation, stem from the conviction that both translators and readers are manipulated and that, consequently, the subject of ideological manipulation through translation could and should become a central area of investigation in Translation Studies.[3] This approach therefore favours the development of an interest in ideological factors which translation scholars had not disregarded but had until then left in the background. The term 'manipulation', conveying the idea of 'conscious intervention', situates translation in a new paradigm where ideology, power and patronage take a leading role.

Lefevere (1992: 1) considers translators as rewriters of literature, "those in the middle, the men and women who do not write literature, but rewrite it", and sees them as a force of literary evolution. According to the scholar, there is "a double control factor that sees that the literary system does not fall too far out of step with the other subsystems society consists of" (ibid.: 14). The first factor acts within the literary system and is constituted by the professionals (i.e., the translators and, more broadly speaking, all the professionals involved in the translation/adaptation process) whose very professionalism gives them status and power.

If we apply this first factor to AVT, there are several agents involved in the case of dubbing—the translator, who transfers the text from one linguistic and cultural system to another; the adapter or dialogue writer; the dubbing director; the dubbing assistant; and also the distributors and broadcasters of audiovisual programmes—because they, too, intervene directly with the text. Even dubbing actors can and often do take part in the process of adaptation as well as the sound engineer and mixer. Texts in the audiovisual industry are products of teamwork, and the particular role of the individual professionals is difficult to clarify (see Chapter 3).

The second control factor detected by Lefevere (ibid.: 15) acts from outside the literary system and is the concept of patronage, which he understands as "the powers (persons, institutions) that can further or hinder the reading, writing, and rewriting of literature". Power is conceived in the Foucaldian sense, not only as something which represses but which has the force to produce things, induce pleasure, disseminate forms of knowledge, and produce discourse (Foucault 1980: 119). In the field of AVT, patronage is represented, for example, by a government authority or organism able to influence translation at an institutional level. In Italy this is best represented by the *Ufficio di revisione cinematografica*, commonly called *ufficio censura* [censorship office], which is part of the *Ministero dei beni e delle attività culturali e del turismo* [Ministry for cultural heritage, activities and tourism] (see Chapter 3 for an explanation of its role). But patronage is also embodied by distribution and broadcasting companies which, in my opinion, can be counted both among the professionals involved in the translation process (Lefevere's first control factor acting from within the system) and as the powers which delegate authority to the professionals (the second control factor acting from outside the system).

There is also a third element that Lefevere recognises as an important factor of control, namely the dominant poetics in a given time and space. Poetics is defined by the author as the range of literary genres, leitmotifs, typical situations and characters that are important at a given time (Lefevere 1992: 26). This third factor, too, can be applied to the audiovisual field, which arguably even more than narrative literature, relies on the division into specific genres and feeds itself with often stereotypical plots and characters.

Lefevere (ibid.: 39) goes on to reflect on the fact that literary histories have had little time for translations, and he reaches the seminal conclusion that "yet on every level of the translation process, it can be shown that, if linguistic considerations enter into conflict with considerations of an ideological and/or poetological nature, the latter tend to win out". We will verify, in the many occasions in which these conflicts surface in dubbing translation, if Lefevere's intuition can be validated in this specific translation process. Even translation choices which apparently seem to be based on a selection of exclusively linguistic options may conceal some ideological motivations, as discussed in Chapter 7, where considerations on gayspeak lexicon are dealt with in detail.

According to Fawcett (2001: 107), ideological interference with the original text, in Lefevere's terms, does not necessarily mean loss since it can also be viewed as an addition of new richness to the work. Various forms of adaptation can be justified as forms of translation and Lefevere (1992: 51) suggests that even faithful translation can be considered another translation strategy that results from "the collocation of a certain ideology with a certain poetics".

22 Theoretical Framework

Two other concepts proposed by the scholar are of substantial importance for this book. Lefevere (ibid.: 92) expounds the first as follows:

> The genre that is dominant in the target culture defines to a great extent the readers' horizon of expectation with regard to the translated work that tries to take its place in the target culture. If it does not conform to the demands of the genre that dominates the target culture its reception is likely to be rendered more difficult.

The term 'horizon of expectations', as conceptualised also by other authors, is discussed in Chapter 3. More specifically, some of the conclusions drawn from the analysis of the different case studies hint at the fact that expectations may induce manipulative practices to make the text fit into an expected genre: this will be especially evident in the analysis of *Life on Mars* (Chapter 6), a detective series which does not quite fulfil the predictable and traditional characteristics of its genre.

The second concept is exemplified by Lefevere (ibid.: 93) as follows:

> The intended audience also plays a part in determining strategies for the translation of Universe-of-Discourse features. If Homer is translated for the young, as he often was in those stages of cultures which relied mainly, if not exclusively, on the book to propagate cultural values, certain aspects of his Universe of Discourse are likely to be omitted.

By 'universe of discourse' Lefevere (ibid.: 41) means the "objects, concepts, customs belonging to the world that was familiar to the writer of the original". It is easy to apply the author's words, referring to classical literature, to AVT texts: the type of target audience (TA) for which the text is intended (by patrons) has a heavy impact on the translation process and product. Although not an aim of the present research, it will be reasonably straightforward to verify whether the universe of discourse of the TA has influenced the translation solutions found in our corpus. Considerations linked to the expected audience are also part of the theory expounded in the following section.

Although the present work is mainly aimed at providing a descriptive account of translating strategies and of translators' regularities, and irregularities, of behaviour, the influence of Lefevere's ideological stance has been strong and can be perceived in two aspects of this research: in the historical chapter on the origins and evolution of dubbing in a totalitarian context but also in the very choice of part of the material selected for the corpus. It was my preliminary hypothesis that some television programmes would be more sensitive than others, more vulnerable to being manipulated. To prove this point it was felt that it would be qualitatively significant to juxtapose a series like *Six Feet Under*, in which so many socially significant issues are openly dealt with, to less overtly charged programmes, ideologically speaking, such as *Friends* and *Life on Mars*.

VERMEER AND THE *SKOPOS* THEORY

Toury himself (1995: 25) has found parallels between his work and Vermeer's (1978) *Skopostheorie*, stressing the temporal coincidence of the first formulations of both target-oriented theories and explaining, at the same time, which are the points of divergence:

> Whereas mainstream *Skopos*-theorists still see the ultimate justification of their frame of reference in the more 'realistic' way it can deal with problems of an *applied* nature, the main object being to 'improve' (i.e., change!) the world of our experience, my own endeavours have always been geared primarily towards *the descriptive-explanatory* goal of supplying exhaustive accounts of whatever has been regarded as translational within a target culture, on the way to the formulation of some *theoretical* laws.

However, the scholar goes on to detect in second-generation *Skopos*-theorists, most notably Nord (1991), attempts to bridge the gap by incorporating the notion of norms in translation into a fundamentally Vermeerian account.

The *Skopos* theory rests on a functional and sociocultural concept of translation, which encourages the consideration of contextual factors surrounding the translation such as "the culture of the intended readers of the target text and of the client who has commissioned it, and, in particular, the function which the text is to perform in that culture for those readers" (Schäffner 2001: 235). However, the fundamental thrust of this theory is to elucidate the purpose (*skopos*) of the translation before beginning the actual translation process, thus adopting a prospective attitude to translation (determined by the client's needs) as opposed to traditional source text (ST)-oriented approaches (ibid.: 235–236).

It should be noted that although the *Skopos* theory can sometimes be seen as synonymous of rather free translations, one of the possible *skopoi* of the TT can also be that of fidelity to the ST.

Knowing why and by whom an ST has been selected for translation and what the function of the TT will be in the receiving culture is of vital importance to AVT, which strongly depends on industrial and marketing factors.

For Vermeer (in Munday 2008: 80), intertextual coherence (i.e., the coherence of the TT with the ST) is hierarchically less important than intratextual coherence (i.e., the internal coherence of the TT), downplaying in this way the role of the ST. The analysis of the case studies will sometimes verify this assumption, showing how a reflection on the intended purpose of a translation commission can shed light on some of the choices in the selection of certain translation strategies. In Vermeer's approach (1989/2004: 235), the commission comprises a goal and the conditions to achieve it, including fees and deadlines, and the role of the commissioner is perceived as being of paramount importance. This is particularly true in the field of AVT, where distribution and broadcasting companies play a decisive part in the distribution of translations. Ignoring the commercial environment, even a descriptive type of analysis based on the search for textual and linguistic norms could lead to a partial and impoverished result.

CONCLUSIONS

It has been noted by some scholars that, despite its growing popularity, AVT shows a lack of systematic theorisation and the reliance on allochthonous rather than autochthonous translation models (Pérez-González 2014: 97) that could properly account for its unique nature and that the orientation of some of the research conducted in this field has been mainly prescriptive, "describing and deciding how and where the subtitle should appear and what are the best techniques for producing a successful product" (Munday 2008: 193). The same author, who probably refers to more traditional accounts of AVT, goes on to enumerate which, in his opinion, would be the best areas to be the subject of further detailed research. He cites Chaume (2004), who stresses the need to incorporate techniques and metalanguage from film studies into AVT research, and Díaz Cintas (2003: 32), in particular his call for more studies that would take into account the macro-level and would focus on issues such as power, culture and ideology to promote a more descriptive rather than prescriptive paradigm of analysis. As for the latter point, the already-cited collection edited by Díaz Cintas (2012) on manipulation in AVT is a step in this direction.

The need for the integration of these two arguably different approaches—drawing from film studies and from pieces of research on ideology in translation—have indeed influenced the general approach to the corpus under scrutiny in the present research. Insights on both matters come to the surface throughout this book, and although this work can be said to be mainly descriptive, it also expresses the need to open up to broader ideological reflections on the data.

NOTES

1. The notion of norms has been explored in its theoretical aspects by other scholars after Toury, notably Chesterman (1993), Hermans (1991, 1993, 1996) and Nord (1991, 1997). Chesterman's (1993: 9) contribution to this fruitful field was to distinguish between 'professional norms', which concern

the translation process, and 'expectancy norms', which "are established by the receivers of the translation, by their expectations of what a translation (of a given type) should be like, and what a native text (of a given type) in the target language should be like". Nord (1991), a scholar working within the general principles of *Skopostheorie*, classifies norms in 'constitutive norms', related to the translation product, and 'regulatory norms', related to the translation process. According to Hermans (1996: 4–5), norms are psychological and social entities which he discusses in relation to the concept of conventions, understood as "regularities in behaviour which have emerged as arbitrary but effective solutions to recurrent problems of interpersonal coordination". In the specific field of AVT, descriptive norms have stimulated several interesting studies, most notably the ones by Ballester Casado (2001), Díaz Cintas (1997), Goris (1993), Karamitroglou (2000), Martí Ferriol (2006).

2. Not many are the books containing the statements of such professionals, which can thus mainly be found in interviews and enjoyed in personal communications which for the author of this book were not hard to obtain as Rome is the city where most dubbing companies are located. However, there are some edited collections which include articles by Italian dubbing adapters and dialogue authors, such as those by Baccolini, Bollettieri Bosinelli and Gavioli (1994), containing, among other contributions, a precious testimony of the modus operandi of Oreste Lionello (1994), one of Italy's historical dubbers; Castellano (2000); Di Fortunato and Paolinelli (1996). For Lionello's work, see also Ranzato (2011). These contributions reflect the points of view of both academics and dubbing professionals. Other books, such as the one by Paolinelli and Di Fortunato (2005)—a rather biased account of the virtues of dubbing versus subtitling—and the one by Giraldi, Lancia and Melelli (2014) are authored by dubbing adapters (the former) and by dubbing experts and film critics (the latter). See also the interesting documentary by Paul Mariano, *Being George Clooney* (2015), an informative, entertaining, detailed account of the dubbing industry in Italy and elsewhere.

3. Translation Studies have shown their concrete motivation in taking Lefevere's cue with studies openly dealing with issues of censorship, manipulation and ideology, such as Álvarez and Vidal's (1996), Billiani's (2007) and, in AVT, Díaz Cintas's (2012).

REFERENCES

Álvarez, Román and M. Carmen-África Vidal (eds.). 1996. *Translation Power Subversion*. Clevedon: Multilingual Matters.

Baccolini, Raffaella, Rosa Maria Bollettieri Bosinelli and Laura Gavioli (eds.). 1994. *Il doppiaggio—trasposizioni linguistiche e culturali*. Bologna: Clueb.

Baker, Mona. 2001. "Norms", in Mona Baker (ed.) *Routledge Encyclopedia of Translation Studies*. London and New York: Routledge, 163–165.

Ballester Casado, Ana. 2001. *Traducción y nacionalismo: La recepcion del cine americano en España a través del doblaje, 1928–1948*. Granada: Editorial Comares.

Bassnett, Susan and André Lefevere. 1990. *Translation, History and Culture*. London: Pinter.

Bassnett, Susan and André Lefevere. 1998. *Constructing Culture: Essays on Literary Translation*. Clevedon: Multilingual Matters.

Billiani, Francesca. 2007. *Modes of Censorship and Translations. National Contexts and Diverse Media*. Manchester: St Jerome.

Castellano, Alberto. 2000. *Il doppiaggio—Profilo storia e analisi di un'arte negata*. Roma: Aidac.
Chaume, Frederic. 2004. "Film Studies and Translation Studies: two disciplines at stake in Audiovisual Translation". *Meta* 49(1): 12–24.
Chesterman, Andrew. 1993. "From 'Is' to 'Ought': laws, norms and strategies in Translation Studies". *Target* 5(1): 1–20.
Díaz Cintas, Jorge. 1997. *El subtitulado en tanto que modalidad de traducción fílmica dentro del marco teórico de los Estudios sobre Traducción*. (Misterioso asesinato en Manhattan, Woody Allen, 1993.) PhD thesis. València: Universitat de València.
Díaz Cintas, Jorge. 2003. *Teoría y práctica de la subtitulación: inglés-español*. Barcelona: Ariel.
Díaz Cintas, Jorge (ed.). 2012. *The Manipulation of Audiovisual Translation*, Meta special issue 57(2).
Di Fortunato, Eleonora and Mario Paolinelli. 1996. *La questione del doppiaggio—Barriere linguistiche e circolazione delle opere audiovisive*. Roma: Aidac.
Even-Zohar, Itamar. 1990a. "The 'Literary System'". *Polysystem Studies* [=*Poetics Today*] 11(1): 27–44.
Even-Zohar, Itamar. 1990b. "The Position of Translated Literature within the Literary Polysystem". *Poetics Today* 11(1): 45–51.
Fawcett, Peter. 2001. "Ideology and translation", in Mona Baker (ed.) *Routledge Encyclopedia of Translation Studies*. London: Routledge, 106–111.
Foucault, Michel. 1980. *Power/Knowledge: Selected Interviews and Other Writings 1972–1977*. New York: Pantheon Books.
Giraldi, Massimo, Enrico Lancia and Fabio Melelli. 2014. *Il doppiaggio nel cinema di Hollywood*. Roma: Bulzoni.
Goris, Olivier. 1993. "The question of French dubbing: towards a frame for systematic investigation". *Target* 5(2): 169–190.
Gutiérrez Lanza, Camino. 1999. *Traducción y censura de textos cinematográficos en la España de Franco: doblaje y subtitulado inglés-español (1951–1975)*. PhD thesis. León: Universidad de León.
Hermans, Theo (ed.). 1985. *The Manipulation of Literature. Studies in Literary Translation*. London: Croom Helm.
Hermans, Theo. 1991. "Translational norms and correct translations", in Kitty M. van Leuven-Zwart and Ton Naaijkens (eds.) *Translation Studies: The State of the Art: Proceedings from the First James S. Holmes Symposium on Translation Studies*. Amsterdam and Atlanta, GA: Rodopi, 155–169.
Hermans, Theo. 1993. "On modelling translation: models, norms and the field of translation". *Livius* 4: 69–88.
Hermans, Theo. 1996. "Norms and the determination of translation", in Román Álvarez and M. Carmen-África Vidal (eds.) *Translation Power Subversion*. Clevedon: Multilingual Matters, 25–51.
Hillis Miller, Joseph. 1987. "Presidential Address 1986: The triumph of theory, the resistance to reading, and the question of the material base". *PMLA*, 102(3): 281–291.
Holz-Mänttäri, Justa. 1984. *Translatorisches Handeln: Theorie und Methode*. Helsinki: Suomalainen Tiedeakademia.
Hönig, Hans G. and Paul Kussmaul. 1982. *Strategie der Übersetzung. Ein Lehr—und Arbeitsbuch*. Tübingen: Gunter Narr Verlag.
Karamitroglou, Fotios. 2000. *Towards a Methodology for the Investigation of Norms in Audiovisual Translation*. Amsterdam and Atlanta, GA: Rodopi.
Lefevere, André. 1985. "Why waste our time on rewrites? The trouble with interpretation and the role of rewriting in an alternative paradigm", in Theo Hermans (ed.) *The Manipulation of Literature*. New York: St. Martin's Press, 215–243.

Lefevere, André. 1992. *Translation, Rewriting and the Manipulation of Literary Fame*. London: Routledge.
Lionello, Oreste. 1994. "Il falso in doppiaggio", in Raffaella Baccolini, Rosa Maria Bollettieri Bosinelli and Laura Gavioli (eds.) *Il doppiaggio. Trasposizioni linguistiche e culturali*. Bologna: Clueb, 41–50.
Martí Ferriol, José. 2006. *Estudio empírico y descriptivo del método de traducción para doblaje y subtitulación*. PhD thesis. Castelló de la Plana: Universitat Jaume I.
Munday, Jeremy. 2008. *Introducing Translation Studies. Theories and Applications*. London: Routledge.
Nord, Christiane. 1991. "Skopos, loyalty, and translational conventions". *Target* 3(1): 91–109.
Nord, Christiane. 1997. *Translating as a Purposeful Activity*. Manchester: St Jerome Publishing.
Paolinelli, Mario and Eleonora Di Fortunato. 2005. *Tradurre per il doppiaggio. La trasposizione linguistica dell'audiovisivo: teoria e pratica di un'arte imperfetta*. Milano: Hoepli.
Pavesi, Maria. 2006. *La traduzione filmica. Aspetti del parlato doppiato dall'inglese all'italiano*. Roma: Carocci.
Pérez-Gonzállez, Luis. 2014. *Audiovisual Translation—Theories, Methods and Issues*. London and New York: Routledge.
Ranzato, Irene. 2011. "Translating Woody Allen into Italian. Creativity in dubbing". *The Journal of Specialized Translation* 15: 121–141.
Schäffner, Christina. 2001. "Skopos theory", in Mona Baker (ed.) *Routledge Encyclopedia of Translation Studies*. London: Routledge, 235–238.
Shuttleworth, Mark. 2001. "Polysystem theory", in Mona Baker (ed.) *Routledge Encyclopedia of Translation Studies*. London: Routledge, 176–179.
Snell-Hornby, Mary. 1988. *Translation Studies. An Integrated Approach*. Amsterdam: John Benjamins.
Toury, Gideon. 1995. *Descriptive Translation Studies and Beyond*. Amsterdam: John Benjamins.
Vermeer, Hans J. 1978. "Ein Rahmen für eine allgemeine Translationswissenschaft". *Lebende Sprachen* 3: 99–102.
Vermeer, Hans J. 1989/2004. "Skopos and commission in translational action", in Andrew Chesterman (ed.) *Readings in Translation Theory*. Helsinki: Oy Finn Lectura, 173–187. Reprinted in Lawrence Venuti (ed.). *The Translation Studies Reader*. London: Routledge, 221–232.

Filmography

Being George Clooney, Paul Mariano, 2015, USA.
Friends, Marta Kauffman and David Crane, 1994–2004, USA.
Life on Mars, Matthew Graham, Tony Jordan and Ashley Pharoah, 2006–2007, UK.
Six Feet Under, Alan Ball, 2001–2005, USA.

3 Censorship and the Film Industry
A Historical Overview of Dubbing in Italy

INTRODUCTION: DEFINING CENSORSHIP AND MANIPULATION

'Censorship' and 'manipulation' are words that naturally go together, and it is easy to overlook possible distinctions between the two. Adaptation for dubbing in Italy is traditionally associated with a creative process which enjoys great freedom. To trace its historical roots, it is necessary to explore the distinction between these two sometimes overlapping concepts. To do that, it may be first useful to follow Díaz Cintas (2012: 284–285) in his definition of technical and ideological manipulation. According to the author, the term 'manipulation' does not necessarily have a negative connotation, and its first meaning of handling something "by manual or mechanical means" provided by the OED (Brown 1993) can suitably be applied in AVT "to refer to those instances where changes and modifications to the original text are incorporated because of technical considerations" (Díaz Cintas 2012: 284). On the other hand, the second meaning of the word 'manipulation' has more negative connotations, being linked to a form of control or influence exerted often in an unscrupulous or unfair way. In this second sense, according to the author (ibid: 285), we find ourselves in the presence of ideological manipulation.

The concept of censorship is, in my opinion, a step forward in this direction as it adds a constructive aspect to the negative one of ideological manipulation. The official censorship apparatus, in fact, does not just suppress information, but as gatekeepers, it also takes a clear stance on how to deal with the moral behaviour, political sympathies and sexual orientations portrayed in the source text. This active, preventive side of censorship has been and is still being used as an effective tool, not only by totalitarian governments but also by liberal ones, to influence the public's consciousness. As Talbot (2007: 5) highlights:

> Any state, but more especially a dictatorship, will rely on censorship to limit the public's horizon of expectation and therefore to shape consensus. It would be naïve to believe that this does not hold to some

extent for democratic states too, but in many ways the process is more visible in democratic states which now have Freedom of Information legislation.

The concept of 'horizon of expectation', a term employed by Jauss (1982: 24) to refer to the readers' general expectations on style, form and content of the text in the translated new version, helps us give shape to the more elusive, although more comprehensive, term of manipulation. Under this prism, it defines the dialectical way in which a text is produced by the translator. The new TT may respond to the expectations of the public while also considering the way in which this new audience will interpret and judge it according to their own beliefs, biases and preconceptions. These constraints can be said to have an impact on the translator and the public from inside, so to speak, whilst, at the same time, prevailing target norms of a linguistic, textual, translational, and sociocultural nature act as constraints from outside. Norms, more than technical constraints, tend to be responsible for the manipulation of the text by translators and adapters. Ideology, but also, as Fawcett (2003: 145) aptly writes, "human randomness and simple cussedness" help give shape to the new text.

Following Fawcett (ibid.), I propose to use the term 'manipulation' both in those cases where the solutions seem to have been caused by mistakes or carelessness as well as those cases in which the decisions have been taken on the grounds of apparently technical and ideological constraints. Censorship, on the other hand, is a declaredly conscious act of suppression and modification of form and content generally exerted from 'above'—that is, by the government and/or by other actors of patronage such as production, distribution, exhibition, and broadcasting companies in the case of AVT.

To pin down the concept of manipulation, it is also useful to introduce what Katan and Straniero-Sergio (2003: 151) call "the comfort factor", that is, the degree to which the TV audience is entertained, a concept which matches the expectations of both broadcasters and viewers. This concept is particularly useful since, as is explored in the following chapters, manipulative practices tend to be more easily detectable nowadays in the translation done for television than for the cinema.

Definitions of a general nature are necessary and helpful as heuristic tools; however, it should not be forgotten that every society has its own history—one that, to some extent, may at times contradict certain general assumptions. The history of Italian translation practice has its own peculiarities that contribute to create a multifaceted reality which makes it hard sometimes to try and fit all the details within the framework of a smooth, unequivocal interpretation.

As Schäffner (2003: 23) points out, "It can be said that any translation is ideological since the choice of a source text and the use to which the subsequent target text is put is determined by the interests, aims, and objectives of social agents". It is then accepted that translations are an important factor in shaping the cultural landscape of a society, and totalitarian governments have always proved to be alert to the dangers that transferring authors from one culture to another may imply.

In Italy, Filippo Tommaso Marinetti (1876–1944), the founder of the artistic and social movement of Futurism, began a campaign against translations in the 1930s, during the Fascist government, attacking publishers who imported foreign literature in newspaper articles and regional conferences. Marinetti, a strong supporter of the *duce*, felt that even if the quantity of translated foreign books had been crucially reduced during Fascism and was minimal (7 percent of the national book production), this input of foreign authors into the Italian market was still far too large for the Fascist autarchic standards (Talbot 2007: 156). Although the censorship of books received very little organised attention (Rundle 2000: 71), a decree law which, in 1935, elevated the state secretariat for the press and propaganda to ministry level, also gave it the authority to confiscate any offending publication and to examine all non-periodical publications. In January 1938, Gherardo Casini, director general for the Italian press at the *Minculpop* (Ministry of Popular Culture), sent a telegram to publishers requiring them to send him, as a matter of urgency, a list of their foreign works in print and those planned for the future (ibid.). A census of translations had begun. Censors were employed by publishing houses to 'correct' dialogue printed in books, substituting, for example, the formal *lei* address form with the informal *voi*.[1] In July 1940, with Italy's entry into the war, a law was passed with the aim of controlling the publication of translations. All proposals for translation now had to be given explicit approval by officials from *Minculpop*. Talbot (2007: 157–158) also cites one of the most famous cases of translation censorship, the writer Elio Vittorini's *Americana* project, which consisted in the translation of several books by US writers. The two-volume anthology was due to be published by Bompiani in 1941 as part of a series of world literature, but the then Minister of Culture Alessandro Pavolini decided against it. As he explains in a letter to Valentino Bompiani (in Talbot 2007: 158):

> I remain however of the opinion that the publication at this time, of the American anthology is inopportune. The United States are a potential enemy. The attitude of their president towards the Italian people is well known. It is not the time for courtesies towards America, not even literary ones. Furthermore, the anthology would only refocus the excessive enthusiasm for recent American literature, which is a fashion to be discouraged.

The anthology was eventually published in 1942, after the suppression of all the footnotes, and was published in its restored form only in 1968.

Alongside this reality, however, it is worth noting other episodes, as a testimony of the disorganised attention given to books. When D. H. Lawrence published *Lady Chatterley's Lover* in Florence in 1928, the sixth year of the

Fascist state, he did not have any problem with the authorities. Ironically, the same book could not be published in democratic Britain until the 1960s. US authorities burned copies of *Ulysses* (Joyce 1922/2010) on the dockside in 1922, while Antonio Pizzuto, an Italian author and translator, member of the elite Italian secret police, entertained plans to translate Joyce's novel into Italian just a few years later. He did not succeed (*Ulisse* was eventually published in 1960), but the Sicilian newspaper *L'Ora* published a translation of Molly Bloom's final monologue in 1926, marking a great literary event in Italy. As Talbot (ibid.) argues, Fascist censorship was considerably and surprisingly more progressive than literary censorship was in the Western democracies, at least in some accounts. It is in this context that we should examine the complexities of the relationship between Fascism and censorship, a relationship which can be traced to the birth of the audiovisual industry in Italy and which has left a legacy in shaping the practice of dubbing in Italy to this day.

THE LEGISLATION ON CENSORSHIP

Mussolini and his Fascists did not invent either censorship or propaganda in Italy. Both had a very long history in the country (Laura 1961: 4–10). Preventive censorship had been practised extensively by the Catholic Church, especially from the Council of Trent onwards.[2] Ecclesiastical censorship on forms of entertainment was not uniform. On one hand, it showed an attitude of strict refusal to accept cinema in particular and entertainment shows in general, as they were occasions and places of vice and immorality.[3] The opinion of an 'expert', printed in the Paduan diocesan bulletin, is symptomatic of this kind of mentality: "Plants kept in obscurity die. So it is for man. A boy shut for two or three hours inside a cinema is robbed of the sun necessary for his development [. . .] Cinema can damage the boy's morality" ("Un esperto parla", *Bollettino diocesano*, Padova, 1928, my translation). On the other hand, religious authorities could be more open and tolerant provided that films were inspired by moral principles (Brunetta 1975: 60). Pope Pius XI, in his encyclical of 21 December 1929, *Divini illius magistri*, warned about the dangers of, among others, cinema shows but also encouraged the possibility to act through these new media to educate people and give them moral guidance by producing morally edifying theatre and cinema shows (Pio XI 1929).

In the 20th century, the first legislative measures on censorship arrived shortly after the circulation of the first audiovisual products. In 1910, a disposition of the *Ministero degli interni* [Home Affairs] gave the prefects the faculty of authorising or rejecting public screenings. A few years later, on 20 February 1913, a memorandum from Prime Minister Giovanni Giolitti[4] gave the prefects the necessary details on the criteria to use in granting or refusing the authorisations for films to be screened. According to the dispositions, it was necessary to ban those films which "make the representatives of the public forces appear hateful and make the criminals appear as nice people", and it advised to look out for "the shameful excitation of sensuality, provoked by scenes where the vividness of the images immediately nourishes the lowest and most vulgar passions, and other films which stir the hatred between social classes or are an offence to national decorum" (in Laura 1961: 5, my translation).

This text is important because it is the first that gives explicit indications on the nature of the prohibitions, and it is remarkable because it already contains two fundamental principles of the type of control which was going to be exerted from then on: moral censorship (criminals should not be nice, and sexuality should be banned because it stirs vulgar passions) and political censorship (exaltation of the public forces, harmony between social classes and affirmation of national dignity). It is equally interesting to note that the provisions perceived that, unlike other modes of expression, cinema has a "vividness" whose effects are more important than those excited by other kinds of representations.

A few months after the Giolitti memorandum, censorship was given a proper legislative organisation. The *Ufficio di revisione cinematografica* [Bureau for Cinematographic Revision] was set up on 1 May 1913 with the specific brief of monitoring and amending the iconic and verbal content—intertitles at the time—of silent films. It carried out an operation of cleansing the films it examined, a task which contributed to conditioning the evolution of the Italian language from the very beginning of cinema and shows how that form of regulatory intervention in linguistic matters, long thought to be unique to the Fascist government, was in fact very much alive at the time of Giovanni Giolitti (Raffaelli 1991: 164). The Law of 25 June 1913, n. 785, gave the state the power of control over film content. The *Regio Decreto* [Royal Decree] of 31 May 1914, n. 532, instituted a censorship commission which was entirely administrative, composed of officers of the public security or police chiefs. This way, it was the *Ministero degli interni* which censored films.

A *Regio Decreto-Legge* of 9 October 1919, n. 1953, set up in addition a preventive form of censorship: the stories and screenplays of the Italian films in production would have to be examined and authorised before filming.

The following law, passed on 22 April 1920, n. 531, is also notable because it changed the composition of the censorship committee. This was to be composed not only of public security officers (which went from four to two members) but also of a judge, a mother of children, an expert in artistic and literary matters, a publicist, and a member to be chosen from among educators or representatives of humanitarian associations for the moral protection of people, young people in particular. For the first time, policemen became a minority on the board, and even if all the other members were to be nominated by the *Ministero degli interni*, censorship showed a sign of opening up, in a slightly more liberal sense, to artistic demands. This evolution towards a more liberal system would be brutally interrupted by Fascism.

When, in October 1922, Fascism came to power, it inherited a sufficiently repressive body of legislation. Nonetheless, the new government felt the need to make it stricter, and it was the prime minister himself, Benito Mussolini, who proposed the adoption of new bills. The *Regio Decreto-Legge* of 24 September 1923, n. 3287, was the most important document on the subject in the whole Fascist period, and it would be the point of reference for all the following provisions.

The document reiterated the existence of double censorship—on screenplays and on finished films—and the obligation to submit a project for censorship revision before and after the film was shot. Censorship was always based on ethical criteria on one hand and on political criteria on the other. What was completely different now was the way in which censorship actually worked and how the control commission was composed. In fact, the latter continued to exist only in the case of appeals. In ordinary practice, screenplays and films were to be revised by individual executives and officers of the *Ministero degli interni*, thus essentially by public security people. This was a very significant change. The commission virtually disappeared as the material was now revised by individual officers of the ministry. The mildly liberal turn taken by the former government in choosing people who were not politicians or policemen was then nullified (Gili 1981: 15–19).

After the fundamental 1923 change, the alterations made in the following years were more limited and concerned mainly the composition of the control commission. Following the protests from various sectors of society—cinema professionals, intellectuals and Catholics, from whose ranks mothers and members belonging to the world of education and to humanitarian organisations usually came—the first degree commission for the control of screenplays and films was restored in 1924, after only one year of having been abolished. And though it became stricter and more repressive through each successive stage of legislation, its oscillations also reveal interesting tendencies and the two souls of the Fascist government: one utterly repressive, the other more sensitive to cultural demands.

The modifications of the Law of 24 June 1929, n. 1103, for example, saw the increase in the commission of the number of members coming from the ministries and from the Fascist Party. On the other hand, it clearly sought to give itself a better professional base by nominating representatives of Istituto Luce,[5] of Enac (*Ente Nazionale per la Cinematografia* [National Board for Cinematography]) and two people who were competent in cinematographic matters. The professional turn, though, was soon abandoned, and the following laws, until 1935, were all in the direction of a more thorough politicisation of the commission and thus of the practice of censorship. With the Law of 10 January 1935, n. 65, the process of fascistisation was completed, and censorship was by now totally administrative and politicised: no more educators, no professionals, no experts or members of Istituto Luce or Enac, and no more mothers or judges.

To sum up, from 1923 to 1939, the various law decrees gave more and more power to censors who were recruited from the ranks of officers of some ministries, and to the representatives of organisms directly linked to the regime, like the Fascist Party and the Fascist university groups. Cinema enjoyed very little freedom and, as argued by Gili (1981: 21–25), the self-censorship applied by authors and producers—who did not want to risk their money and then see their films banned—probably worked as a mechanism of self-regulation even before the actual control by the commission.

Luigi Freddi, who was nominated *Direttore Generale per la Cinematografia* [general director for cinematography] in 1934, was the champion of preventive censorship.[6] He saw the advantages of a full preventive censorship from the very early stage of screenplay writing and, from the moment he became general director, he applied it in the strictest possible way (ibid: 28–30). Even if he had great respect and admiration for the Hays code,[7] what Freddi had in mind was especially the German system because it privileged the political aspect of censorship, as he thought censorship was essentially a political institution. He saw the participation of 'simple' citizens in the commission (mothers, art experts, etc.) as a serious mistake as it was, in his opinion, only a demagogic concession to call people who did not have a sense of the moral, social and educational policies of the state to perform a task which was essentially technical (ibid: 40).

CENSORSHIP AND FOREIGN FILMS: THE BIRTH OF A DUBBING INDUSTRY

There are relatively few examples of silent movies which had problems with censorship in the 1920s. The content of these first fiction films was generally based on classical works of literature, the words of explanation or dialogue in the intertitles were limited to just a few, and the attention of audiences and reviewers seemed very much captured by the music played by the orchestras in the background (Quargnolo 1986: 8–13).[8] As Quargnolo (1970: 68) also notes, a notable exception in terms of attention by Italian censors were Rodolfo Valentino's films, whose distribution was banned in 1925 for a very brief period because Valentino had apparently made outrageous comments about his native country.

With the arrival of sound films, in 1927 in the USA and in 1929 in Italy, the situation changed. The mainstay of the Italian Fascist political economy was its drive for autarchy, that is, for an economic self-sufficiency and independence from foreign cultural influence. The answer of the authorities to the threat of the possible penetration of films spoken in foreign languages was a total prohibition on screening them in Italy. From 1929 to 1931 the absence or the purely experimental character of dubbing gave way to incredible solutions, and many sound films were actually muted and screened without sound. According to Gili (1981: 34), the justification of such a policy—wanted, as it seems, by Mussolini himself—was that this way it was possible to prevent Italians from learning foreign languages by going to the cinema.

These muted films were left with only the music and sound effects tracks, while the film sequences were continuously interrupted by intertitles, sometimes very long ones, containing the translations of the dialogue. Among these films, to name but a few of the most famous, were *Der blaue Engel* (*L'angelo azzurro* 1930) by Josef von Sternberg, *Halleluja!* (*Alleluja* 1929) by King Vidor, and *Sous les toits de Paris* (*Sotto i tetti di Parigi* 1929) by René Clair. *The Show of Shows* (*La rivista delle nazioni* 1929), by John Adolfi, was presented without the sequence where one could see (and hear) John Barrymore reciting the monologue from *Richard III* (Quargnolo 1970: 68–69).

The problem was finally solved when dubbing became technically viable in 1931. The films were then dubbed into Italian either in their original country, normally the USA, or in Italy. But the government was quick to react, and the *Regio Decreto-Legge* of 5 October 1933, n. 1414, prohibited the importation of films which had been dubbed elsewhere than in Italy. It was now possible for the censor to view the film in the original version and to suggest the alterations in the dialogue that needed to be introduced in the dubbing so as to modify the unpleasant sequences. With this policy the government achieved a greater control over the 'purity of the language', which added to other, more overtly political advantages: manipulation of content, deletion of unwanted references and, in some cases, addition of more 'pleasant' references. The government could, from then on, exert without difficulty a linguistic control which aimed first of all at the disappearance of Italian dialects, regionalisms and accents in the final dubbed version. US films—the majority of the films imported—were to be dubbed in an abstract Italian, thus contributing to the effort of cultural and linguistic homogenisation which was one of the aims of Fascism. From this point of view, the foreign film to be dubbed was a more flexible and controllable product than an original Italian film (Gili 1981: 35–37).

This system was ideological in design because it enacted an ongoing imperative of fascist cultural policy, that is, the defence and promotion of national identity. Indeed, dubbing attempted to protect the Italian public from exposure to foreign influence through the manipulation of language and images, and in this respect it can be seen as the cinematic equivalent to the central goal of the *Istituto Nazionale Fascista di Cultura* [Fascist National Institute of Culture], founded in 1926. Under the directorship of Giovanni Gentile, the institute was set up to "preserve for our intellectual life its national character according to the genius and the tradition of our race, and also to favor its expansion abroad" (in Mack Smith 1959: 418). The ideological character of state-mandated dubbing cannot be overstated.

Such was the force of the purification campaign that even at times of extreme technical limitations, the dubbing requirement always remained in place.

Once the technical infrastructure was set up, dubbing became a very effective vehicle for mediating between the ideological mandates of Fascism and the commercial interests of the film industry. The case of *The Adventures of Marco Polo* (Archie Mayo 1938) illustrates the balance between political and economic imperatives. The Fascist censorship board initially blocked the film's importation because it felt that Gary Cooper was an inappropriate representative of the legendary Venetian explorer. After pressure was brought to bear on behalf of the film's distributor, the ideological problem was solved by changing Cooper's fictional nationality. The film's title became *Uno scozzese alla corte del Gran Khan* [*A Scotsman at the Court of the Great Khan*]. Any changes in the film's dialogue that were needed to make the narrative conform to the protagonist's new national identity could then be made during the dubbing process.

When Luigi Freddi, after a long disagreement with the minister of popular culture, left his position as general director for cinema in 1939, cultural transformations were also beginning to affect the general debate on censorship. There was a new generation of artists and intellectuals, even within the Fascist structures, which the regime had difficulty keeping under control. The industry journals *Cinema* and *Bianco e Nero* published articles which questioned the conformism of Italian film production, and a slow evolution of censorship policies in a more liberal sense was soon underway (Gili 1981: 58–59). This new turn was favoured by political events such as Italy being at war and Mussolini approaching his fall and being thus weaker and less alert.

It is worth mentioning here the different but parallel situations in the other two large European countries under dictatorship and united by similar protectionist and linguistic preoccupations: Spain and Germany.

With regard to the Spanish cinematographic world, and following Díaz Cintas (2001: 64–66), the first attacks on the freedom of expression on screen started with the creation of the *Junta Superior de Censura Cinematográfica* [High Board of Cinema Censorship] on 18 November 1937. Its main goal was to reduce the pernicious influence that foreign and national cinema could exert on the education and thought of the masses. In keeping with Hitler's policy and following closely the example of Mussolini's Italian legislation, the *Ministerio de la Industria y Comercio* [Ministry of Industry and Commerce] on 23 April 1941 issued a decree prohibiting the screening of films in any language other than Spanish. And, as in Italy, dubbing had to be carried out by firms based on Spanish territory and by Spanish nationals. In this country too, the law aimed at the homogenisation of the Castilian national language by not only prohibiting foreign languages on screen but also by eliminating virtually any expression in Catalan, Galician or Basque. On 31 December 1946, following the general discontent of intellectuals against dubbing and in an attempt to highlight the intention of the government, after the defeat of European fascism, to be seen as detaching itself from any link to authoritarian regimes, dubbing ceased to be compulsory. Nevertheless, a general public taste had been formed, and dubbing continues to this day to be preferred by Spanish audiences, despite a recent surge in subtitling provision. With the arrival of democracy, censorship was abolished in 1977.

As Danan (1991: 612) states, "Hitler's ruthless pangermanic policy was an effort to recapture Germany's past grandeur and unity, briefly achieved between 1890 and 1914". The Nazi law on cinema of 16 February 1934 submitted all films—and all screenplays before them—to a strict censorship control concerned with linguistic purity and especially content. Propaganda films received a great impulse by the Nazi government, unparalleled in the rest of Europe in terms of quantity and, sometimes, artistic value, as in director Leni Riefenstahl's famed achievements.

CINEMA AS ART AND ENTERTAINMENT— CINEMA AS AN INDUSTRY

For more than a century, images of America have exerted their charisma on Italian imagination. Following Ricci (2008: 126), the penetration of American culture into Italy began just a decade after the country's formation as a unified nation-state back in 1870. It was initially brought to Italy in the form of news and letters from the more than 4 million immigrants who arrived in the United States between 1880 and 1920. Its pre-eminence within the Italian society remains strong to the present day and is immediately recognisable by the dominance of American audiovisual programmes in both Italian cinemas and television channels. As a term of reference within the public discourse, America was second only to the Fascist regime itself, and today it can be said to be second to none.

Fascist cultural practices and the pervasive presence of American culture were then two of the most visible components of the social lexicon available to audiences during the fascist *ventennio*.[9] They are inextricably linked together in the repressive formation of state censorship guidelines and the state's political economy in the field of cinema. The state, Mussolini and Hollywood were the paradigmatic authorities for both cultural production and cultural reading in the period (Ricci 2008: 14). Hollywood values, regulated by the Hays code, became contentious for Fascist Italy only when international relations deteriorated from 1935 because of Ethiopia, the Spanish Civil War and Italy's alliance with the Nazis. As pointed out by Talbot (2007: 7–8), it was only then that these values came to be perceived as a threat to the Fascist way of life because they represented America, potentially an enemy. Newspapers were then advised not to publish articles about Hollywood because, in the words of Gaetano Polverelli (in Tranfaglia 2005: 169), "we have in Italy a film industry of our own to praise".[10]

Cinema was Mussolini's *arma più forte*, literally 'its strongest weapon', in indoctrinating the public, but Mussolini's regime (1922–1943) inherited a sector which lacked appropriate technology, capital and a robust infrastructure. There was no national film industry. If Italy's film industry before World War I had been a commercial and critical success at home and abroad, its economic basis was badly damaged in the war, and to make matters worse, nostalgia for a golden age was hampering innovation. In this general atmosphere, public taste turned most naturally to Hollywood. American films flooded into the country, introducing a thrill of modernisation which crossed all class and regional divisions. American film distribution networks expanded rapidly in the 1920s, attracting investment and loans from American banks. The Fox Corporation was the first to set up offices in Italy in 1921. MGM followed, establishing a distribution office in Rome in 1923, thus facilitating the penetration of US films into the Italian marketplace. Italian production companies became dependent on American technology, especially once the talkies arrived in 1929. American studios were able to increase their foreign market share by using domestic revenue to subsidise overseas sales. All this, combined with a growing appetite in Italy for the American dream, meant that American posters and publicity were ubiquitous. Between 1925 and 1930, it is estimated that 80 percent of the films screened in Italian cinemas were American (Talbot 2007: 144–146).

The first move of the Fascist state was, in November 1925, the nationalisation of Istituto Luce, which had the task of producing news, propaganda, education and culture for the home market. However, the support made available to production companies was modest, and with isolated exceptions, at the beginning there was little or no interest shown by the Fascist hierarchy in cinema as entertainment. Certainly, there was no strategic plan. Unlike the earlier grasp of other cultural industries,[11] more than a decade would pass before the Fascist state took any significant control over the production and distribution of fiction films as focus in the early years was centred on non-fiction and newsreels.

A number of studies have analysed the apparently anomalous relationship between this totalitarian regime and cinema. As Ricci (2008: 54) points out, the state's slow entrance into the country's cinematic affairs served to disjoin readings of Italian cinema during Fascism from Fascism itself. Even though Fascism intended to tackle the problem since the mid-1920s, it could not create a Fascist art which could break away from the forms of tradition. Besides, in the early years, the need to consolidate power meant that the government neglected the intellectual and artistic fields. The censorial apparatus was managed and controlled almost personally by Mussolini, and all cultural activities were sidelined, priority being given to the establishment of order and the reinforcement of power. In a famous speech on 26 May 1927, known as *Discorso dell'Ascensione* [Ascension Discourse], Mussolini (in Brunetta 1975: 31, my translation) clarified the terms of the issue:

> *Signori: è tempo di dire che l'uomo, prima di sentire il bisogno della cultura, ha sentito il bisogno dell'ordine. In un certo senso si può dire che il*

poliziotto ha preceduto, nella storia, il professore, perché se non c'è un braccio armato di salutari manette, le leggi restano lettera morte e vile.

[Gentlemen: it is time to say that men, before feeling the need for culture, felt the need of order. In a way one could say that, in history, the policeman preceded the teacher, because when one is not armed with a pair of safe handcuffs to use as weapons, laws remain just dead and cowardly words.]

The Fascism of the 1920s, founded on an ideology of violence and action, did not feel the need to foster collaboration with intellectuals as it actually viewed any form of intellectual activity with suspicion and even disdain.

Fascism started to get interested in cinema in a systematic and important way after the period of *squadrism* of the 1920s,[12] when it sought the support of a few intellectuals. They helped to project a new, interclassist image of Fascism and sought the middle classes as privileged interlocutors. It was at this moment that Fascism started to intervene in cinema with a series of provisions and aids to the industry, provisions which were quite useful to give credit to the open and tolerant image that the regime assumed in those years and which somehow were in contrast with the repressive legislation on censorship which, as discussed above, was being developed (Brunetta 1975: 29–32).

ITALIAN ON FILM

The passage from silent to sound movies can be considered a revolution both from a sociolinguistic standpoint and from the point of view of the power of cinema to influence and represent a dominant linguistic model for the language of the Italian people. When the industry took the first steps in sound cinema at the end of the 1920s, a fifth of the Italian population was illiterate. And for 20 years afterwards dialect would be, for four Italians out of five, the normal form of communication.

There were no common models or points of reference for a national language: the bureaucratic and institutional language could not be considered a model, as it would remain till the present day virtually a foreign language for many. The language used in the translations of American films started to create the reference model for spoken Italian. It is thanks to the cinema, and to dubbing in particular, that a certain way of speaking and communicating became common in language, losing gradually its direct affiliation to the more formal language of theatre and literature (Brunetta 1997: 12–14).

According to data presented by De Mauro (1991: 119–120), sound cinema in the post-World War I years attracted 48.6 percent of the population. A survey conducted by the Italian National Institute of Statistics (ISTAT) in 1958 gave an even higher percentage, 64.9 percent. According to the same survey, cinema's force of penetration in the poorest classes and regions is evident when we compare newspaper readers and cinemagoers: in the three regions of Puglia, Basilicata, and Calabria they were respectively 34.3 and 58.7 percent; in Sicily 38.4 and 64 percent; in Southern Lazio and Campania 45.9 and 63 percent; in Sardinia 50.9 and 69 percent. For a large portion of the Southern population, sound cinema was then the first source for learning the national language. Radio and television show the same characteristics, but their percentages are even higher: in the post-World War II years, those who listened to the radio and watched television were 80 percent of the population above 12 years of age.

Cinema reinforced in the general public the sense that dialects were forms related to what was still provincial, old-fashioned, oppressive and laughable in Italian society—forms, then, to be dismissed, to be considered as relics of the past. Twentieth-century *romanesco* (the Roman dialect, which has strong influences from Southern dialects) was increasingly used in cinema to give a cinematographic shape to popular, 'low-brow' content (De Mauro 1991: 124).

The problem of linguistic correctness started to be felt with the arrival of an industrially and culturally significant cinema, that is, with the passage from short to medium and long feature films in the 1910s. As films became longer, intertitles were also longer and more frequent, sometimes ridden with linguistic mistakes. It became a commonplace, for critics and members of the general public, to make comments in newspapers not only on the mistakes but also on foreign, exotic words seen (and later heard) on screen. These are for example the words of a reader of *La Grande Italia*, a weekly magazine, who, in 1911, anticipates the linguistic xenophobia of the Fascist *ventennio*.

> I would like to remark something which has lately become disgusting for viewers and humiliating for our national pride. I would like to mention several Italian companies and especially a notable one from Turin, which in all of their productions never forget to include that exotic 'something' without which they would not be welcome with clients [. . .] abroad. So we see that dear *police* [in English in the text] popping up everywhere in capital letters, and those signs, those notices written in any language but ours. (in Raffaelli 1991: 166, my translation)

The dubbed versions of foreign films gradually gave birth to that *italiano medio* that was suitable for "primary communicative functions" (Brunetta 1975: 427). They usually rejected dialectal solutions as a way to translate the linguistic varieties of the original works. Freddi (1929), for example, had an early phobia of dialects and vehemently opposed regionalisms and foreign words in favour of a more standard Italian. All English-language films were to be translated into 'pure'—that is, non-accented, non-dialectal—Italian. The suppression of accent and dialect in the Italian cinema during the 1930s provides one of the reasons why the national cinema of neorealism, developed between the 1940s and the 1950s, was considered a radical break from the past. Neorealism's use of non-professional actors speaking accented and dialectal Italian, that defined them in terms of their diverse regional identity, was therefore also a reaction against the very specific tenets of Fascist cultural policy (Talbot 2007: 60–64).

Another linguistic target of the Fascist government was address forms. As documented by Raffaelli (1991), the measures taken in this field, too, would have important consequences for the Italian language that was spoken in films. The polite pronoun *lei* was banned from use on 11 April 1938, a provision which concerned all state employees; from June of the same year the prohibition was extended to the cinema, so *lei* started to be excluded from both national and foreign productions. Another law of 9 June 1939 prohibited children from being given foreign names, which led to the preoccupation of Italianising the names of characters in films.

In April 1937, *Bianco e nero* published a long article by Ettore Allodoli on Italian language in cinema. His judgement is generally positive regarding Italian films but is quite critical of the dubbing of foreign films. He especially notes:

> We still hear continuously in conversation the pronoun *voi*, a polite form of address which is not common any longer, not familiar, not really ours, and which gives the dialogue a snobbish society tone, an exaggerated and false tone. [. . .] And what should we say of the extremely long imperfect tenses in the second person plural, which confer an excessively worldly character, that false worldliness I mentioned above, *mi amavate, mi baciavate, mi baciucchiavate*, [. . .] which would disappear with the integral restoration of the *lei* polite form of address. (Allodoli 1937: 10–11, my translation)

This position was completely reversed in an article by the same author written the following year:

> The opportune official dispositions on the abolition of *lei* and on the use of *voi* and of *tu* have concluded an interesting debate where the three famous monosyllables have each stepped forward to say, to defend, to demonstrate their verbal personality. *Lei* has been defeated, and rightly so, and its disappearance is an affirmation of *cameratismo* [Fascist comradeship] and of sharing of a faith which binds together so many millions of Italians in the expressions of speech and writing. (Allodoli 1938: 341, my translation)

In the period between the two articles, as the author himself remembers, one of the most important linguistic attacks of Fascism had taken place, started on 15 January 1938 with an article by Bruno Cicognani on the *Corriere della sera*. Fascist Italy was encouraged to abandon the use of *lei*, considered as a testimony of centuries of slavery, and to go back to the Roman and Christian *tu*, and to *voi* as a mark of respect and acknowledgement of hierarchy.

Accused of *lesa romanità*, that is an 'insult to Romanity', of being of foreign descent and a peculiarity of the hated bourgeois, *lei* rapidly became the object of a violent opinion campaign, and after a few weeks, its use was gradually prohibited for the members of the *Gioventù Italiana del Littorio* (the Fascist youth organisation) and the *Partito Nazionale Fascista* as well as in the schools, the army, the public offices, and the press.

While it is doubtful that this new habit was actually followed in the daily use of Italian, cinema was quick to react and eliminated immediately this criticised form, even though it was not the object of direct provisions on this particular theme. From then on only *voi* could be heard on the screens. From a form of snobbish elegance, *voi* had become an expression of consensus towards the regime, while *lei* sounded as the distinctive mark of antifascism (Ruffin and D'Agostino 1997: 69–74).

In 1937, the critic Giacomo Debenedetti (in Briareo and Debenedetti 1937: 155, my translation) wrote that dubbing was "defeating old *birignao* [drawl] and substituting the bad habit of 'acting' with the more precise and concrete habit of 'talking'". On the other hand Alberto Savinio (in Raffaelli 1996: 85, my translation) wrote in the newspaper *La Stampa*, on 7 January 1938, that dubbing was a

> language with neither character nor gender [. . .] insipid and colourless [. . .] Except for a very few cases, the Italian that these Anglosaxon shadows moving on the screen pretend to speak is so very palely 'Italian' that, in contrast, the Italian comically deformed by Laurel and Hardy becomes somehow genuine.[13]

Dubbing maintained the linguistic features developed by the Italian language in the 1930s, that is, the full respect of the Roman-Florentine pronunciation, a substantial adherence to the grammatical norm, the use of the conditional (which in Italian is considered, as is the subjunctive, more educated, thus not commonly used in the most popular dialectal forms) and the adoption of a standard and widely comprehensible lexicon. Italian dubbing remained virtually unaltered, both in the cinema and on television until the beginning of the 1970s. Only then can we register a remarkable turning point in dubbing, when dialects started to appear in the translation of the big American productions. The first important film where characters speak Sicilian is *The Godfather* (Francis Ford Coppola, 1972).[14] From then on, film dialogue has been marked at times by expressions in dialect, thus the linguistic gap between national productions and foreign imported productions has not been, since those years, as wide as in the previous decades (Raffaelli 1996: 27–28).

Apart from very few examples (e.g., the dubbing of *Il trono di sangue* [*Throne of Blood*], Akira Kurosawa, 1960), the only notable instance of a temporary digression into nonstandard forms of Italian is the following: in the early 1940s and immediately after the war, dubbing production in Italy ceased, and films started to be dubbed in the USA again by Italian

American actors before they were eventually distributed in Italy. The actors, especially those playing the minor characters, kept their marked original dialect pronunciations. One of the most remarkable examples is the comedy masterpiece *The Shop Around the Corner* (*Scrivimi fermo posta*, Ernst Lubitsch, 1940) which was dubbed by the Italian American couple Augusto and Rosina Galli, the latter a well-known actress in the USA. Augusto, who dubs James Stewart in the film, speaks a remarkably exotic Italian, the language of someone who has lived in the United States all his life. The effect is definitely foreign, but as the story is set in Budapest, the exoticism is not disturbing and is somehow in the nature of the film.

However, these are only a few exceptions in the history of dubbing in Italy prior to the 1970s. Overall, dialects and less-formal linguistic expressions gained ground only after the 1970s and are sometimes used today especially in comedy but also in dramatic films for the cinema as well as in television series.

TECHNICAL CONSTRAINTS IN DUBBING

As a form of revoicing, dubbing requires the substitution of the original voice of the actors by the voice of other actors in a different language. Although it can be considered a practice similar to voice-over in the sense that the original soundtrack is affected in the process, dubbing is, however, different from voice-over in two respects. Firstly, because the original soundtrack containing the dialogue is totally erased and substituted by a new one in the target language (TL). Secondly, because dubbing must adhere to lip synchronisation; that is, to sound 'natural' and authentic, the performed translation must match, as closely as possible, the lip movements of the speaker on the screen.

As in other forms of AVT—namely subtitling, surtitling, voice-over, interpreting and audio description—dubbing texts present an interrelation of two main different codes, the visual and the auditory, which in turn give rise to four communicative dimensions that need to be considered when translating: (1) verbal signs transmitted acoustically, (2) non-verbal signs transmitted acoustically, (3) verbal signs transmitted visually, and (4) non-verbal signs transmitted visually (Delabastita 1989). What changes in comparison with other forms of AVT is the type of relationship established among the different codes. According to Cary (1960), dubbing is a form of "total translation", as it requires the translator to take into account not only the semantic and pragmatic aspects of the dialogue and the gestures but also the phonological dimension—intonation, word length and prosody—so that technical lip synchronisation can be attained in a way that conveys the right illusion to the target viewers.

Lip-synch is generally regarded as one of the strongest constraints for dubbing translators: "In a hierarchy of priorities, synchronies take precedence over a faithful rendering of the ST content" (Chaume 2012: 72).[15] In the standard way the industry works, the adapter receives the rough translation carried out by the translator and has to modify some of the utterances to match them with the length of the original utterance (isochrony) and the lip movements of the person seen on the screen (phonetic or lip synchrony). Another important type of synchrony is the kinesic or body movement synchrony which seeks to come up with a translation that is in tune with the movements of the actors (ibid.: 68–69).

Pavesi (2006: 15–16) maintains that not all translators/adapters and actors respect all the constraints of synchronisation. Similarly, in his analysis of five dubbed films into French, Goris (1993) finds considerable variation in the behaviour of adapters concerning lip-synch. He concludes that phonetic lip-synch was respected in only 15 percent of extreme close-ups in one of the films analysed. On the whole, close phonetic lip-synch occurred in variable percentages, which are often very low. Meanwhile, isochrony is maintained in 100 percent of all close-ups in the five films, and it is often respected even in the case of long shots.

Over the years, dubbing for cinema in Italy has changed substantially in the area which Chaume (2012: 69–70), discussing Whitman-Linsen (1992), knows as "character synchrony". In this respect, dubbing practice has developed a marked tendency to imitate the vocal properties of the original voices, a feature which was not present in the early decades of this professional practice. Although this aspect has not been discussed in depth in the relevant literature, this evolution is, in my opinion, a fundamental dividing line between films that were dubbed before and after (roughly) the 1970s. More importantly, this dubbing trend has given rise to a schism between dubbing for cinema and dubbing for television, in the sense that mimicking the vocal qualities of the original actors does not seem to be a translational priority on TV.

Dubbing voices from the early decades to the 1970s were often characterised by the so-called *birignao,* a term which in theatre and cinema indicates a nasalised vocal rendition often accompanied by prolonged vowels and other phonetic alterations of natural speech. *Birignao* makes voices sound artificial, affected and only mockingly elegant. It is a dubbing mannerism which has still many aficionados among lovers of early cinema but is now out of fashion.[16]

Another characteristic of film dubbing in early cinema, which has now disappeared, was its tendency to consistently perpetuate character stereotypes: positive heroes had one typical kind of voice, villains had another one, whilst mothers and vamps were dubbed with yet other recurrent voices (Ottoni 2000: 8).

The current trend in cinema today, and for many years now, has been to choose dubbing actors who are even physically close to the original actors to reproduce their tones of voice as faithfully as possible. Although the imitation is not always perfect, the differences that a hearer can detect between the original and the dubbing actors, for example by switching to the original audio on a DVD, are often very slim and are mainly related to the different nature of the languages spoken and not to the dubbers' voices or their ways of acting. Such is the case, for example, of the unique voice adopted by Tom Hanks in *Forrest Gump* (Robert Zemeckis 1994), whose typical mannerisms and tone were seamlessly reproduced by Francesco Pannofino.[17]

In this respect, the difference between cinema and television dubbing actors is striking: although some dubbing actors may occasionally work in both media, this is not the norm, and some actors seem to prefer the more glamorous cinema productions over the more prosaic TV soap operas or sitcoms. For reasons probably linked to the different status of television productions when compared to cinematographic ones, dubbers for television do not appear to seek the kind of mimical reproduction which is now current in cinema, and TV voices and acting styles often show a considerable departure from the original.

TRANSLATORS/ADAPTERS: THE CASE OF ITALY

The spatial and temporal constraints typical of all modes of AVT have long influenced the attitude of translation scholars towards it in such a way that for many years, it was always considered a form of adaptation rather than proper translation (Díaz Cintas and Remael 2007: 9). In the particular case of dubbing, this perception is also mirrored in the way the professional practice is conducted, with the dichotomy between the figures of the translators and the dialogue writers or adapters. The former are the first to tackle the language transfer of the dialogue and generally have a tendency to stick to a more semantic translation, while the latter are traditionally perceived—by the general public and even by themselves—as freer from the constraints of semantics and, at the same time, more bound by the technical constraints and synchronies of dubbing. The result is that adapters often change greatly the text of the translations provided by the translators.

This duality between the translator and the adapter is particularly significant in dubbing in Italy (again with similarities in countries like Spain and Germany, see for example, Chaume 2004), where the "fuzziness" of the translation/adaptation/dubbing process has been well documented by Pavesi and Perego (2006). Translation for dubbing, as well as for subtitling, has always been the work of a team, and the individual role played by any of the professionals involved is generally difficult to ascertain. On many occasions, the researcher can only guess what the individual contributions may have been. Outside inner professional circles and apart from occasional interviews, little is known about who the actual translators of the films are in Italy, how many there are and how the translation work is distributed among them. Pavesi and Perego's study represents a preliminary step to bridge this lack of information. This invisibility of the translators makes it difficult to embark on a potentially interesting line of research, that is, one which would compare the actual translation carried out by the translator with the final version the audience hears on the screen.[18]

Adaptation is generally perceived by some professionals in the dubbing industry as a more prestigious task than translation, to the point that many Italian adapters often refuse to be considered translators and prefer to emphasise the artistic, creative and, to some extent, the most glamorous aspects of their professional activity (ibid.: 100).[19] This is generally an attitude taken by adapters who are not translators and may have a limited knowledge of the source language, which in Italy happens to be the case most of the time. Pavesi and Perego (ibid.: 104) conducted a survey by means of questionnaires and interviews, and according to their findings, "adaptors hardly ever hold a degree in translation, and their proficiency in the language(s) they translate and adapt from ranges from very low to very high and has, if at all, been acquired informally", while some of their interviewees stated that some of the most notable adapters do not know the language they translate from at all (ibid: 111).

The case of Tonino Accolla, one of the most prestigious Italian adapters, and one who would be on top of the hierarchical structure of dubbing professionals that Pavesi and Perego (ibid.: 102–103) infer from their data, can be considered exemplary. As well as being one of the most popular dubbing actors, having lent his voice to actors such as Jim Carrey, Eddie Murphy, Mickey Rourke, Kenneth Branagh and Homer Simpson, to name but a few of his impersonations, he was also in great demand as a dubbing director and adapter. His credits as a dialogue writer of Italian dubbed films are not limited to blockbusters and include for example a Shakespearean production, *Looking for Richard* (*Riccardo III—Un uomo, un re*, Al Pacino 1996). In a personal communication, Tonino Accolla (May 2006) acknowledged that he had never studied English formally, that his knowledge of the language had been acquired over the years and could not be defined as proficient, and that he used a pool of translators and advisers to translate the scripts that he later adapted.

It is evident that the adaptation process in Italy is traditionally associated with a creative work which enjoys great freedom. A quotation from the cited study by Pavesi and Perego (2006: 104) may give the picture of the socio-historical singularity of this professional category:

> The peculiarity of this profession is evident also in its history: the 'founding fathers' of today's adaptors were navy officers with a wide experience at all levels, who were open-minded and highly proficient in English—a competence acquired through the contact with native speakers—people who had travelled the world and had lived in several countries and in some cases had been war prisoners. Back in Italy after the Second World War, they were among the very few people capable of dealing with a foreign language and with foreign (American) producers (Paolinelli and Di Fortunato 2005: 17–19). Furthermore, they were the right people in the right place: most proposals for becoming dialogue translators and adaptors came from relatives working in the cinema industry. (Biarese 2000: 103–104)

This brings out an important issue, namely the centrality of family or acquaintance relations for entering the dubbing world, which apparently seems to be a decisive factor in this professional environment.

Although the authors go on to state that the family-business nature of the professional field of adapters was apparent especially in the past (ibid.: 105), my perception, based on long working experience in the cinema field, is that the dubbing business, whether family run or not, is still a very restricted circle hardly accessible to outsiders. The situation may be more varied today, especially in the case of dubbing for television, with smaller companies springing up every day, but it still remains closed as most of the dubbing directors and adapters in charge of these companies are professionals (often also dubbing actors) who have worked in the field for years.

In this type of translation, because there is hardly ever an individual translator, it may be more appropriate to refer to the professionals involved in the dubbing process (translators, adapters, dialogue writers, dubbing directors and dubbing actors) as the authors of the translation, working individually or in a team on the target version of an audiovisual product.

The problem of authorship, explored in recent years by scholars interested in the many declinations of the concept of 'voice' in translation studies (Buffagni, Garzelli and Zanotti 2011; Taivalkoski-Shilov and Suchet 2013), is all the more complex when the 'inhabitants' of a text (*inquilinos*, as Pérez López de Heredia 2003, calls the different participants in the creation of a text) are as many and sometimes as difficult to identify as in the case of dubbed dialogues.

CONCLUSIONS: CENSORSHIP TODAY

Films to be distributed in today's Italy, of either foreign or local production, need to be submitted to a censorship commission at the *Direzione generale cinema* [General Directorate for Cinema] of the *Ministero dei beni e delle attività culturali e del turismo* [Ministry for cultural heritage and activities and for tourism]. The legislation which rules its activities fundamentally dates back to 1962, the year in which law 161 on the revision of films and plays was approved. As in earlier times, the censorship commission is variously composed of a magistrate or law scholar, educators, psychologists, cinema professionals (distributors and producers), cultural experts in cinema, representatives of parents' associations and, if there are animals in the film, also representatives of animal rights' associations. Censorship is mainly concerned with the protection of minors, and after its verdict, distributors have 20 days to make an appeal or make the necessary cuts and editing to the film. No film can be screened in theatres without a 'certificate of revision', that is the formal approval of the cinematographic revision commission.[20]

Television policies on the other hand are not so overtly and uniformly regulated, and because of this, censorship and manipulation in this medium are slippery notions. Apart from a few references to broadcasting companies' internal regulations and guidelines, it is through the analysis of the data from the corpus that this issue is tackled in this book. By looking into the different translation strategies applied, the task is to detect whether these may reflect some type of technical or ideological manipulation in varying contexts.

It is, however, important to stress that what now stands out as authorial freedom, as the sometimes overly bold visibility of adapters involved in creating the Italian versions of films and programmes, is in fact rooted in a practice of intervention on audiovisual texts dating back to the early days of the dubbing industry.

NOTES

1. This linguistic operation, promoted by the Fascist government, is more thoroughly dealt with in the section of this chapter: "Italian on film".
2. The Council of Trent or Tridentine Council started in 1545 and closed, after several interruptions, in 1563.
3. This attitude dated back to the pre-Tridentine times and was traditionally linked to patristic studies such as Tertullian's *De Spectaculis* (*On the Spectacles*, written between 197 and 202 AD, www.the-faith.org.uk/tertullian1.html).
4. Giovanni Giolitti (1842–1928) was the prime minister of Italy for five times until 1921. In spite of the errors committed during his last mandate, his serious commitment and remarkable achievements in developing the new democratic state have earned the period in which he was in charge the label of *età giolittiana* [the age of Giolitti]. At the end of his last mandate, Giolitti tolerated the actions of the Fascist *squadre*, private armies engaged in brutal repression and violence, believing that their violence would finally be reabsorbed by the democratic system.
5. Istituto Luce, founded in 1924, was the first public institution in Italy responsible for the dissemination of didactic and informative audiovisuals. It later became a fiction film production and distribution company. As well as keeping up with these activities, it is today an important historical archive of audiovisual materials.
6. Luigi Freddi is a leading figure in the history of Italian cinema. He was a journalist and had been connected to the movement of Futurism. He became a member of the Fascist Party and editor of Mussolini's newspaper, *Popolo d'Italia*, in 1920. From 1922 he became director of the Propaganda Office of the *Partito Nazionale Fascista* and then *Segretario dei Fasci all'Estero* [Fascist secretary for foreign affairs]. From 1934 until 1939 he was the first general director for cinematography. Fallen in disgrace for a short period, he held a prestigious position again at the beginning of the 1940s as president of Cinecittà, of Enic (*Ente Nazionale Industrie Cinematografiche* [Cinematographic Industries National Organism]) and of the production and distribution company Cines. After September 1943 he moved to Venice, where he continued his relentless activity as an organiser of cinema productions. After the war, in 1949, he wrote a book of memoirs in two volumes, *Il Cinema*, which includes various official documents and is an invaluable source for the history of cinematography.
7. Particularly strict censorship guidelines were in vigour in the USA from 1930 to 1968, originally created by William H. Hays, president of the Motion Picture Association of America.

8. More information about the role and composition of intertitles can be found in Marie (1977) and Van Wert (1980).
9. It is one of the customary ways in which historians refer to the period Italy was ruled by the Fascist government of Mussolini, which lasted roughly 20 years, between 1922 and 1943.
10. Gaetano Polverelli was head of the *Ufficio stampa*, the press office of the Fascist government, from December 1931. He went on to become minister for popular culture in 1943.
11. In June 1925, the government founded the National Fascist Institute of Culture, headed by Giovanni Gentile. Six months later it called for the establishment of an Italian Academy. In 1926, the *Federazione Italiana delle Biblioteche Popolari*—the sprawling network of left-leaning local libraries—was placed under direct Fascist control. In the same year, a special commission on Fascist education banned 101 of the 317 history textbooks that were being used in Italian classrooms. And, by the end of 1926, all major non-Fascist newspapers had been totally suppressed.
12. See note 4.
13. Laurel and Hardy were in fact the inventors of their peculiar diction in the Italian dubbing of their films. They dubbed and acted their lines in various languages, including Italian, as in *Pardon Us* (1931) by James Parrot, their first long-length feature film. Their Italian was of course mispronounced to say the least. As the Italian version of the film, *Muraglie*, was very successful thanks to Laurel and Hardy's funny (mis)pronunciation, the Italian dubbers tried to imitate it in other films by the pair and in the redubbing of this same film (Quargnolo 1986: 30).
14. Another popular American film, Disney's *The Aristocats* (Wolfgang Reitherman 1970) played with different accents in Italian: the main cat character, Romeo, speaks in *Gli Aristogatti* with a heavy Roman accent (in original the cat is of Irish descent, but its accent sounds as General American) (see also Bruti 2009 on this film). This is, however, an animation film, so the impact was far less influential than that exerted by the realistic setting and characters of *The Godfather*.
15. Opinions against this assumption are mainly based on artistic, rather than technical, grounds. To mention one of the most authoritative, Federico Fellini did not think perfect lip-synch was very important and did not take any particular measure to respect the length of his actors' lines in redubbing (or, more precisely, revoicing by intralingual post-synchronisation), a practice which is customary in his films (Lionello 1994: 50).
16. Although there are no linguistic studies on *birignao* as such, the term is often referred to in essays on dubbing and theatre speech (see, e.g., Buttafava 1996: 126; D'Amico 1996: 212).
17. For a detailed account of the influence of dubbing on the perception of the characters, see Palencia Villa (2002).
18. Outside Italy, this topic has been explored by Richart Marset (2010).
19. This attitude is exemplified by the following excerpt from the *Contratto collettivo nazionale di lavoro del settore doppiaggio* [National collective contract of work in the field of dubbing] (2008); it is stated that "at the moment of signing the individual contract, the Adapter-dialogue author is given the text of the original dialogues in paper format or on a digital support as well as a copy of the film [. . .]. Such material should be kept with utmost care in order to safeguard the property of the work and cannot be given to third parties under any title, form or way, with the exception of the temporary transfer of the text only, for the time necessary to create a literal translation" (*Contratto collettivo nazionale*: 17, my translation).

20. *Ministero per i beni e le attività culturali* in collaboration with Cineteca di Bologna has recently launched a research programme on its own history of censoring practices by setting up an archive of censored film files and a data bank of deleted scenes, which can be accessed online: Italia Taglia—Progetto di ricerca sulla censura cinematografica in Italia: http://www.italiataglia.it (see also Mereu 2012).

REFERENCES

Allodoli, Ettore. 1937. "Cinema e lingua italiana". *Bianco e nero* 4: 4–11.
Allodoli, Ettore. 1938. "Voi, tu, lei". *La lettura: rivista mensile del Corriere della Sera*, 341–346.
Biarese, Cesare. 2000. "I dialoghi dell'ammiraglio. Intervista a Ferdinando Contestabile", in Alberto Castellano (ed.) *Il doppiaggio: profilo, storia e analisi di un'arte negata*. Roma: AIDAC, 103–108.
Briareo, Gustavo and Giacomo Debenedetti. 1937. "Il doppiaggio in Italia". *Cinema* 29: 154–156.
Brown, Lesley. 1993. *Oxford English Dictionary*. Oxford: Oxford University Press.
Brunetta, Gian Piero. 1975. *Cinema italiano tra le due guerre: fascismo e politica cinematografica*. Milano: Mursia.
Brunetta, Gian Piero. 1997. "Introduction", in Valentina Ruffin and Patrizia D'Agostino (eds.) *Dialoghi di regime*. Roma: Bulzoni Editore, 11–32.
Bruti, Silvia. 2009. "From the US to Rome passing through Paris—accents and dialects in The Aristocats and its Italian dubbed version", in Michela Giorgio Marrano, Giovanni Nadiani and Christopher Rundle (eds.) *The Translation of Dialects in Multimedia*, InTRAlinea special issue, http://www.intralinea.org/archive/article/1713.
Buffagni, Claudia, Beatrice Garzelli and Serenella Zanotti (eds.). 2011. *The Translator as Author: Perspectives on Literary Translation*. Berlin: LIT Verlag.
Buttafava, Giovanni. 1996. "Il doppiaggio è veramente un male minore?", in Eleonora Di Fortunato and Mario Paolinelli (eds.) *Barriere linguistiche e circolazione delle opera audiovisive: la questione doppiaggio*. Roma: Aidac, 124–126.
Cary, Edmond. 1960. "La traduction totale: cinéma". *Babel*, 6(3): 110–115.
Chaume, Frederic. 2004. "Film Studies and Translation Studies: two disciplines at stake in Audiovisual Translation". *Meta* 49(1): 12–24.
Chaume, Frederic. 2012. *Audiovisual Translation: Dubbing*. Manchester: St Jerome.
Cicognani, Bruno. 1938. "Abolizione del 'Lei'". *Corriere della Sera*, 15 gennaio: 3.
Contratto collettivo nazionale di lavoro del settore doppiaggio. 2008. www.fia-actors.com/uploads/SAI%20doppiaggio%202008.pdf, last accessed 31st March 2015.
D'Amico, Masolino. 1996. "Dacci un taglio, bastardo! Il doppiaggio dei film in Italia", in Eleonora Di Fortunato and Mario Paolinelli (eds.) *Barriere linguistiche e circolazione delle opere audiovisive: la questione doppiaggio*. Roma: Aidac, 209–216.
Danan, Martine. 1991. "Dubbing as an expression of nationalism". *Meta* 36(4): 606–614.
Delabastita, Dirk. 1989. "Translation and mass-communication". *Babel* 35(4): 193–218.
De Mauro, Tullio. 1991. *Storia linguistica dell'Italia unita*. Bari: Laterza.
Díaz Cintas, Jorge. 2001. *La traducción audiovisual: el subtitulado*. Salamanca: Ediciones Almar.
Díaz Cintas, Jorge. 2012. "Clearing the smoke to see the screen: ideological manipulation in audiovisual translation", in Jorge Díaz Cintas (ed.) *The Manipulation of Audiovisual Translation*, *Meta* special issue 57(2): 279–293.

Díaz Cintas, Jorge and Aline Remael. 2007. *Audiovisual Translation: Subtitling*. Manchester: St Jerome.
"Un esperto parla". 1928. *Bollettino diocesano*. Padova.
Fawcett, Peter. 2003. "The manipulation of language and culture in film translation", in María Calzada Pérez (ed.) *Apropos of Ideology. Translation Studies on Ideology-ideologies in Translation Studies*. Manchester: St Jerome, 145–163.
Freddi, Luigi. 1929. "Dei dialetti". *Il popolo d'Italia*, 14 August.
Freddi, Luigi. 1949. *Il Cinema*. Roma: L'Arnia.
Gili, Jean. 1981. *Stato fascista e cinematografia: repressione e promozione*. Roma: Bulzoni Editore.
Goris, Olivier. 1993. "The question of French dubbing: towards a frame for systematic investigation". *Target* 5(2): 169–190.
Italia Taglia—Progetto di ricerca sulla censura cinematografica in Italia: www.italiataglia.it, last accessed 31st March 2015.
Jauss, Hans Robert. 1982. *Toward an Aesthetic of Reception*. Brighton: Harvester Press.
Joyce, James. 1922/2010. *Ulysses*. London: Wordsworth; Italian translation: 1960. *Ulisse* (translated by Giulio De Angelis). Milano: Mondadori.
Joyce, James. 1926. "Il monologo di Molly Bloom" (translated by Antonio Pizzuto). *L'Ora*: 3.
Katan, David and Francesco Straniero-Sergio. 2003. "Submerged ideologies in media interpreting", in María Calzada Pérez (ed.) *Apropos of Ideology. Translation Studies on Ideology-ideologies in Translation Studies*. Manchester: St Jerome, 131–144.
Laura, Ernesto G. 1961. "Vicende legislative della censura in Italia", in Ernesto G. Laura (ed.) *La censura cinematografica: idee, esperienze, documenti*. Roma: Edizione Bianco e Nero, 4–17.
Lawrence, D. H. 1928/2010. *Lady Chatterley's Lover*. London: Penguin.
Lionello, Oreste. 1994. "Il falso in doppiaggio", in Raffaella Baccolini, Rosa Maria Bollettieri Bosinelli and Laura Gavioli (eds.) *Il doppiaggio. Trasposizioni linguistiche e culturali*. Bologna: Clueb, 41–50.
Mack Smith, Denis. 1959. *Italy: A Modern History*. Ann Arbor: University of Michigan Press.
Marie, Michel. 1977. "Intertitres et autres mentions graphiques dans le cinéma muet". *Image et son* 316: 68–74.
Mereu, Carla. 2012. "Censorial interferences in the dubbing of foreign films in Fascist Italy: 1927–1943", in Jorge Díaz Cintas (ed.) *The Manipulation of Audiovisual Translation*, Meta special issue 57(2): 294–309.
Ottoni, Filippo. 2000. "Introduzione", in Alberto Castellano (ed.) *Il doppiaggio: profile storia e analisi di un'arte negata*. Roma: Aidac, 7–9.
Palencia Villa, Rosa María. 2002. *La influencia del doblaje audiovisual en la percepción de los personajes*. PhD thesis. Barcelona: Universitat Autònoma de Barcelona.
Paolinelli, Mario and Eleonora Di Fortunato. 2005. *Tradurre per il doppiaggio. La trasposizione linguistica dell'audiovisivo: teoria e pratica di un'arte imperfetta*. Milano: Hoepli.
Pavesi, Maria. 2006. *La traduzione filmica. Aspetti del parlato doppiato dall'inglese all'italiano Disponibilità immediata*. Roma: Carocci.
Pavesi, Maria and Elisa Perego. 2006. "Profiling film translators in Italy: a preliminary analysis". *The Journal of Specialised Translation* 18: 99–144.
Pérez López de Heredia, María. 2003. "Las rescrituras españolas del teatro norteamericano: textos, paratextos, metatextos", in Ricardo Muñoz Martín (ed.) *Actas del I Congreso Internacional de la Asociación Ibérica de Estudios de Traducción e Interpretación*. Granada, 12–14 de febrero de 2003. AIETI 1, 469–493.

Pio XI. 1929. *Divini Illius Magistris.* http://w2.vatican.va/content/pius-xi/it/encyclicals/documents/hf_p-xi_enc_31121929_divini-illius-magistri.html, last accessed 23rd July 2015.
Quargnolo, Mario. 1970. "La censura cinematografica da Giolitti a Mussolini". *L'Osservatore politico letterario* 7(July): 65–76.
Quargnolo, Mario. 1986. *La parola ripudiata.* Gemona: La Cineteca del Friuli.
Raffaelli, Sergio. 1991. *La lingua filmata. Didascalie e dialoghi nel cinema italiano.* Firenze: Le Lettere.
Raffaelli, Sergio. 1996. "Un italiano per tutte le stagioni", in Eleonora Di Fortunato and Mario Paolinelli (eds.) *Barriere linguistiche e circolazione délle opere audiovisiva: la questione del doppiaggio.* Roma: Aidac, 25–28.
Ricci, Steven. 2008. *Cinema & Fascism, Italian Film and Society, 1922–1943.* London: University of California Press.
Richart Marset, Mabel. 2010. *La alegría de transformar.* Valencia: Tirant Lo Blanch.
Ruffin, Valentina and Patrizia D'Agostino (eds.). 1997. *Dialoghi di regime.* Roma: Bulzoni Editore.
Rundle, Christopher. 2000. "The Censorship of Translation in Fascist Italy". *The Translator* 6(1): 67–86.
Savinio, Alberto. 1938. *La Stampa*, 7th January.
Schäffner, Christina. 2003. "Third ways and new centres—Ideological unity or difference?", in María Calzada Pérez (ed.) *Apropos of Ideology. Translation Studies on Ideology—ideologies in Translation Studies.* Manchester: St Jerome, 23–41.
Taivalkoski-Shilov, Kristiina and Myriam Suchet (eds.). 2013. *La traduction des voix intra-textuelles / Intratextual Voices in Translation.* Montréal: Éditions québécoises de l'œuvre.
Talbot, George. 2007. *Censorship in Fascist Italy, 1922–43.* London: Palgrave Macmillan.
Tertullian. n.d. *De Spectaculis (Of Spectacles).* Transl. by T. R. Glover. www.the-faith.org.uk/tertullian1.html, last accessed 31st March 2015.
Tranfaglia, Nicola. 2005. *La stampa del regime 1932–1943. Le veline del Minculpop per orientare l'informazione.* Milano: Bompiani.
Van Wert, William. 1980. "Intertitles". *Sight and Sound* 49(2): 98–105.
Whitman-Linsen, Candace. 1992. *Through the Dubbing Glass: The Synchronization of American Motion Pictures into German, French, and Spanish.* Frankfurt am Main: Peter Lang.

Filmography

The Adventures of Marco Polo (*Uno scozzese alla corte del Gran Khan*), Archie Mayo, 1938, USA.
The Aristocats (*Gli aristogatti*), Wolfgang Reitherman, 1970, USA.
Der blaue Engel (*The Blue Angel/L'angelo azzurro*), Josef von Sternberg, 1930, Germany.
Forrest Gump, Robert Zemeckis, 1994, USA.
The Godfather (*Il padrino*), Francis Ford Coppola, 1972, USA.
Halleluja! (*Alleluja*), King Vidor, 1929, USA.
Kumonosu-jo (*Throne of Blood/Il trono di sangue*), Akira Kurosawa, 1960, Japan.
Looking for Richard (*Riccardo III—Un uomo, un re*), Al Pacino, 1996, USA.
Pardon Us (*Muraglie*), James Parrot, 1931, USA.
The Shop Around the Corner (*Scrivimi fermo posta*), Ernst Lubitsch, 1940, USA.
The Show of Shows (*La rivista delle nazioni*), John Adolfi, 1929, USA.
Sous les toits de Paris (*Under the Roofs of Paris/Sotto i tetti di Parigi*), René Clair, 1929, France.

4 Culture Specific References

DEFINITIONS

The first problem in defining a culture specific reference derives from the fact that, in a language, everything is practically culture specific, including language itself (Franco Aixelá 1996: 56–57).

Relatively few scholars in Translation Studies, and even less in AVT, offer systematic definitions of CSRs. In what follows, an overview is offered of the most relevant academic approaches to these cultural elements, which have been referred to using a vast array of terms: 'culture specific,' 'culture bound references/elements/terms/items/expressions', *'realia'*, 'allusions' or, more generally, 'cultural references'. 'Culture specific' (or, interchangeably, 'culture-bound') is the preferred definition of this kind of elements in this work, although the more general term of 'cultural references' may occasionally be used.

One of the earliest scholars who attempted to pinpoint the characteristics of CS terms and expressions is Finkel (1962: 112), for whom these elements "stand out from the common lexical context, they distinguish themselves for their heterogeneity, and consequently they require a reinforcement of attention in order to be decoded".

Only a few years later, Vlahov and Florin (1969: 438), defining more precisely the nature of CSRs, which they termed *'realia'*, offered a now classical definition, according to which these elements are words or composed locutions typical of a geographical environment, of a culture, of the material life or of historical-social peculiarities of a people, nation, country, or tribe and which, thus, carry a national, local or historical colouring and do not have precise equivalents in other languages. Tomaszczyk (1983: 289) argues that even if, by definition, the set of culture-bound lexical units should include only those items which represent "objects, ideas, and other phenomena that are truly unique to a given speech community", the boundary between culture-bound terms and non-culture specific vocabulary is a fuzzy one and depends merely on a matter of degree.

CSRs could be included in the wider group of untranslatable words, as Leemets (1992: 475) defines them:

> Every language has words denoting concepts and things that another language has not considered worth mentioning, or that are absent from the life or consciousness of the other nation. The reasons are differences in the ways of life, traditions, beliefs, historical developments—in one word, the cultures of the nations. Also, differences can be observed on conceptual level. Different languages often nominate concepts from different viewpoints, and they also tend to classify them slightly differently.

Although Leemets focuses more generally on all lexical gaps between two languages, her emphasis on culture makes the quotation perfectly suitable to culture-bound material. The last part of the quotation in particular—"different languages often nominate concepts from different viewpoints"—synthesises an aspect which is not always stressed by other scholars: similar concepts or objects may exist both in the SC and in the TC, but the *viewpoint* from which the two cultures involved look at them may be different.

Mailhac (1996: 133–134), on the other hand, is more specifically concerned with the nature of CSRs, which he defines even more interestingly by stating that: "by cultural reference we mean any reference to a cultural entity which, due to its distance from the target culture, is characterized by a sufficient degree of opacity for the target reader to constitute a problem". This definition is particularly useful because, by referring to the degree of opacity, Mailhac emphasises how the interpretation of cultural references is characterised by a varying degree of subjectivity. His mention of the distance between TC and SC indicates the relativity of the concept, which is the main cause of the difficulty in finding univocal and unambiguous strategies for the translation of these references.

It can also be safely stated that the understanding of these particular elements may constitute a problem even for a part of the SA or readership since not all people from a given country or community will necessarily know the meaning of a given reference, even if it is supposed to belong to their own culture. This may be due to different educational and social backgrounds or generation gaps, as people belonging to a given social class or age group may be completely ignorant of an item which is extremely popular for another class or age group. Nevertheless, however ignorant part of the SA may be, that does not imply that these elements are not at least potentially retrievable by the culture of origin, while only a small or negligible portion of the TA might have easy access to the same reference.

Another scholar who refers explicitly to the problem these items constitute in translation is Franco Aixelá (1996: 58) for whom these references are

> those textually actualized items whose function and connotations in a source text involve a translation problem in their transference to a

target text, whenever this problem is a product of the non-existence of the referred item or of its different intertextual status in the cultural system of the readers of the target text.

His definition clearly states how the translation problems may stem from two different situations: an objective one (the "non-existence of the referred item") and a relative one (the "different intertextual status" of the TT with respect to the ST). The latter situation is relative as the intertextual status keeps shifting and varying because the relationship between two cultures can change in a very short period of time. In other words, because of their dynamic nature, "no two elements retain the same relationship over a sufficient period of time" (ibid.: 57). Hence, the translation strategies used at some point in time may not be appropriate at other time.

The problems of translating CSRs are also underlined by the influential scholar Leppihalme (1997). This author prefers to refer to a particular set of CSRs which may create a culture 'bump' to the translators, that is, a small-scale culture shock which may cause problems in finding the right cultural equivalent. Although the term 'allusion' is given considerable latitude by other scholars, Leppihalme (ibid.: 3) uses it in the sense of a "pre-formed linguistic material (Meyer 1968) in either its original or a modified form, and of proper names, to convey often implicit meaning". The author goes on to state that her focus is less on allusions as a literary phenomenon and more on them as a translation problem requiring the use of appropriate translation strategies. The great quantity of examples she provides shows that what Leppihalme means by allusions is a wide range of possibilities from simple quotations (which may or may not be obscure to the TC or even the SC) to more oblique hints. An important aspect of allusions is literature's ability "to create new literature out of the old" (Johnson 1976: 579), that is to say, to involve the reader in a recreation by alluding to partly hidden meanings that the readers should be able to get and then use to achieve a deeper knowledge of the work. Since the 1980s, the growing interest of researchers in audience reception and in the role of the reader has made this a particularly relevant point (Leppihalme 1997: 8). Readers who recognise a creative allusion, that is, an allusion which has not become stereotyped because of too many repetitions, attain a deeper understanding of a text, which means that they are in some way participating in its creation and can consequently feel a sense of fulfillment because they feel part of a restricted circle of readers who are on the same wavelength as the author (ibid.: 32–33). As Cuddon (1999: 27) also states:

> It is often a kind of appeal to a reader to share some experience with the writer [. . .]. When using allusions a writer tends to assume an established literary tradition, a body of common knowledge with an audience sharing that tradition, an ability on the part of the audience to 'pick up' the reference.

56 Culture Specific References

Kosunen and Väisänen (2001) consider "culture-bound terms" as a form of allusion, and Gambier (2001: 230–233) discusses examples of allusions that could also be classified as culture specific items. For her part, Ruokonen (2010: 34) considers that

> on the whole, it seems that the overlap between the three concepts of allusion, quotation and culture-specific item is more of [sic] a question of delimitation (keeping the material manageable) than of definition (establishing essential differences between the concepts).

Although, as we have seen, Leppihalme awards the term 'allusion' a wide scope, making it coincide in fact with CSRs, it is also true that the focus of her study appears to be limited to literary references. The quoted definition by Cuddon also supports the view that the term 'allusion' is privileged when made in connection with literary or, more broadly, artistic works. Without theoretically excluding other objects (i.e., commercial products, celebrity names etc.), the term 'allusion' is preferred, in the studies on this subject, when it refers to more complex intertextual elements and concepts. Allusions create two kinds of links in the extratextual world: they connect the alluding text to previous literary tradition (Irwin 2002: 521) and create a sense of connection between the author and the reader, "cultivating intimacy and forging a community" (ibid.: 522).

In the field of AVT, few are the authors who have provided definitions of CSRs. Among the scholars who have tackled this problem in reference to dubbing is Agost Canós (1999). For this author, cultural elements are those items "which make a society different from another, so that each culture has its idiosincracies" (ibid.: 99, my translation). She goes on to write that cultural elements are

> specific places of any city or country; aspects related to the history, the art and the customs of a given society and age (songs, literature, aesthetic concepts); very popular characters, mythology; gastronomy, institutions, currencies, systems of weight and measurement; etc. (ibid., my translation)

One of the downsides is that the groupings she proposes are quite generic. However, her analysis becomes far more interesting when she underlines the importance of the context in understanding these elements and when she draws our attention to the references which are shared by the SC and the TC, which makes them less exclusively rooted in the SC (ibid.: 100). She also contends that the cultural power that some cultures exert on others—for example, the ubiquitous USA culture on the rest of the world—may contribute to reducing the cultural gap between two given cultures. In Chapter 3, I discussed the historic pervasiveness of the US culture in Italy and within the field of cinema in particular.

Always in the field of audiovisuals but in reference to subtitling, Santamaria Guinot (2001: 237, my translation) defines cultural references as

> the objects and events created within a given culture which have a distinctive cultural capital, intrinsic to the whole society and with the potential of modifying the expressive value conferred to the individuals who are related to that value.

Although the focus of this definition is on elements created within a given culture, the author also calls the attention to the fact that all cultural references should be taken into account when conducting an analysis and not only those which can diverge between the SC and the TC (ibid.: 239).

In the discussion of these items, and again in a study on subtitling, Pedersen (2005: 2) coins yet another term:

> Extralinguistic Culture-bound Reference (ECR) is defined as reference that is attempted by means of any culture-bound linguistic expression, which refers to an extralinguistic entity or process, and which is assumed to have a discourse referent that is identifiable to relevant audience as this referent is within the encyclopedic knowledge of this audience.

Although the author explains his choice of the term 'extralinguistic' by considering these cultural items as not being part of a language system, thereby explicitly excluding what he calls "intra-linguistic culture-bound references, such as idioms, proverbs, slang and dialects" (ibid.: 1), the term 'extralinguistic' would exclude not only the linguistic features mentioned by the author but also expressions relative to concepts and customs—for example, 'when the ball drops', in reference to a New Year's Eve tradition in the USA—or, more importantly, to quotations and allusions to other texts which would be difficult to define as extralinguistic entities. It could be argued that we could not possibly consider a reference to the "Yes we can" speech by Barack Obama or to "two houses both alike in dignity" from Shakespeare's *Romeo and Juliet* as 'extra' linguistic, and it would seem inappropriate not to consider them as CSRs as they are in fact quintessential cultural references specific to a given culture. The difference which does exist between this kind of intertextual references and the other types of CSRs will be discussed more thoroughly in the following sections of this chapter.

Díaz Cintas and Remael (2007: 200) also define these elements as extralinguistic, and in fact, in the classification they propose, quoted in the following section, they list such extralinguistic items grouped under the headings of geographical, ethnographic and socio-political references, thereby excluding what I term 'intertextual references' (also discussed in the same section), that is, the realm of allusions.

The subjective, dynamic and relative nature of CSRs is underlined by Ramière (2007). These items create networks of associations which are specific to the culture in which they are rooted. The fruition of cultural elements is based on shared experiences, and this is the first reason for the difficulties encountered when translating them. Besides, seeing that cultures are dynamic systems, the complexity of the translation process is emphasised by the fact that these networks of semantic and intertextual associations are continually changing (ibid.: 63).

Chiaro (2009: 156), in reference to both dubbing and subtitling, gives the following definition:

> CSRs are entities that are typical of one particular culture, and that culture alone, and they can be either exclusively or predominantly visual (an image of a local or national figure, a local dance, pet funerals, baby showers), exclusively verbal or else both visual and verbal in nature.

Chiaro is one of the few scholars to address explicitly the visual, and not exclusively verbal, nature of some CSRs; a concept which has been somehow taken for granted by AVT scholars in their definitions of these elements. At the same time, Chiaro's reference to "one particular culture, and that culture alone" seems to be too limiting as, unless we embark on a philological and etymological research into their origin, on many occasions cultural elements may belong to more than one culture.

To conclude this section on some of the working definitions of CSRs, I would like to stress the importance of the concept of 'cultural embeddedness' for AVT in general and for the translation of CSRs in particular. Quoting Pym (2010: 107–131), but see also Ramière (2010), "texts belong", that is to say that they are rooted in a context of space and time in which they are best comprehensible.[1] Similarly to books, to which Pym mainly refers, films are the product of a specific context, and this is evident not only in the verbal language used but also in the components that make part of the image: geographic place, historical period, dress code, non-verbal signs of communication, cinematographic conventions, editing, formal qualities, and so on. Thus the concept of belonging refers to a complex network of relations which links the original film to its context of production. This raises the issue of cultural specificity and of its transfer into another sociocultural universe. As Pym (ibid.: 127) again underlines, the more a text "presupposes its place of production", the more it is difficult to transfer it to another culture. The privileged relationship between author and SA allows the latter to understand all or almost all of the signs contained in the text. The task of the translator is then to loosen the "bonds of belonging" (ibid.: 145) of a text to its original culture and to find strategies to embed it in the TC. In what concerns the different types of AVT, dubbing seems to be the one that most promotes this new embedding because, by deleting the ST linguistic component and replacing it with that of the TT, it tends to favour the acceptability of the new text by the TC. Nonetheless, the problems linked to the necessity of blending harmoniously the different communication channels and the different filmic codes (Chaume 2004) are still highly relevant and can be considered to be most peculiar of AVT when compared to other types of translation.

CLASSIFICATIONS OF CULTURE SPECIFIC REFERENCES

Sapir (1949/1985: 36) describes the close connection between vocabulary and culture in these terms:

> Vocabulary is a very sensitive index of the culture of a people and changes of the meaning, loss of old words, the creation and borrowing of new ones are all dependent on the history of culture itself. Languages differ widely in the nature of their vocabularies. Distinctions which seem inevitable to us may be ignored in languages which reflect an entirely different type of culture, while these in turn insist on distinctions which are all but intelligible to us.

Thus, every language has different semantic ranges and different ways of grouping objects and concepts. If this is true for the general vocabulary, it is even truer for culture specific vocabulary which carries with it a whole world of images and associations. Some of the leading scholars who have dealt with the study of CSRs have proposed classifications to group them. From a translational perspective, taxonomies of CSRs have also been put forward by various scholars, including some of the ones whose definitions have been discussed in the previous section.

The cultural categories proposed by Newmark (1988: 95), and adapted from Nida (1945), are well known, and they are often quoted in the relevant literature. They are based on various lexical fields associated to a culture specific lexicon:

- Ecology (such as terms relating to flora, fauna, geography, etc.)
- Artefacts (material culture including references to food, clothes, house, towns and means of transportation)
- Social culture (words referring to work and leisure)
- Organisations, customs, activities, and so on (such as political and administrative references, religious, historical or artistic terms)
- Gestures and habits

Although, as Ramière (2007: 49) points out, this classification is useful to organise these kinds of elements, the truth is that it has been criticised for its rigidity and lack of contextualisation (Mailhac 1996: 137–139; Kwiecinski 2001: 129–134).

Other authors provide even more general lists divided into various categories. For example, Bugarski (1985: 159) refers to "cultural elements and systems—ranging from food, clothing, work, leisure, and sports to economy, politics, religion, law, and philosophy"; whilst Rantanen (1990: 55–58) puts forward a taxonomy based on Newmark's, in which CSRs are listed in terms of lexical fields with a general lack of systematicity. A more detailed taxonomy, however, is included in Díaz Cintas and Remael (2007: 201), who distinguish among the following:

Geographical References

- Objects from physical geography: savannah, mistral, tornado
- Geographical objects: downs, Plaza Mayor
- Endemic animal and plant species: sequoia, zebra

Ethnographic References

- Objects from daily life: tapas, trattoria, igloo
- References to work: farmer, gaucho, machete, ranch
- References to art and culture: blues, Thanksgiving, Romeo and Juliet
- References to descent: gringo, Cockney, *Parisienne*
- Measures: inch, euro, pound

Socio-Political References

- References to administrative or territorial units: county, *bidonville*, state
- References to institutions and functions: *Reichstag*, sheriff, Congress
- References to sociocultural life: Ku Klux Klan, Prohibition, landed gentry
- References to military institutions and objects: *Feldwebel*, marines, Smith & Wesson

These classifications include mostly lexical categories, although the reference to Romeo and Juliet in the art and culture field, as the title of the play or as character names, seems to broaden the concept by possibly including quotations and allusions to works of art and literature.

Being one of the most detailed, this list of categories has been considered as a point of reference in this work, although as we will see, this book focuses on the relationship between references and a given culture or cultures more than on finding clear-cut categories for each item.

Pedersen (2007: 109) proposes a non-exhaustive list, limited to the purpose of his study, which includes "domains" deduced from the corpus he analysed and "taken into consideration inasmuch as they can be used to explain subtitling regularities" (ibid.: 108). Pedersen's comment to his taxonomy is important in that it emphasises how even if these categories overlap to a certain extent, and thus compiling an exhaustive taxonomy is probably utopian and futile, domains are still useful if employed more generally to explain subtitling behaviour (ibid.: 110). In other words, taxonomies cannot be used to determine without ambiguity whether a given element belongs to one particular category or another, but they can be very useful to analyse the nature of CSRs.

In discussing the parameters which influence the choices of the translators, Pedersen (2005: 10–15) introduces the terms of 'transcultural' and 'monocultural' references and the notion of the 'centrality of reference', all of them invaluable concepts for the present reflection on the nature of CSRs.

One of Pedersen's fundamental parameters is 'transculturality', that is the way in which, in the modern world, cultures are interconnected one to the other. This implies that cultural elements which were once familiar only to one culture are now accessible at a global level and thus are not, strictly speaking, culture specific, if by this term we mean 'specific to a single culture'. That is the case of references which today can be considered universally known. Pedersen proposes to make a distinction between (1) transcultural elements, which are globally known and "retrievable from common encyclopedic knowledge of the ST and TT audience", for example, Jacques Cousteau (ibid.: 10–11); (2) monocultural elements, of which Pedersen does not provide an example in the quoted study, but which, unlike the former, "can be assumed to be less identifiable by the majority of people of the TT audience than it is to the relevant ST audience, due to differences in encyclopedic knowledge" (ibid.: 11); (3) microcultural elements, which are so specific that they are known only to a limited part of even the SA, for example, the name of a street of a given area.

The second parameter proposed by Pedersen (ibid.: 11–12) is "extratextuality", which determines if a CSR exists outside the ST (as most cultural references do) or not. If they do not, then references are considered "text internal"; that is, they are created ad hoc for the text at hand. In our corpus, for example, the fictional café Central Perk in *Friends* is text internal as it does not exist in reality and is a fictional element of the text.

The third parameter is the "centrality of reference", which Pedersen (ibid: 12–13) rightly considers one of the most influencing. It refers to references which either on a macro or micro level, or both, are central to the text; that is, they may represent a central theme or leitmotif of the text. He mentions the example of the film *The Bridges of Madison County* (Clint Eastwood, 1995) in which the CSR contained in the title, the bridges of that particular USA county, are central to the plot of the film. This centrality obviously influences the choices of the translators.

The four following parameters proposed by Pedersen (ibid.: 13–14) are conceived especially for subtitling. 'Intersemiotic redundancy' derives from the polysemiotic nature of audiovisual texts in which the information carried by the different channels may sometimes overlap, so that, for a subtitler, there may be no need to translate verbal information that is also conveyed by images or the soundtrack, particularly when faced with the need of reducing the ST. In dubbing, intersemiotic redundancy is rarely an influencing parameter as theoretically all the verbal information can be translated.

'Cotext', as a further influencing parameter, is also thought of with the subtitling process in mind: redundant information may be contained in the rest of the text (e.g., repetitions in a dialogue), and thus there is no need to translate them if this information is otherwise conveyed. In dubbing, all redundancies are theoretically translated, and any manipulations or omissions are due to considerations which are in fact the object of the present analysis.

'Media-specific constraints' are also conceived by Pedersen as constraints on the subtitling process. This parameter, however, may also be applied to dubbing in the form of lip-synch and isochrony (see Chapter 3).

The final parameter quoted by Pedersen (ibid.: 14–15) concerns 'paratextual considerations', that is, issues related to the *Skopos* theory (see Chapter 2): TT audience-related issues such as age groups, familiarity of the audience with the main theme of the programmes, and so on; broadcasting-related issues such as the nature of the broadcaster, the time of programming, and so on; and issues related to pragmatic matters such as deadlines and remuneration of the translators.

Most of Pedersen's parameters, especially the first one involving transculturality, have influenced the proposed categories on the nature of CSRs used in the present work and illustrated in the following section.

Chiaro (2009: 155) also refers to the problem of translating CSRs in audiovisuals by including them in what she terms "translational hurdles", which she divides into the following:

1. Highly culture-specific references (e.g., place names, references to sports and festivities, famous people, monetary systems, institutions, etc.)
2. Language-specific features (terms of address, taboo language, etc.)
3. Areas of overlap between language and culture (songs, rhymes, jokes, etc.)

Interestingly, Chiaro considers three macro categories of which only the first directly refers to CSRs. However, the third, the areas of overlap between language and culture, is also related to cultural elements. To my knowledge, she is the first scholar in AVT to tackle the problem, however in passing, of the difficult categorisation of some cultural elements due to their linguistic nature and not, as it is customarily defined, extralinguistic nature. The "songs" she mentions in the third subdivision, for example, are certainly cultural elements, although a chorus from *Grease* (Randal Kleiser 1978) or an aria by Rossini would hardly be included in a taxonomy composed of mainly lexical items.

The need for a functional division into domains that might help define the nature of the CSRs analysed in the present corpus has also guided my attempts to find a suitable classification, which is discussed in the next section.

The Point of View of the Target Culture

The different classifications discussed so far mainly propose groupings into lexical fields. Moreover, although most scholars stress that culture specificity depends on the relationship between SC and TC, the relative nature of this relationship does not appear to be reflected in their lists, which consider the elements as specific of a single culture and objectively problematic.

The taxonomy proposed in this book is mainly concerned with conceptual rather than lexical groupings and, as in the case of Pedersen's, is meant to be used as a practical tool for analysis. It is an attempt to account for frequent overlappings between categories and has been primarily conceived by taking the point of view of the TA in its relationship with the ST. Only this relationship is important or at least can be taken into account by the translator and the researcher, as these professionals cannot make objective statements on the degree of problematicity or even on the degree of familiarity of a given item by any given culture. In other words, to consider the word 'Brooklyn' as globalised or, in Pedersen's words, transcultural, because most people in the Western world are familiar with this area of New York thanks to US films, TV shows and today's easier travelling conditions, increases the already high risk played by subjectivity in defining CSRs. Their location within the boundaries of the TC's encyclopedic knowledge is in fact hard to determine: if we consider, for example, the Italian TC involved in this analysis, it can be highly problematic to define the degree of dissemination even of a widely known term such as 'Brooklyn', let alone other items which may be equally transcultural but do not enjoy the same degree of popularity. The present classification thus takes into account the nature of CSRs within the relationship between TT and ST and from the exclusive point of view of the TC.

Acknowledging that a concept like 'national identity' may still have meaning in today's globalised world, in this work I will refer to British culture, Italian culture, US culture and so on, as to entities to which a given cultural element belongs. This means that it has its origin and has been absorbed as a cultural concept or object and is felt as an integral part of that culture by the SC itself, while it is felt as exotic in various degrees by other cultures. This exoticism results from the intimacy or the distance that exists between a culture and a given element. There can be a very low degree of exoticism in a CSR which has long found its way outside its country of origin (e.g., Halloween), a medium degree of exoticism (e.g., falafel), or a high degree of exoticism (e.g. Massimo Troisi, one of the most popular, but seldom exported, Italian comedians), but these varying degrees can only be assessed in the relationship between the TC and the other cultures (SC and any other third culture). In this sense, no objective claim can be made on the supposed exoticism of a given element which in fact may be exotic for the TC but far from exotic for a third culture: there are books, songs, films and so on, which are popular in their country of origin and exported only to selected countries where they may enjoy a high degree of success while remaining completely unknown elsewhere (e.g., the horror film director Dario Argento is very famous in Italy and Japan, while he may be completely unknown to non-*cinéphiles* elsewhere). The concepts of 'specialistic' and 'elitarian' are also problematic as virtually any CSR can be very well known to a small or large portion of specialists. The relative nature of CSRs is thus considered in this analysis as a quintessential quality pertaining to these items.

The present classification also introduces a distinction between real-world and intertextual references. The former are references to non-fictional persons, objects and events: living or once living people, food, currency, institutions, celebrations and everything which composes our reality. The latter are intended as explicit or indirect allusions to other texts, which create a bond between the translated text and other literary, audiovisual or artistic texts. The nature of these references is different from the nature of real-world references, and allusions to and quotations from other fictional works are included here in the domain of CSRs more explicitly than it has been done in the classifications discussed above. Their different nature, however, is acknowledged, as allusions create a special relationship between the audience and the text itself, and to a certain extent, they presuppose a disposition on the part of the TA to retrieve information and make associations which are usually more than general as they require a certain degree of specialist knowledge. The nature of textual references such as 'pizza' or 'Pavarotti' is conceived in this work as being of a different nature than a quote such as "Ground control to Major Tom" (from *Space Oddity*, David Bowie 1969) or images of red shoes and a rainbow alluding to *The Wizard of Oz* (Victor Fleming 1939).

The following categories to classify CSRs are thus proposed in Table 4.1:

Table 4.1 Classification of CSRs[2]

Real-world references
1. Source culture references
2. Intercultural references
3. Third culture references
4. Target culture references
Intertextual references
5. Overt intertextual allusions
6. Covert intertextual allusions
7. Intertextual macroallusions
All of the above can be:
• Verbal or non-verbal cultural references
• Synchronous or asynchronous cultural references

Culture Specific References 65

In this classification, conceived for methodological purposes, the first comment to make is relative to the macro division. Although intertextual references naturally participate in the same categories as real-world references—that is, they may belong to the SC, to a third culture and so on—their origin is considered here as a secondary aspect compared to their universal nature and potentially timeless status of works of art, literature and popular culture. This status makes them, in a way, super cultural. Whatever the origin of *Hamlet, Mona Lisa,* the *Odyssey,* Super Mario, *Mr Tambourine Man* and Mikey Mouse, it is the intertextual relationship created between two cultural texts, and the effect this relationship has on the audience, that sets these elements apart from the others.

The second, more important comment on this classification is that it assumes without ambiguities the point of view of the TC audiences and potential translators and categorises CSRs from this point of view. The focus is on the target recipients and on the relationship they establish with the ST. What this means in practice is more fully explored in the following sections.

Source Culture References
Source culture references are those belonging to the SC, despite their degree of popularity outside the boundaries of their original culture. In many cases they may coincide with those that Pedersen (2005: 11) terms 'monocultural' references and 'microcultural' references, which can be references to people, things and places who or which have remained only locally known. They can also be references to the history, the politics or some social aspects of the SC, which are historically and socially embedded in it in such a way that their "bonds of belonging" (Pym 2010: 145) are particularly hard to cut. SC references as conceived here can also cover a part of the transcultural area. Transcultural elements are for Pedersen (2005: 10–11) those which, though specific to the SC in its original usage, have also become so widely disseminated that they can safely be considered of global knowledge. More specifically, transcultural elements are generally known to the people of the TC, who have developed a good degree of acquaintance with the elements in question, be they the name of a famous person (Madonna), a brand (McDonald's), a place (Cambridge), an institution (the CIA) and so on. By a 'good degree of acquaintance' it is meant that the reader or the member of the audience is fully aware of most of the cultural echoes and interconnections that the element has created in the collective imagination. The name 'Cambridge', for example, will trigger in the mind of an Italian educated person a network of associations which are generally shared by people in England and in the rest of the world: small English town, prestigious university, upper-class education, Received Pronunciation, importance of sports like rowing and so on, although other, more local references will inevitably be lost to an international audience.

However, for the present classification, and in keeping with the aim of selecting the point of view of the TA, cultural echoes and associations are not objective enough parameters to define a category. SC references are thus terms which are strictly embedded in the SC, and however well-known in the TC, they do not have a direct, provable, objective bond with the TC, something concrete which is not merely connections and associations that some members of the TA, however many they may be, can make thanks to their personal knowledge of the SC. In other words, no matter how famous the commercial chain Starbucks is, it is considered here as an SC reference as none of its stores has so far been opened in Italy and the associations an Italian can make relative to it are linked to films and travels abroad. This cannot be said of many other brand names which, whatever their origin, may in fact be included in other categories, as the following section explores.

If we assume the point of view of the TC, many elements which are generally and quite vaguely defined as 'transcultural' can find a more definite categorisation. However, if we abandon the point of view of the TC, we may tread on very slippery ground: for example, how global is a 'globalised' element? How can we measure its degree of transculturality? As it is indeed very hard to answer these questions, it is safer to assume the point of view of the TC and classify a given item in terms of its distance from the TC itself.

Intercultural References

An intercultural reference is a reference which has forged a dialogue between the SC and the TC. This relationship can be objectively verified not only in terms of vague notions such as 'popularity', or 'associations' but rather by measurable and proven facts: an SC singer whose records are distributed in the TC, a brand which is commercialised in the TC and so on. The name 'Mc Donald's', for example, would stimulate in the TA a web of associations which are not only linked to its country of origin, the USA. It would be associated, by someone from Rome, to a long queue of teenagers waiting for their hamburgers in Piazza di Spagna and to the complaints of the nearby Valentino's *haute couture* firm about the smoke coming from the restaurant's chimney more readily than to any drive-through in a Californian boulevard. In other words, intercultural references are those originally SC references which have been absorbed, in various degrees, by the TC, which has, to some extent, made them their own. Intercultural references are also those few elements which both the SC and the TC consider their own, no matter their origin which, in certain instances, can be debatable (e.g., Santa Claus).

I would argue that classifying a reference as either SC or intercultural reduces the risk of excessive subjectivity in classifying and then translating CSRs, meaning that an objective classification would arguably guide the translator towards a choice that would mirror the actual relationship of the TC with the given element. Choosing this type of classification, instead of thinking in more subjective terms, would mean relying not too much on the translator's education and personal associations and more on an objective evaluation of the audience's means to understand the meaning of a CSR. What Fawcett (1998: 114–123) calls the "presuppositional knowledge"; that is, the background assumptions of the translator in the act of translating may not coincide, in fact, with the TC's or part of the TC's actual knowledge. Often, an element that was considered monocultural the first time it was translated into a given TL may have become more widespread by the time subsequent translations are required. The matter is not secondary as it does influence the choice of translation strategy to a great extent, and using less subjective categories such as SC reference and intercultural reference may help to overcome some of the problems.

Third Culture References

This category refers to elements which do not originally belong either to the SC or the TC but to a third culture. References to third cultures are not generally quoted as a category in itself, and other researchers, like Pedersen (2005: 10–11), prefer to include them in the wider sector of transcultural references. I consider that they deserve a category of their own as the challenges they pose to the translator are of a different nature than those created by the SC or intercultural references illustrated earlier. In this sense, third culture references rely on the degree of familiarity of the SC with a given third culture (or at least with the particular element taken from it), which may be different from the TC's degree of familiarity.

Food and festivities, but also celebrities, often belong to this category, and it is safer to make assumptions on these particular elements from the point of view of the (Italian, in this case) TC. Hence, when translating a US production, even words like 'scone' or 'Victorian age' can be considered elements belonging to a third culture, the British, even if language and history make the British and the US cultures particularly close. Even popular British food such as scones, widely diffused in the USA, is felt as exotic to a certain degree in that country, if we have to judge from the following excerpt from *Friends*:

EXAMPLE 4.1: *FRIENDS* SEASON 5 EPISODE 12

CONTEXT: Ross is upset because he has learnt that his English ex-wife is getting married again.

ORIGINAL FILM DIALOGUE

GUNTHER: Here's your **scone**.
ROSS: Oh, thanks Gunther. (*He takes it, hands the plate it's on to Rachel, sets it down on the table, and proceeds to destroy it.*) STUPID **BRITISH SNACK FOOD!**
CHANDLER: Did they teach you that in your anger management class?

68 Culture Specific References

> PHOEBE: Hey. You know what might help you deal with it? You two are in the past. You can't be mad about the past. Are you still mad about, you know, the **Louisiana Purchase**?

ITALIAN ADAPTATION	BACK-TRANSLATION
GUNTHER: Il tuo **plum cake**. ROSS: Stramaledetto **cibo inglese**. CHANDLER: Te l'hanno insegnato nei corsi di autocontrollo? PHOEBE: Sai che cosa può aiutarti? Prova a ragionare così. Tu e Emily siete il passato e non puoi prendertela per il passato. Sei ancora arrabbiato per **le rivolte degli indiani**?	GUNTHER: Your **plum cake**. ROSS: Super-damned **English food**. CHANDLER: Did they teach you that in self-control courses? PHOEBE: You know what can help you? Try to reason this way. You and Emily are the past, and you can't take it out on the past. Are you still angry about **the Indian revolts**?

The fact that scones belong to a culture different from the North American one is presented as established. However popular in the USA, they are ordered by Ross as food exemplifying the British culture he now hates. The point of view of the Italian TC is different since scones are felt even more exotic and cannot normally be found in Italian stores. To find a still British but less exotic item, translators have resorted to 'plum cake', which on the other hand is a quite popular snack in the TC. Incidentally, the final SC reference to the historical event of the Louisiana Purchase, the acquisition by the USA of the French territories in 1803, has been substituted by a more generic but still SC-oriented reference to 'the Indian revolts'. Thus, in this excerpt, CSRs have not changed categories in translation, but strategies have been adopted to bring them nearer to the TA.

To sum up, third culture references, together with the TC references that follow, are those which best demonstrate the importance of taking the point of view of the TC in dealing with CSRs as they are the ones in which the distance between SC and TC is best exemplified.

Target Culture References

This category includes references which are, to a certain extent, exotic for the SC but are far from exotic for the TC as, in fact, they belong to its own cultural landscape. It is essential that in these cases translators take into account the effect caused by the reference on the TA, which may be very different from the effect the same element had on the SA.

I will give here an example not taken from the present corpus as the not very frequent but interesting references in this field are best illustrated in all their implications in the respective analyses of the case studies.

Culture Specific References 69

The example proposed here is taken from James Ivory's 1985 transposition of E. M. Forster's *A Room with a View* (1908/2006), which is paradigmatic because it is a film full of Italian references:

EXAMPLE 4.2: *A ROOM WITH A VIEW (CAMERA CON VISTA,* JAMES IVORY 1985)

CONTEXT: Lucy, a young English girl, has mentioned a novel written by a friend to her fiancé Cecil and to George Emerson, who is in love with her.

ORIGINAL FILM DIALOGUE

LUCY: No wonder the novel's so bad. Still, one ought to read it, I suppose.
CECIL: There's an absurd account of a view.
LUCY: Do read it. Do you like our view, Mr. Emerson?
GEORGE: My father says there's only one perfect view—the view of the sky over our heads.
CECIL: I expect your father has been reading **Dante**.

ITALIAN ADAPTATION	BACK-TRANSLATION
LUCY: Non stupisce che sia un brutto libro, però si dovrà leggerlo, immagino, avendola conosciuta.	LUCY: No wonder it is a bad book, but one will have to read it, I imagine, having known her.
CECILIO: C'è un'assurda descrittiva ambientale che ti risparmierei.	CECILIO: There's an absurd ambient description that I would spare you.
LUCY: Leggila. Lei che ne pensa del nostro paesaggio?	LUCY: Read it. What do you think of our landscape?
GEORGE: Mio padre dice che esiste solo un panorama perfetto—il panorama del cielo sulle nostre teste.	GEORGE: My father says that only one perfect panorama exists—the panorama of the sky above our heads.
CECILIO: Immagino che suo padre abbia letto **l'Alighieri**.	CECILIO: I imagine your father has read **Alighieri**.

The authors of the Italian version have felt the need to adjust the reference to Dante in transferring it to the TT, not simply leaving it as a loan. In a film full of references to Italy and to Italians, the substitution of Dante's name with his more pompous, though less used surname, Alighieri, contributes, if not to render the element as exotic as it was for the SA then at least to transmit the grandiloquence of the character of Cecil. Thus Cecil's idiolect is defined more in the details of his sterile intellectualism and artificiality than in his being an 'Italianate', as he loves to call himself.

It is important to stress that this category tends to be more sensitive in dubbing than in other types of AVT as any CS reference to the TC and/or language risks to be lost in translation if uttered in the TL. Although this is also true with other types of AVT, the presence of the original soundtrack in subtitling allows the audience to notice the code switching between the two languages and forces the translator to activate different solutions in the subtitles, whereas in dubbing, the acoustic channel must convey both the semantic and the paralinguistic import of a phrase, and the audience is not necessarily alerted to any code switching. A careful evaluation of the diegetic value of these rhetorical devices in the original is thus mandatory before proceeding to their translation.

Even more than with the third culture references already discussed, TC references emphasise the relative status of CSRs which acquire their full meaning only in the interaction between the two cultures involved in the translating process.

Overt Intertextual Allusions

Allusions are CSRs of a different nature when compared to those already illustrated as they do not establish a link with a cultural element from reality as such but an intertextual connection with items from other fictional texts and works. These can range from the great works of art and literature to popular art and culture: from Tolstoy's *War and Peace* (1865–69/2006) and Picasso's *El Guernica* to the most recent pop song, comic book, video game, soap opera and so on. As it has been argued earlier, these CSRs create a special relationship between audiences and texts, and that is why they are considered of a different import from the references previously illustrated. The referents of allusions belong to a body of "assumed shared knowledge" (Kaskenviita 1991: 77), which may be general or specialised, part of the SC, of the TT or of any third culture but whose nature is different from real-world CSRs.

The category of overt allusions includes intertextual references explicitly quoted in the text. Formal implicitness or covertness is traditionally considered a defining characteristic of allusions (Pucci 1998: 6). Genette (1982: 8), for example, adopted this view in his influential overview of the different types of intertextuality. In contrast, other researchers studying allusions have argued for a more flexible approach highlighting that allusions can also appear as exact quotations or proper names (Ben-Porat 1976: 110) or otherwise "preformed linguistic material" (Leppihalme 1997: 3) and even state openly their source reference (Irwin 2001: 287).

When elements of this nature are widely known, there is the further difficulty for the translator of having to refer to the title or quotation as it was officially translated in the TL, with the risk of losing the meaning/reference of the original allusion in the new context. In this sense, it is particularly difficult to adopt a suitable strategy in the translation of song titles and lyrics if they are not familiar to the TC. In cases where the content of the song is necessary to understand the joke, the adoption of a localising strategy, that is, the use of a song which belongs to the TC or is at least better known to it, is often chosen to get the message effectively across.

Whether highbrow or lowbrow, these references are generally perceived as having a sophisticated quality to them. They represent a sensitive category in translation because of what could be termed 'the presumed ignorance' of the TA on the part of some translators. In other words, presuming that the TA might be ignorant of a particular content, translators may feel the need to simplify or otherwise alter the content itself for the audience to understand. This is true with excerpts from the great literature, as in the case of a theatre director of a contemporary play yelling angrily at his actors, "A plague on both your houses", from Shakespeare's *Romeo and Juliet* (*Friends*, Season 3 Episode 22)—arguably a quote not immediately detectable even by a sizeable portion of the SA—but also with much simpler references to titles of popular songs, films or TV programmes.

Covert Intertextual Allusions

From what has been illustrated in the former subparagraph, we may derive that covertness is the quintessential characteristic of allusions, while overt allusions may be classified as allusions by extension. As Irwin (2001: 287) states, it is clear that an allusion is a type of reference, but in "what way it must be covert, implied, or indirect is a matter of some dispute".

This category includes indirect references and more or less covert allusions to other texts. They are often felt as problematic and sometimes too cryptic to be kept unaltered in the TT, even when an official translation may already exist. The series *Life on Mars* contains a few examples of this kind. The following exchange shows how hard it can be for the translator to detect such echoes in a text:

EXAMPLE 4.3: *LIFE ON MARS*, SEASON 1 EPISODE 1 (PILOT)

CONTEXT: Sam, a police investigator of our time, has just mysteriously plunged into the year 1973 and has met his rude, new boss.

ORIGINAL FILM DIALOGUE

SAM: Alright. Surprise me. What year is it supposed to be? [. . .] Who the hell are you?
GENE: Gene Hunt, your DCI, and it's 1973. Almost dinner time. I'm havin' 'oops.

As is more extensively illustrated in Chapter 6, this is part of one of the series' covert intertextual allusions to other audiovisual programmes, in this particular case a British police series of the 1970s, *The Sweeney* (I. K. Martin 1975–1978), which informs much of the show's visual and verbal style. Gene's phrase is a hint to one of *The Sweeney*'s most quoted replies: "We're the Sweeney son, and we haven't had any dinner". It is doubtful that the majority of the SA would have got this allusion had the writers of the show not mentioned the influence that the 1970s programme exerted on them. This illustration shows how important the role of the paratext as well as that of the cotext are in understanding the nature and value of CSRs in general and of covert allusions in particular.

Intertextual Macroallusions

Sometimes it is an entire programme which, at a macro level, turns out to be an allusion to another text, playing from beginning to end with the presumed familiarity of the public with a given hypotext.[3] This operation can be carried out overtly, when a work is explicitly based on the ST—for example, Season 4 Episode 5 of *South Park* (Trey Parker and Matt Stone 1997-in production), which states from the very first lines of the script that it is an adaptation of Charles Dickens's *Great Expectations* (1861)—or it can also be carried out covertly, disseminating hints and clues for the members of the audience so that they can recognise the hypotext(s) behind the hypertext. This is the case, for example, of the film *Bridget Jones's Diary* (Sharon Maguire, 2001)—a covert macroallusion to Jane Austen's novel *Pride and Prejudice* (1813 /2012)—and, even more covertly, of the film *Bridget Jones: The Edge of Reason* (Beeban Kidron 2004), a subtle allusion to Jane Austen's *Persuasion* (1818 /2007). As in the case of these two films, macroallusions are grasped by the audience by capturing dialogue excerpts, character and plot similarities, as well as visual hints, and by joining all the pieces to get a bigger picture. However, macroallusions appear to be more than just the sum of several overt and covert allusions, and they can be fully grasped and appreciated in the wider context of the entire text which, only when taken as a whole, will fully clarify its bonds with the hypotext.

To sum up, macroallusions do not work so much (or not only) as accumulation of details but as a general concept of the film or programme, which might be expressed in either the visual or verbal style, or in a series of details, or in an explicit parody of plot, characters and contents. Macroallusions can be overt—for example in declared parodies—but they are more often covert and quite subtle.

In this corpus, intertextual macroallusions have been found in the series *Life on Mars*, and they are discussed in depth in Chapter 6.

Non-verbal Cultural References

As mentioned in the categories breakdown, all the references mentioned can be either verbal or non-verbal as well as synchronous or asynchronous. This section looks into those quintessentially audiovisual references which are non-verbal.

Non-verbal CSRs can be visual and/or acoustic, and their impact can be markedly exotic: even the ringing tone of a telephone, which can vary from country to country, will tell us that the home we see on the screen is far away from ours. These elements are, in audiovisual programmes, some of the most characterising in terms of place and time. Their embeddedness into the SC cannot be rooted out, and these elements cannot be transferred into the TT by any translation strategies other than by eliminating them, that is, muting or editing them out, by adding an explicitating caption on screen, or by simply leaving them untranslated as signs of foreignness. When the addition of a caption is not deemed necessary, the latter is generally

Culture Specific References 73

the policy resorted to by adapters, while muting and cutting are somehow extreme options, seldom chosen in nowadays cinema but still resorted to in television. The series *Life on Mars* is an example discussed in Chapter 6.

Often neglected by adapters, the potential of non-verbal references should be fully grasped as these signs are sometimes part of more complex verbal and non-verbal communicative acts. In the field of humour, this is what Zabalbeascoa (1996: 251–255) knows as "complex jokes", which combine the acoustic and the linguistic codes to achieve their humoristic effect. Díaz Cintas (2001: 122) adds noise as one of the dimensions to this category, by which he means not only noise in itself but also suprasegmental and paralinguistic information such as intonation and regional accents. Non-verbal signs are easier to deal with in subtitling than in dubbing as they may provide information which does not need to be repeated in a verbal form in the subtitle.

Nonetheless, as highlighted by Díaz Cintas and Remael (2007: 46) when discussing all types of AVT, "the most difficult situation arises when a linguistic sign, a phrase, refers metaphorically to an iconographic sign or image that the source and target culture do not share". Visual and, I would argue, some acoustic references may be hard to grasp for the TA, and adapters often choose creative ways of conveying the information, as in the following example, which includes a complex joke in the broader sense intended by Zabalbeascoa (1996: 251–255).

EXAMPLE 4.4: *SIX FEET UNDER*, SEASON 1 EPISODE 2

CONTEXT: Nate is mocking his brother David, whom he suspects of having had sex the night before.

ORIGINAL FILM DIALOGUE

NATE: (*speaking in a robot voice, similar to HAL in* 2001: A Space Odyssey) Morning, Dave. Aren't those the same clothes you had on yesterday?
DAVID: Everything I own looks alike.
NATE: I sense you're not being completely honest with me, Dave.
DAVID: Have you changed any since you were 14?
NATE: (*laughs*) Hey. **I'm all for you getting laid,** believe me. (. . .)
NATE (*always keeping the HAL voice*): We are looking quite spiffy in that suit, Dave.
DAVID: That's so clever. **You're talking like the computer in the movie.** Wow, you're funny.

ITALIAN ADAPTATION	BACK-TRANSLATION
NATE *(parla con voce normale):* Buon giorno, David. Che è successo, hai messo gli stessi vestiti di ieri?	NATE (*speaks with a normal voice*): Good morning, David. What happened, are you wearing the same clothes as yesterday?

> DAVID: Sono quelli del lavoro, tutti uguali.
> NATE: Strano ma sento che mi stai nascondendo qualcosa, David.
> DAVID: Hai smesso di crescere quando avevi quattordici anni, vero?
> NATE: Se c'è una donna faccio il tifo per te. (. . .)
> NATE *(parla normalmente)*: Con quel completino sei un vero schianto, David.
> DAVID: **Grazie mille Mr 2001 Odissea nello strazio.** Non sei divertente.
>
> DAVID: They are work clothes; they're all the same.
> NATE: Funny, but I feel you're hiding something from me, David.
> DAVID: You stopped growing up when you were 14, right?
> NATE: If there's a woman, I'm all for you. (. . .)
> NATE *(speaks normally)*: With that little suit you're a real knockout, David.
> DAVID: **Thank you very much, Mr 2001 A Pain Odyssey.** You're not funny.

The allusion to Stanley Kubrick's classic film *2001: A Space Odyssey* (1968) is quite subtle as in the original dialogue the film is only evoked by Nate's intonation, in his imitation of the computer Hal, by David's vague words ("you're talking like the computer in the movie"), and by the fact that the main character in Kubrick's film is also called David. In Italian, though, Nate speaks with a normal voice, and it is by manipulating the film title in David's last line—*Grazie mille Mr 2001 Odissea nello strazio* [Thank you very much, Mr 2001 A Pain Odyssey]—that the dialogue manages to achieve, by compensation, its goal of sarcastic humour.[4] The dynamics of the joke change completely from a joke containing a paralinguistic element to one based on a wordplay on allusion.

In conclusion, whether they refer to elements deeply embedded in the SC or to more universally spread items, non-verbal CSRs are felt as problematic in dubbing. In this type of translation, the substitution of the original voices with those of the dubbing actors, and sometimes also the replacement of ambient and other diegetic sounds and noises with a different soundtrack (see Chapter 5), may result in distancing the target audience from the CSR.

Asynchronous References

Scholars have tended to discuss cultural references almost exclusively as objects and people set in a certain place and in terms of their geographical distance from the TC. However, elements are also set in a specific time as well as place, and in this respect they are time specific as well as culture specific. Time-specific references, that is cultural elements viewed as not only embedded in a specific culture but also in a specific time, tend to grow more opaque as years go by, when they do not become accepted and are absorbed by culture(s) in such a way as to become virtually timeless. In translating a Jane Austen novel, for example, a translator will encounter innumerable CSRs which today's (source and target) readership may not be able to appreciate if it were not for the occasional footnotes: dances, foods, clothes and so on which belong to a given historical period. However, if all CSRs are also potentially time specific, this category may be useful to analyse films and TV programmes whose specific aim is to depict another (past/future) era, notably costume dramas and the so-called period TV fiction programmes which have become so popular in recent years. What makes this situation interesting is that cultural references depicted in these programmes do not belong to the same time in which the members of the audience live, thus they are 'asynchronous references' in relation to their point of view. The closer to our time the depicted epoch is, the more we realise how relatively short the lifespan of some CSRs is in people's memories. That is to say, although it may seem normal that the customs and mores of a 16th-century person feel remote to us, it is perhaps surprising that the way of life of people from the 1960s or 1970s should feel as distant as it does sometimes and to see how much we have forgotten about our collective past. The main concern with this category being the point of view of the TC, it is also important to acknowledge that some of these elements may not be recognised by some members of the SC. In encountering these elements that belong to their own culture but come from a different time, some SC viewers may experience the type of culture shock felt when travelling to a remote country. As explored in Chapter 6, most of the fascination that period programmes exert is due to their inherent and universal exoticism—an exoticism that, I would argue, is felt more poignantly the less, and not the more, remote the series is as the relative closeness of the period will facilitate the audience's identification.

The category of asynchronous references will be useful in the analysis of the period series included in the present corpus, *Life on Mars*, and it can also serve as a tool to read CSRs that come from other texts and from a different generational perspective. In this order of ideas, the same sense of vertigo in encountering asynchronous CSRs may be experienced when dealing with futuristic films and series, only that in this case the elements will be most probably fictional and would thus have only a diegetic reality which sets them apart in a category of their own.

The strategies that can be used to translate CSRs are discussed in the following sections and serve as a methodological tool for the subsequent analysis of the present corpus.

STRATEGIES FOR THE TRANSLATION OF CULTURE SPECIFIC REFERENCES

Taxonomies of translation strategies to deal with CSRs are mostly discussed, directly or indirectly, within more general studies on translation. Among these, one of the most influential is Vinay and Darbelnet's taxonomy (1958/2002: 128–137), first published in 1958 in their *Stylistique comparée du français et de l'anglais*. Although it is not applied to CSRs in particular, it has been taken as a point of reference by numerous scholars also in this specific field. The authors use the terms 'methods' and 'procedures' rather than 'strategies', but the terms appear to be used synonymously by them and by other scholars also mentioned in this chapter. Their two umbrella translation strategies are direct and oblique translation, each of them covering a range of procedures:

Direct Translation

1. Borrowing
2. Calque
3. Literal translation

Oblique Translation

4. Transposition
5. Modulation
6. Equivalence
7. Adaptation

The scholars' comments for each procedure contain insights which are directly useful for the present analysis. The authors note, for example, that though borrowing is the simplest translation method, it merits discussion because translators often use it as a stylistic method to foreignise a text by introducing and leaving unaltered terms that would sound exotic to the TC. Calque is explained as a special kind of borrowing which translates literally each of the elements of an expression from the ST, as in 'skyscraper' = *grattacielo*. The third direct procedure, literal translation, appears to have much in common with calque, but the authors seem to apply it to longer phrases transferred into the TL by observing the latter's grammatical norms, as in 'to be or not to be, that is the question', translated in Italian with: *essere o non essere, questo è il problema*.

Among the oblique translation procedures, Vinay and Darbelnet list transposition (the replacement of one word class with another without changing the meaning of the message) and modulation (a variation of the form of the message by a change in point of view and a different expression of the same concept), which are both types of grammatical recategorisation. The first can be exemplified by the Italian equivalent of the proverb 'where there is a will, there is a way' = *volere è potere* [to want is to be able to], where 'will' is a noun and *volere* is a verb, although the meaning of the phrase remains virtually the same. An example of modulation is for instance: 'I don't think I'll come' = *Credo che non verrò* [I think I won't come].

As for the last two oblique translations, they generally involve more complex procedures. Equivalence is used to render a situation using completely different structural and stylistic methods. The authors note that a feature of equivalence is that it is often of a syntagmatic nature and affects the whole range of a message, with the result that most equivalences are fixed (idioms, clichés, proverbs, etc.). An example would be: 'curiosity killed the cat' = *tanto va la gatta al lardo che ci lascia lo zampino* [the cat gets so close to the lard that it loses its paw]. The seventh and last method, adaptation, is considered as the extreme limit of translation. According to the authors, it is used when the SL message is unknown to the TC, in which case translators have to create a new, equivalent situation. Thus adaptation can be described as a form of situational equivalence. For example, 'Pass me the peanut butter' was translated with the phrase: *Passami il formaggio* [pass me the cheese] in the Italian version of *Some Like It Hot* (*A qualcuno piace caldo*, Billy Wilder 1959) at a time when peanut butter was still an exotic product in Italy.

The term 'adaptation', as used by translation scholars, can encompass in fact different translational situations, from situational equivalence, to localisation, to an extreme form of rewriting. Moreover, the term assumes different nuances in AVT, in film and television as well as in theatre studies (Hutcheon 2006). It often involves a rethinking and rewriting of the whole text for either technical or artistic purposes; that is, a text needs to be adapted following the technical constraints of subtitling, a play is adapted for artistic reasons to a new place and time, or a novel is adapted to become a film.

As mentioned, Vinay and Darbelnet's taxonomy has been highly influential, and many of their concepts have found their way into new taxonomies by later scholars. However, as noted by Pedersen (2007: 113), one of its downsides is that it is largely based on syntax and a very common strategy based on semantics, generalisation, is excluded from it. In this sense Chesterman's (1997) taxonomy of translation strategies is much more exhaustive as it includes syntactic, semantic and pragmatic strategies, but it is far too detailed to be a user-friendly tool for analysis.

As for the translation of CSRs, Ivir (1987: 38) proposes the following list of seven strategies:

1. Borrowing
2. Definition
3. Literal translation
4. Substitution
5. Lexical creation
6. Addition
7. Omission

Of these procedures, (1) borrowing and (3) literal translation are terms taken directly from Vinay and Darbelnet, while by (2) definition the scholar means a form of explicitation in the body of the text or in a footnote, which is mainly used in combination with borrowing. (4) Substitution is the replacement of an SC element with a TC one which is likely to have a similar impact on the reader, whilst (5) lexical creation is the coining of a new term in the TL "when the communicative situation rules out a definition or literal translation, when borrowing is sociolinguistically discouraged, and substitution is not available for communicative reasons" (ibid.: 45). The (6) addition of words is often used, according to Ivir (ibid.: 47), to translate implicit elements of a culture, and finally, the (7) omission of a CSR can be justified in the case of untranslatable references or in cases of redundancy.

Newmark (1981: 75–77), who does not discuss CSRs as such but deals with the "translation of proper names and institutional and cultural terms", proposes a detailed taxonomy only for "national institutional terms". His attempt is asystematic and contains some incongruities. For example, among the translation strategies we find acronyms and metaphors which are not strategies and are not explained by Newmark as such. In his *Textbook of Translation* (1988), the same scholar devotes a whole chapter to literal translation (ibid.: 68–80) and then lists other translation procedures (ibid.: 81–93). In spite of being translation procedures applicable for general purposes, Newmark's explanations show his focus on cultural terms as most of the examples are related to them. His taxonomies clearly show the scholar's interest in the translation of institutions and proper names. The latter are also the subject of Hermans's taxonomy (1988), whose list of four ways to transfer proper names—to copy them, to transcribe them, to replace them and, if they have a meaning, to translate them—is followed by a discussion on other possible strategies such as non-translation by means of omission and the replacement of a proper noun by a common noun (generalisation) as well as by strategies of compensation.

More useful for the purposes of the present work are Leppihalme's (1994) categories for rendering proper name allusions and key-phrase allusions, that is, explicit quotations and more covert allusions, to other texts. Her strategies (ibid.: 106) to deal with proper name allusions include the following:

1. Retention: as such or with guidance, that is, addition of information to guide the TT reader, including footnotes
2. Replacement by another name
3. Replacement by a common noun which serves as a sort of explanation; for example, 'Fangio', if thought unfamiliar, may be replaced by 'Formula driver'
4. Omission

Leppihalme's taxonomy is very simple, but it is a useful heuristic tool for analysis as it includes the basic strategies that could be applied, with some further elaboration, to the translation of CSRs in general.

Her taxonomy for the translation of keynote phrases is also important for the purpose of translating quotations, which have been included in this

Culture Specific References

analysis as they are considered CSRs (ibid.: 107, 114–126). This taxonomy is not easy to summarise because Leppihalme explains each strategy by relating them to different types of allusions:

1. Treating them like idioms: in the case of dead and dying allusions
2. Standard translation and minimum change: when an official translation exists in the TC
3. Guidance or external marking: which means explicitation and the possible addition of markings such as inverted commas or italics to signal the presence of the quotation
4. Internal marking or simulated familiarity: which consists of signaling an allusion by using stylistic contrast
5. Replacement of an SL allusion by a TL-specific allusion
6. Reduction to sense by rephrasing: whereby the TL synthetic image is abandoned in favour of a rephrasing which both explicitates and tries to save some components of the original
7. Omission
8. Re-creation: creation and addition of new material to convey as much of the meaning and tone of the original allusion

In spite of its apparent lack of systematicity—this listing is derived from the scholar's extensive reflections on a series of examples—this classification has the merit of proposing strategies to translate longer and more complex units than the generally single-word terms which have so far been included in the taxonomies of CSRs. As these longer units are included in our study, Leppihalme's methods of translating keynote phrases is a valuable instrument which contributes further insights into the analysis of CSRs.

Leppihalme (2001, 2011) later proposed a taxonomy for translating *realia* in which she re-elaborated and extended her 1994 list of strategies for proper names. This list of strategies is conceived as follows:

1. Direct transfer
2. Calque
3. Cultural adaptation
4. Superordinate term
5. Explicitation
6. Addition
7. Omission

In this new taxonomy, the author prefers to refer to direct transfer and cultural adaptation rather than use the 1994 terms of 'retention' and 'replacement' by another name respectively. In the definition of 'calque' she also includes literal translation; a superordinate term is a form of generalisation;

and 'explicitation' is conceived as paraphrase and/or addition (ibid: 143), while the term 'addition' refers to extratextual information given through footnotes and the like. Finally, by 'omission' the author means the deletion of the CSR.

In 1996 Mailhac (1996: 134–136) proposed a list of procedures which combines terms from the previous literature but also suggests a tripartite model regarding the procedures to be applied to the text as a whole and not only to isolated CSRs, which may be useful to consider the challenges in a larger context:

1. Cultural transplantation: the systematic attempt to convert the SC setting into a TC one
2. Exoticism with minimum presence of the translator: translation which offers no more information than could be reasonably given to the source reader
3. Exoticism with maximum presence of the translator: who overtly adds information which is clearly for the benefit of the target reader

A completely different approach is Katan's (2004: 147), who introduces the concept of 'chunking' (changing the size of a unit), and states that, to handle CSRs, translators may opt for either: (a) 'chunking up' and making CSRs in the target language more general than those in the source language through the adoption of hyperonomy; (b) 'chunking down' by replacing them with more specific references in the target language; or (c) 'chunking sideways' and replacing CSRs with same-level equivalents. These three strategies can be combined in various ways. This model, borrowed by Katan from neuro-linguistic programming and computing, is mainly meant as a tool for teaching translators: "translators need to be able to chunk up and down to establish the wider and narrower frames of reference of the source text [. . .]. [They] must be able to chunk sideways to find equivalent frames in the target culture" (ibid.).

Regarding the strategies proposed for the area of AVT in particular, these have been put forward by scholars mainly dealing with subtitling. Nonetheless, most of these taxonomies can only be called 'media-specific' in the sense that they are illustrated by examples taken from subtitles and not because they mention any influence of the medium itself on the translation of CSRs. This is true, for instance, of Nedergaard-Larsen's (1993) taxonomy for culture-bound problems, which is loosely based on Vinay and Darbelnet's (1958) methods for translation.

Gottlieb (1994: 294), on the other hand, was one of the first to propose a set of 10 strategies specific to the context of screen translation, some of which (transcription, dislocation and condensation) appear to be "more common in subtitling than in printed translation" (ibid.: 295). More specifically for our purposes, Gottlieb (2009: 31) dealt in a later study with the translation of localisms and compared the strategies devised by Nedergaard-Larsen

(1993), Leppihalme (1997), and Pedersen (2005) with his own proposal. His chosen terminology, based on the cited scholars, is the following:

1. Retention
2. Literal translation
3. Specification
4. Generalisation
5. Substitution
6. Omission

In the same study, Gottlieb (2009: 32) makes an interesting point by stating:

> As always in the arts and humanities, classification is bound to be somewhat arbitrary, but three major concerns when establishing ways to discern patterns in one's data must be that:
>
> (1) categories are established to accommodate all findings,
> (2) different categories reflect significant differences in one's findings, and
> (3) the number of categories reflect the number of findings: a small set of data does not tally with a great number of categories.

He goes on to state that in his study, which comprises analyses of a relatively small corpus made up of five Danish films and three US films, the presence of only six strategies is justified but that for larger corpora these categories may deserve further subdivisions (ibid.).

If Gottlieb focuses on subtitling, Ballester Casado (2001), in López Rodríguez (2003: 154), proposes a classification based on Franco Aixelá (1996), which she applies to dubbing. Her model is divided into three basic macrostrategies with further subdivisions:

Macrostrategies	*Procedures*
SL culture-oriented translation	Identity
Explication + identity	
Imitation (literal translation)	
General	Explicitation
Paraphrase	
TL culture-oriented translation	Cultural adaptation

This taxonomy was used by the author as a tool for teaching translation from English to Spanish using the film *American Beauty* (S. Mendes, 1999).

Following Gottlieb's remark, it is my contention that the analysis of a large corpus should require a slightly more detailed set of procedures. Pedersen (2005) has proposed a taxonomy that, as he states, can be applied to other types of AVT as well as subtitling, and although he lists seven categories, two of them, specification and substitution, have further subdivisions. In some measure, he extends the former taxonomies, especially the ones put forward by Leppihalme (1994: 94–102) and Nedergaard-Larsen (1993: 219). In a cline ranging from the most foreignising to the most domesticating strategies—except for the official equivalent which is considered by the author as "different in kind from the other strategies" (Pedersen 2005: 3)—he proposes the following seven strategies for the translation of what he calls 'extralinguistic references' (ECRs) (ibid.: 3–9):

1. Official equivalent
2. Retention
3. Specification (through either explicitation or addition)
4. Direct translation
5. Generalization
6. Substitution (cultural substitution or paraphrase)
7. Omission

The difference between addition (even in the restricted sense proposed by Pedersen, who conceives the added material as latent in the ST ECR) and generalisation (replacement of an ECR referring to something specific by something more general) seems to be too subtle for the two categories to be really productive in an analysis. Pedersen (ibid.: 6) himself states that there are similarities between the two in the sense that the information added in addition is often a hypernym. Apart from this detail, Pedersen's taxonomy is a useful point of reference. Even though he, as most other AVT scholars, only applies it to his corpus of subtitles and the examples he presents are directly linked to the problems presented in this translation mode, his classification can be easily extrapolated to other corpora and case studies.

Díaz Cintas and Remael (2007: 202–207) propose a more clear-cut set of strategies based on Díaz Cintas (2003) and Santamaria Guinot (2001). As this will serve as the basis for the set of strategies proposed in the present work, a brief explanation of each procedure is provided, quoting some of the examples given by the authors:

1. Loan: the word or phrase of the ST is left unaltered in the TT. Examples can relate to food, drinks, place names and historical events, such as muffin, cognac, San Francisco and perestroika.
2. Calque: it is a literal translation of a CSR, generally when there is no exact equivalent in the TL. An example is the Spanish calque translation *Secretario de Estado* for secretary of state, instead of the more common *Ministro de Asuntos Exteriores* [minister of foreign affairs].
3. Explicitation: the text is made more accessible by a specification or a generalisation. Generalisations or hypernyms, the authors explain, are very frequent in subtitling as they have an explanatory function. An example can be *Le Soir* translated with 'a Belgian (quality) newspaper'.
4. Substitution: because of technical constraints, a reference is substituted with another one which deviates more or less from the source one. The authors present this strategy as a variant on explicitation,

by which a long reference that could be translated literally may be substituted by a shorter one to gain space and save reading time. An example given by the authors is the Hungarian dish *goulash* which will sometimes become 'stew'.
5. Transposition: the cultural term is replaced by a cultural term belonging to another culture. The British Marks & Spencer might be replaced by the Dutch HEMA.
6. Lexical recreation: it is the creation of a neologism, which may be inevitable if in the ST there is a made-up word as well. The authors quote the Spanish neologism *rarezametro* [oddity-meter] to account for the English 'weird shit-o-meter'.
7. Compensation: a loss somewhere in the translation is compensated by an addition in another point of the same translation. A "popular strategy in subtitling even though it may not always be practical due to the oral-visual cohabitation of the source and target languages" (ibid.: 206).
8. Omission: it is not considered by the authors as a proper strategy, but it is sometimes unavoidable either because of space–time limitations or because there is no corresponding term in the TL.
9. Addition: it is always a form of explicitation and occurs when CS references might cause comprehension problems. An example can be the word 'chair' in the phrase 'you can send him to the chair', translated into Spanish as *silla eléctrica* [electric chair].

This classification has the merit of being both detailed and agile enough to serve as a valid tool for analysis due to the absence of encumbering subdivisions and to the presence of well-defined clarifications. It is thus a good basis for the taxonomy used in the present work, although its focus on subtitling makes a few adjustments necessary for it to be applied to a corpus of dubbed material.

Corpus-Based Taxonomy of Translation Strategies

As already mentioned, Díaz Cintas and Remael's (2007) taxonomy of translation strategies for cultural references in AVT, conceived for subtitling in particular, can be adjusted to dubbing, a field in which this subject has seldom been specifically tackled. This revised taxonomy will help analyse the case studies presented in the subsequent chapters.

The following is the list of the 11 strategies chosen as a heuristic tool for the present analysis, explained in the following sections and exemplified by dialogue excerpts from the corpus:

1. Loan
2. Official translation
3. Calque

84 *Culture Specific References*

4. Explicitation
5. Generalisation by hypernym
6. Concretisation by hyponym
7. Substitution
8. Lexical recreation
9. Compensation
10. Elimination
11. Creative addition

Compared to Díaz Cintas and Remael's taxonomy, this one has the category of official translation added to it; the terms 'explicitation' and 'substitution' are conceived as quite different concepts compared to the previous taxonomy; 'transposition' is no longer in the list, although its meaning has been absorbed by other categories; the labels of 'generalisation by hypernym', 'concretisation by hyponym', 'elimination' (instead of 'omission') and 'creative addition' (in the place of simple 'addition') have been introduced.

Loan
As previously stated, a loan is the verbatim repetition of the CSR as it was found in the ST. It is left unaltered in the TT as in the following example:

EXAMPLE 4.5: *FRIENDS*, **SEASON 5 EPISODE 12**

CONTEXT: Chandler's boss, Doug, is making one of his jokes.

ORIGINAL FILM DIALOGUE	
DOUG: But seriously, I believe that we should all support President **Clinton**. And her husband **Bill**.	

ITALIAN ADAPTATION	BACK-TRANSLATION
DOUG: Sul serio, credo che tutti noi dovremmo dare il nostro appoggio al presidente **Clinton**. E a suo marito **Bill**.	DOUG: Seriously, I believe that all of us should give our support to president **Clinton**. And her husband **Bill**.

It is worth remembering Vinay and Darbelnet's (1958/2002) opinion on loan, which in the English translation of their essay is termed 'borrowing', as they only considered it a translation procedure because of the fact that translators may use it as a stylistic method to foreignise a text. The use of loans as a foreignising strategy is a concept that I will question and discuss in the chapters devoted to the case studies, showing evidence that foreignisation is in fact not necessarily the natural result of this strategy.

In Chapter 5 I will also draw the attention to loans which underwent a semantic change in their transfer to the receiving culture—words referring to a CSR in the SL which are related to a different concept in the TL.

Official Translation

This category was not included in Díaz Cintas and Remael's (2007) taxonomy, but the concept it expresses is part of classifications by other scholars who call it "recognized translation" (Newmark 1988), "standard translation" (Leppihalme 1994) or "official equivalent" (Pedersen 2005). Although including 'official translation' in the number of strategies may be objectionable, as the term which is 'officially' translated is actually transferred by using one of the other strategies in the list (i.e., loan, calque, substitution, etc.), I believe it is important to set this operation apart from the others in a category of its own, as the use of a recognised term, a term which is already available in the TL, involves a different kind of *modus operandi*, on the part of the translators, from any of the others. This is in fact a non-strategy or, better, a ready-made strategy. It may involve a certain amount of research on the part of the translator to find the established equivalent of an element in the TC. As a result, the use of this strategy usually contributes to create an impression of thoroughness in a translation and favours the prompt response by the TA to the associations triggered by the element:

EXAMPLE 4.6: *LIFE ON MARS*, SEASON 1 EPISODE 2

CONTEXT: Gene is mocking a distressed Sam, who asked to be sent back where he came from.

ORIGINAL FILM DIALOGUE	
GENE: Hello, is that the **Wizard of Oz**? The **Wizard**'ll sort it out. It's because of the wonderful things he does.	

ITALIAN ADAPTATION	BACK-TRANSLATION
GENE: Pronto, è il **Mago di Oz**? Il Mago di **Oz** è uscito. Sai, ha un sacco di cose da fare.	GENE: Hello, is it the **Wizard of Oz**? The **Wizard** of Oz has gone out. You know, he has a lot of things to do.

The reference to the Wizard of Oz—and, in Italian, its official translation, *il Mago di Oz*—is particularly important in this programme as it is an element of the macroallusions contained in the script of the show (see Chapter 6). In this case, the official translation is also a literal translation, though this is not always the case, especially when the titles of films, novels or plays, or quotes from them, have been officially translated into Italian with an adaptation which greatly departs from the original text. In the 1970s, for example, it was traditional, in the Italian cinema industry, to choose lengthy titles for films, a procedure which was also applied to imported films. The title of Nicolas Roeg's 1973 film *Don't Look Now*, to mention just one of the many examples, was officially translated into Italian as *A Venezia... un dicembre rosso shocking* [In Venice... a hot pink December], a title

86 *Culture Specific References*

which had the added bonus of containing the word 'shocking' in it, a perfect catch term for a thriller.

Long-established official translations may cause problems to the translator if the original text contains, for example, wordplay or other significant linguistic or semantic features.

Calque

The word 'calque' implies the literal translation of the CSR (Díaz Cintas and Remael 2007: 202), but to deal with allusions and quotations, it may be useful to indicate that the term 'calque', in this book, also means the word-by-word literal translation of lengthy excerpts, as in the following example:

EXAMPLE 4.7: *FRIENDS*, **SEASON 1 EPISODE 3**

CONTEXT: The group of friends is reminiscing about Monica's ex-boyfriend, whom they were all fond of.

ORIGINAL FILM DIALOGUE

JOEY: Know what was great? The way his smile was kinda crooked.
PHOEBE: Yes, yes! Like the man in the shoe!
ROSS: ... What shoe?
PHOEBE: From the nursery rhyme. "There was a crooked man, Who had a crooked smile, Who lived in a shoe, For a ... while ..."

ITALIAN ADAPTATION	BACK-TRANSLATION
JOEY: Sai che cos'ha? Il modo di sorridere. Un po' storto.	JOEY: You know what he has got? The way of smiling. Slightly crooked.
PHOEBE: Sì, sì, come l'uomo della scarpa.	PHOEBE: Yes, yes, like the man of the shoe.
ROSS: Che scarpa?	ROSS: What shoe?
PHOEBE: La poesia per bambini. "C'era un uomo storto che aveva un sorriso storto e visse in una scarpa storta per un po' di tempo ..."	PHOEBE: The children's poem. "There was a crooked man who had a crooked smile and lived in a crooked shoe for a while ..."

Unlike the former strategy of official translation, calque is a way to preserve any wordplay or double entendre that may be present in the ST as the elements of the sentence all remain in place. Arguably, it could be termed a 'non-creative' strategy as it does not show any real effort to convey the CSR to the TA. For instance, in this example, the literal translation of the English will not resonate in the minds of the TA, and the nursery rhyme's implicit popularity will have to be inferred.

Explicitation
According to Perego (2003: 68), "the status of explicitation in relation to addition, in terms of which of the two is the more general, overriding concept" is a matter of controversy. Explicitation is here understood differently from the sense put forward by Díaz Cintas and Remael (2007), which is closer to the strategy of generalisation by hypernym. The meaning of explicitation in the present taxonomy is nearer to Ivir's definition (1987: 38), and it is, in fact, a form of definition of the CSR by means of an explanation, of addition of information, mainly used in combination with borrowing. Nida, too, understands explicitation as a type of addition by which "there is no actual adding to the semantic content of the message" (Nida 1964: 231).

However, the following example is a good illustration of the fact that, in explicitation, *some* information more than those present in the original text can actually be added:

EXAMPLE 4.8: *SIX FEET UNDER*, SEASON 3 EPISODE 8

CONTEXT: Arthur, the new live-in worker at the Fishers' funeral home, has a crush on Ruth despite the remarkable age difference and tries to find ways to speak to her about love.

ORIGINAL FILM DIALOGUE

ARTHUR: They don't believe in romance.
RUTH: Where did all those children come from?
ARTHUR: We didn't get into it. But romantic love wasn't even invented until the 14th century.
RUTH: I never heard that.
ARTHUR: **Petrarch. He was Italian.**

ITALIAN ADAPTATION	BACK-TRANSLATION
ARTHUR: Non credono nel romanticismo.	ARTHUR: They don't believe in romanticism.
RUTH: Da dove vengono allora tutti quei figli?	RUTH: Where do all those children come from then?
ARTHUR: Non abbiamo approfondito. Ma dopotutto l'amore romantico è nato prima del XIV secolo.	ARTHUR: We didn't get into it. But after all, romantic love wasn't born before the 14th century.
RUTH: Questo non lo sapevo.	RUTH: I didn't know that.
ARTHUR: **Petrarca. Un poeta italiano.**	ARTHUR: **Petrarch. An Italian poet.**

88 *Culture Specific References*

It may appear unusual that in a translation into Italian, one would feel the need to explicitate that Petrarch was an Italian poet, when the original only states the nationality of the artist—an explanation comparable to stating that Shakespeare was a playwright for a British audience. However, this strategy was probably, and suitably, used by the adapters to emphasise Arthur's bookish fastidiousness.

Explicitation also occurs in the cases in which a term for a CSR is replaced by another, more popular or generic, term to define the same item:

EXAMPLE 4.9: *SIX FEET UNDER*, SEASON 3 EPISODE 2

CONTEXT: In one of the rare moments in which Ruth manages to let go, she makes wild plans with her friend Bettina.

ORIGINAL FILM DIALOGUE

RUTH: We could head up to **Frisco**!

ITALIAN ADAPTATION	BACK-TRANSLATION
RUTH: Sì, magari ce ne andiamo a **San Francisco**!	RUTH: Yes, we might even go to **San Francisco**!

Explicitation, as it is conceived in this taxonomy, is closer to Díaz Cintas and Remael's (2007: 207) addition, who in fact state that "additions are always a form of explicitation". This strategy is not always easily viable in dubbing due to isochrony constraints which limit the amount of words a translator can add to the text.

Generalisation by Hypernym
This definition is used here for a specific kind of explicitation which does not add meaning to a CSR but rather replaces it altogether with one or more words having a broader meaning than the given element (hypernym). The following is an example:

EXAMPLE 4.10: *FRIENDS*, SEASON 3 EPISODE 4

CONTEXT: Ross is worried about his son playing with a Barbie and tries to divert him to more 'manly' toys.

ORIGINAL FILM DIALOGUE

ROSS: I'm **G.I. Joe**! Drop the **Barbie**; drop the **Barbie**.

ITALIAN ADAPTATION	BACK-TRANSLATION
ROSS: Sono **Big Jim**! Molla la **bambola**, molla la **bambola**.	ROSS: I'm **Big Jim**! Drop the **doll**; drop the **doll**.

The generalisation by using a hypernym—the Barbie doll has become a generic doll—appears to be quite unjustified here as Barbies are very popular dolls in Italy. And it cannot be explained with the TC's antipathy for including brand names in translations as the other doll Ross mentions, G.I. Joe, is substituted with the more popular Big Jim. Generalisations often lead to loss of colour as the images conveyed by the original CSR may become diluted in the process.

Concretisation by Hyponym

Concretisations or specifications mean that a more general concept is rendered more specific by the use of a hyponym. This strategy is not very frequent in AVT, and in fact, only three occurrences have been found in the corpus. All of them are relative to the established habit among Italians of referring to British people and objects by the term *Inglese* [English], thus translating a more general term with a hyponym, as in the following example:

EXAMPLE 4.11: *FRIENDS*, **SEASON 5 EPISODE 2**

CONTEXT: Ross is referring to their recent trip to London.

ORIGINAL FILM DIALOGUE	
ROSS: Y'know, I think they have those at that **British** pub near the Trade Center.	

ITALIAN ADAPTATION	BACK-TRANSLATION
ROSS: Sono quasi sicuro che la servono in quel pub **inglese** vicino al Trade Center.	ROSS: I'm almost sure they serve it in that **English** pub near the Trade Center.

As the use of hyponyms has been detected in these few instances and only in *Friends*, specification can be considered irrelevant in terms of translation strategies contained in the corpus.

Substitution

With regard to substitution, the definition proposed by Díaz Cintas and Remael (2007: 204) has had to be altered to make it operative in the case of dubbing. According to these scholars, this strategy is typical of subtitling and used sometimes for reasons of spatial and temporal constraints: a long reference which could be translated literally may have to be substituted by a shorter one to gain space and save reading time. In the case of Italian dubbing, there is a high incidence of forms of substitution of an element with another one which may be longer or shorter than the original term and may

90 *Culture Specific References*

even have only a remote link with it or none at all. To my knowledge, this type of substitution—which is neither functional nor cultural and often not justified by technical constraints such as lip-synch—has not been covered by scholars who have dealt with the translation of CSRs, and it may well be considered peculiar to dubbing, which in Italy has traditionally allowed for greater departures from the ST when compared to other forms of AVT. Thus we may encounter substitutions which are evidently dictated by medium constraints, as in the following case:

EXAMPLE 4.12: *LIFE ON MARS*, SEASON 1 EPISODE 4

CONTEXT: Sam Tyler is ironically addressed by a criminal.

ORIGINAL FILM DIALOGUE

WARREN: So, you're **the Caped Crusader**, Mr Tyler.
SAM: I saw a man assaulting another man. I did my job.

ITALIAN ADAPTATION	BACK-TRANSLATION
WARREN: E così lei è **il capo dei crociati**, signor Tyler? SAM: Ho visto un uomo assalire un altro uomo, ho fatto solo il mio dovere.	WARREN: So you're **the leader of the crusaders**, Mr Tyler? SAM: I saw a man assaulting another man. I only did my duty.

The Caped Crusader is another way to refer to the comic superhero Batman. The Italian translation, chosen for the evident, alliterative similarity of the words that will easily fit the lip movements of the actor on screen, has nothing to do with comics and refers to the historical crusaders to the Holy Land. In both cases the reference is used to conjure up the image of a morally driven avenger.

Besides these technical substitutions, however, we may easily find in the corpus these other kinds of occurrences:

EXAMPLE 4.13: *SIX FEET UNDER*, SEASON 1 EPISODE 8

CONTEXT: Claire and her friend Topher are gossiping about a common friend.

ORIGINAL FILM DIALOGUE

CLAIRE: So who do you think plays Parker in the movie of her life? **Sandy Bullock** or **Julia Roberts**?
TOPHER: Oh, please, she'd never rate that high. She'd get one of those *Buffy* or *Dawson's Creek* chicks, tops!

ITALIAN ADAPTATION	BACK-TRANSLATION
CLAIRE: In un film sulla vita di Parker, chi sarebbe la protagonista? Ci vedi **Sandra Bullock** o **Julia Roberts**? TOPHER: Secondo me miri troppo in alto. Io ci vedrei al massimo una delle **scimmie di Tarzan**, niente di più.	CLAIRE: In a film on Parker's life who would you see as the protagonist? Do you see **Sandra Bullock** or **Julia Roberts**? TOPHER: In my opinion you're aiming too high. At best I would see in her one of **Tarzan's monkeys**, no more.

This far-fetched and unjustified substitution replaces very popular television shows like *Buffy* (Joss Whedon, 1997–2003) and *Dawson's Creek* (Kevin Williamson 1998–2003)—well-known in the TC by the same loan titles—with a reference to Tarzan's monkeys. It is true that the audience would probably think of Tarzan as of the protagonist of popular telefilms, thus remaining, in a way, in the same area of the original, but the substitution is still hardly explainable. Substitutions of this kind cannot be ascribed either to technical constraints, such as the ones discussed in Díaz Cintas and Remael's (2007) taxonomy, or to cultural considerations, such as the need to substitute an exotic or unknown term for one that will be familiar to the new audience.

Substitutions (and eliminations, discussed later) are normally justified in various ways by professionals in the field, who sometimes refer to the technical constraints imposed by dubbing, namely the need to lip-synch or to keep isochrony with the original, and other times mention considerations linked to the reception of the programme which leads to the replacement of a lesser-known CSR with one more popular for the TA. The following passage contains two CSRs that have been substituted with various solutions:

EXAMPLE 4.14: *LIFE ON MARS*, SEASON 1 EPISODE 1

CONTEXT: Gene is interrogating a suspect, Dora, in his usual gentlemanly manner.

ORIGINAL FILM DIALOGUE

GENE: Let's play **hopscotch** or **pin the tail on the donkey**. You pick, Dora.
DORA: I want a lawyer.
GENE: I wanna hump **Britt Ekland**. What are we gonna do?

ITALIAN ADAPTATION	BACK-TRANSLATION
GENE: **Giochiamo** a campana, anzi, no, a **rubabandiera**.	GENE: Let's play **hopscotch** or rather **capture the flag**.

DORA: Voglio un avvocato. GENE: E io scoparmi la regina madre, come la mettiamo?	DORA: I want a lawyer. GENE: And I want to fuck the Queen Mother. What are we going to do?

One of the games mentioned by Gene, 'pin the tail on the monkey', has been replaced by the more popular *rubabandiera* [capture the flag]; more markedly, the name of the actress Britt Ekland, popular in the 1960s and 1970s, has been replaced by a reference to the Queen Mother. As for the merits of the latter solution, the CSR remains more or less place specific—Britt Ekland is Swedish but has long been a British resident and is mostly associated with British films, and the Queen Mother is of course a member of the British royalty—but the time specificity of the element has not been considered in the substitution. The name of Britt Ekland, which may not be widely known among the younger generations of both the SC and the TC audiences, is one of the many chosen by the authors of this period series to capture the atmosphere and the mood of the 1970s in which the story is set. The timeless Queen Mother, who died in 2002, cannot serve this purpose and hence the departure from the ethos of the original series.

Substitution, as conceived in this taxonomy, encompasses Díaz Cintas and Remael's (2007: 204) transposition, by which a "cultural concept of one culture is replaced by a cultural concept from another". The term 'substitution' is preferred here for several reasons: it emphasises more clearly and defines better the far-fetched, 'creative' and sometimes incongruous substitutions which often occur in Italian dubbing and of which the case studies will offer plenty of examples. Secondly, the term 'transposition', despite its established tradition in Translation Studies since Vinay and Darbelenet (1958/2002), is also widely used in other contexts such as Film Studies to refer to intersemiotic adaptation, and using it to define two different concepts, both related to films, might create confusion.[5] More importantly, as has been illustrated, substitution in this taxonomy encompasses a wider range of possibilities than transposition.

Lexical Recreation
As in Díaz Cintas and Remael's taxonomy, lexical recreation implies the coining of a neologism and is generally used when the ST itself contains a neologism. There are no instances of lexical re-creations in the corpus analysed in this work. Outside the corpus, the widely known case of *luccicanza*, from the Italian version of Stanley Kubrick's film *The Shining* (1980), is an example: the choice of the word *luccicanza* (a previously nonexistent noun in Italian, deriving from *luccicare* = to glitter) is a neologism introduced in the official dubbing of Kubrick's film to translate 'the shining'. The following instance

may also serve as an illustration for this strategy, which, in this case, is also used in combination with creative addition:[6]

EXAMPLE 4.15: *MANHATTAN MURDER MYSTERY (MISTERIOSO OMICIDIO A MANHATTAN)* **(WOODY ALLEN 1993)**

CONTEXT: Carol is sure she has just seen her supposedly dead neighbour alive, on a bus, and she is telling her disbelieving husband about it.

ORIGINAL FILM DIALOGUE

CAROL: I'm telling you I saw Mrs House.
LARRY: Yes I know, on **the dead persons' bus**. No car fare.

ITALIAN ADAPTATION	BACK-TRANSLATION
CAROL: Io ti dico che ho visto la signora House.	CAROL: I'm telling you I saw Mrs House.
LARRY: Sì, lo so, su **un mezzo mortorizzato**, l'ultima corsa gratis.	LARRY: Yes I know, on **a rigor mortorised vehicle**. Last ride for free.

In this case, the Italian adapters have chosen to create a neologism when the original text contained none: *un mezzo mortorizzato* plays with the words *morto* [dead] and *motorizzato* [motorized] to create the image of a vehicle carrying dead people.

Compensation
Similarly to Díaz Cintas and Remael's approach, compensation occurs when a loss in one point of the translation is compensated for in another point of the same translation. It is a strategy which requires a certain amount of creative effort on the part of the translator and, according to the corpus, it is not often resorted to in dubbing, possibly also because of technical lip-synch constraints which limit the possibilities of dislocations within a text. A good instance of compensation was illustrated in Example 4.4, in which the film *2001: A Space Odyssey* was evoked in the ST by the actor imitating the voice of the Hal computer. In the TT, the imitation disappeared, but a wordplay on Kubrick's title (*Grazie mille Mr 2001 Odissea nello strazio* [Thank you very much Mr 2001 A Pain Odyssey]), not present in the original text, compensated for the loss and kept the intertextual allusion.

Elimination
The term 'elimination' is preferred here instead of 'omission', used by Díaz Cintas and Remael and by many other scholars to define the instances in

94 Culture Specific References

which a CSR, present in the ST, is not transferred to the TT and disappears. If omission in subtitling is often resorted to to avoid redundancy (naming a CSR which is also clearly visible and comprehensible on screen may be avoided in subtitling to respect time and space limitations), this will seldom occur in dubbing. The case studies demonstrate how in a great number of instances, CSRs are omitted in dubbing due to arbitrary or questionable choices, hardly justifiable by technical or other forms of constraints. That is why the term 'elimination'—which suggests the voluntary act of making an element disappear from a text without replacing it with another CSR—is preferred to the more customary word 'omission'. See, for example, the next excerpt from a series which is not included in the present corpus:

EXAMPLE 4.16: *SKINS* (J. BRITTAIN AND B. ELSLEY, 2007–2013), SEASON 3 EPISODE 3

CONTEXT: The gangster Johnny is threatening Thomas, who had the bad idea of squatting in one of Johnny's flats.

ORIGINAL FILM DIALOGUE

JOHNNY: I want £300 deposit **by *Desperate Housewives* on** Thursday. And don't bother trying to move flat, cos they're all mine. **And that'll be £400 by *X Factor*.** We wouldn't want that, would we?

ITALIAN ADAPTATION	BACK-TRANSLATION
Voglio che mi porti 300 sterline di caparra **per giovedì sera**. E non provare a cambiare appartamento. Perché sono tutti miei. Se cerchi di fare il furbo . . . **diventano 400**. E non vogliamo che accada, vero?	I want you to bring me 300 pounds deposit **by Thursday evening**. And don't try to change flat. Because they are all mine. If you try to play smart . . . **it becomes 400**. And we don't want that to happen, right?

The elimination of the titles of two TV programmes mentioned in the TT appears to be quite arbitrary as both of them are very popular in Italy by the same original title. No technical consideration seems to have provoked the adapter's choice as, in fact, the loss of the two titles may have created some lip-synch problems.

It is worth mentioning that this category also encompasses what other scholars (Newmark 1988; Ballester Casado 2001; Pedersen 2005) define as 'paraphrase', as the rephrasing of the CSR by this strategy may result in the omission of the element itself by a paraphrase which fits the context; for example, in the following instance, the CSR is eliminated, and a suitable paraphrase has taken its place:

> **EXAMPLE 4.17: *SIX FEET UNDER*, SEASON 1 EPISODE 8**
>
> **CONTEXT:** Claire's friend, Parker, admires the old hearse Claire uses as a car.
>
> **ORIGINAL FILM DIALOGUE**
>
> PARKER: This car is like total **Graceland** on wheels.
>
> | ITALIAN ADAPTATION | BACK-TRANSLATION |
> |---|---|
> | PARKER: Questa macchina è enorme. | PARKER: This car is enormous. |

As we can see, the CSR is eliminated, and it is not substituted with another CSR but with a paraphrase which, while explaining the meaning of Parker's words, does not contain a new CSR and arguably impoverishes the conveyed image.

Pedersen (ibid.: 9) admits that the situational paraphrase can result in quasi-omission since "when using this strategy, every sense of the ST ECR is completely removed, and replaced by something that fits the situation, regardless of the sense of the SC ECR".

Creative Addition

For Díaz Cintas and Remael (2007: 207), addition is mainly chosen in subtitling to bypass any technical constraints imposed by the medium. In dubbing, and arguably in subtitling as well, the reasons for this choice can also be subjective and dictated by the personal taste of the translator and/or adapter. The adjective 'creative' to define this type of addition has been deemed necessary to distinguish it from the additions included in the taxonomies put forward by some scholars quoted in this chapter. Creative addition is not a form of explicitation, as implied in Díaz Cintas and Remael (ibid.), but a form of authorial intervention by the adapter. In this sense, it is an example of translation close to the concept of rewriting postulated by Lefevere (1992). The following excerpt, again from *Skins*, serves as an illustration of what can be considered an extremely manipulative practice:

> **EXAMPLE 4.18: *SKINS*, SEASON 1 EPISODE 8**
>
> **CONTEXT:** Tony has been left alone by his friend. For the first time the gang leader is feeling blue and quite lonely.
>
> **ORIGINAL FILM DIALOGUE**
>
> KENNY: Where's all your mates then, Tone? **Fallen on hard times, have you, shag?**
> TONY: Something like that.

KENNY: **Well, no offence** but the sooner I get these sold, the sooner I get to the missus for cocoa and cuddles. And I'm not going to get much sold standing next to a posh lad, am I?

ITALIAN ADAPTATION	BACK-TRANSLATION
KENNY: E i tuoi amichetti dove sono, Tony? Forse **il grande regista non ha più i suoi attori?** TONY: Sì, più o meno. KENNY: **Senza offesa, Fellini**, ma prima sbologno queste copie, prima posso tornare dalla mia bella per coccole e cioccolata.	KENNY: Where's all your mates, Tony? Perhaps **the great director has lost his actors?** TONY: Yes, more or less. KENNY: **No offence, Fellini**, but the sooner I get rid of these copies, the sooner I get to my babe for cuddles and chocolate.

The addition of the TC reference to the Italian director Federico Fellini is an example of creativity in dubbing. This addition is introduced by the line: *il grande regista non ha più i suoi attori?* [the great director has lost his actors?], which replaces, more than translates, the line: 'fallen on hard times, have you, shag?'. After this introduction, Kenny continues to play on the theme of film directors by calling Tony 'Fellini' in his last line.

Creative additions can be used, and in fact are often used, as the analysis of the corpus will show, to enhance the humorous effect of the programme. This category can be considered typical of dubbing, and especially of Italian dubbing, as its use in other forms of AVT is quite limited. The fact that the original soundtrack can be heard renders the implementation of this strategy riskier in subtitling and voice-over translation, for example.

Following the definition and illustration of the strategies that are to be used in this analysis, the next section briefly dwells on the type of CSRs that have been found and considered in the corpus.

CULTURE SPECIFIC REFERENCES IN THE CORPUS

The present corpus has been gathered for the purpose of analysing culture specific references, and to my knowledge, it is one of the largest corpora considered for the quantitative and qualitative analysis of CSRs in AVT. Among the corpora used by other scholars, Ramière's studies (2006, 2007) are based on three films and one film, respectively, of which she analysed both the dubbing and the subtitling; Gottlieb (2009) analysed the subtitles of five Danish films and three US films; Pedersen's (2007) corpus is composed of 100 films and TV programmes in English, of which he compared the Danish and Swedish subtitling. The present corpus is composed of

187 television fiction programmes of various lengths (from 22 minutes to 1 hour), totalling more than 95 hours. All of the CSRs appearing in the corpus have been considered and not only a random selection.

The excerpts which contain the CSRs have all been transcribed in their original English and in the Italian dubbed solutions, and they have been back-translated in English, highlighting in various colours, for easier detection, the different translation strategies used by the adapters. To clarify this procedure, in the following example I have included in brackets the chosen colour for the strategies (blue for elimination and red for substitution), following the word in bold, which appears in colour in the original tables:

EXAMPLE 4.19: *LIFE ON MARS*, SEASON 2 EPISODE 5

ORIGINAL FILM DIALOGUE

SAM: Well, someone thinks he's innocent.
GENE: Don't start! I've come at this from more angles than **Linda Lovelace**. He's not innocent; he confessed. Worse, he gloated about it.
SAM: Well, obviously someone wants him out. How about Graham's family?
GENE: Oh, quick thinking, **Van der Valk.**

ITALIAN ADAPTATION	BACK-TRANSLATION
SAM: Qualcuno lo pensa innocente.	SAM: Someone thinks he's innocent.
GENE: Senti, non cominciare. Ho studiato la faccenda **da più punti di vista** [BLUE]. Non è innocente, ha confessato. Peggio, era contento.	GENE: Listen, don't start. I've studied the matter **from several points of view**. He's not innocent, he confessed. Worse, he was glad.
SAM: Allora ovviamente qualcuno lo vuole fuori. Forse la famiglia di Graham.	SAM: Then obviously someone wants him out. Maybe Graham's family.
GENE: Perspicace, **Perry Mason** [RED].	GENE: Clever, **Perry Mason**.

It is important to point out that the approach to the analysis is both quantitative and qualitative. The calculation of the number of different translation strategies is instrumental when drawing statistical conclusions. In addition to this, the previous discussion on the nature of CSRs will serve as an aid for a qualitative analysis which takes into account both the strategies used and the specific nature of the cultural elements. The elimination or substitution of an element has a very different impact depending on its nature: one thing is eliminating, from a text translated into Italian, the name of UK's Prime Minister David Cameron, and another thing is eliminating the name of Italy's Prime Minister Matteo Renzi. The choice, which might be dictated by various reasons, including ideological ones, may have a very different bearing in the two cases. These variables have been considered in the qualitative analysis of the case studies.

The present investigation has purposely chosen not to include the important category of invented cultural elements which have been created specifically for the fictional stories of the programme, for example, the already cited name of the café where the characters in *Friends* gather, Central Perk. Interesting as it would be to analyse, this category would take us into a different realm. The present analysis deals only with pre-existing CSRs, whether real or fictional, but not invented for the diegetic purposes of the text at hand.

The inclusion of currency (dollars and pounds), measures (inches and gallons) and geographical terms (Ohio and London) has been considered carefully. They are CSRs traditionally included in analyses of this type, but unlike most of the others, these particular elements have long had an established, fixed way of translating them in Italian dubbing. Currencies in Italian are translated, with very few exceptions, with the official translation of the terms *dollaro* [dollar] and *sterlina* [pound]. Imperial measures, on the other hand, are translated by roughly calculating their equivalents in the metric system used in the TC; hence, 5 inches become an average of 12 *centimetri*, and 15 stones are more or less equal to 95 *chili*. Geographical places are translated, as a rule, with a loan or with an official translation if one already exists: *Las Vegas* [Las Vegas] or *Barcellona* [Barcelona]. Ruling these references out would have been an extreme decision, and I have rejected it, but it is important to underline that the high incidence of these elements and the relatively fixed way they are translated tend to unbalance the statistical figures in the sense that these data—less meaningful because of being long established—can render the reading of the rest of the data more opaque (see, e.g., the dozens of times that the loan word 'New York' is mentioned in *Friends*).

Part of the corpus allows the drawing of some diachronic considerations, and an interesting aspect of this type of research is the monitoring of the evolution of a given CSR. In this sense, a reference which was originally restricted to a particular culture may have been exported systematically during the years with the result of being known today by other cultures, including the target one. Certain elements can thus be monitored, through the analysis of some television programmes, in their evolution from being specific to a particular culture and slowly becoming more international. The long-running series of *Friends* is good ground for such considerations in relation to festivities such as Halloween and Thanksgiving (see Chapter 5).

Non-verbal references have been included in the corpus when they are relevant to the meaning of the dialogue. That is to say that posters in the street, product labels, TV programmes and so on are visual CSRs which have not been considered if the characters do not refer to them in their dialogue. This is because this study is focused on translation strategies, and non-verbal elements are usually considered by dubbing adapters only insofar as they affect the dialogue exchanges.

Finally, some conclusions on the distribution of CSRs among the different genres can be drawn and will be drawn in the different case studies as the occurrence of these items sensibly varies from series to series, as do the ends they are used for.

CONCLUSIONS

As it has been discussed, the definition of 'culture specific references' can encompass a wide range of elements. The taxonomies presented, those classifying the items according to their nature and those listing the possible translation strategies, have mostly been applied to subtitling when working in AVT. Although most of them can be also used for the analysis of dubbing, some adjustments have been deemed necessary to deal with the specific challenges of this form of AVT. Following the lead of other scholars who have dealt with these particular elements, my taxonomies were not pre-formed but are based on the corpus under scrutiny, a corpus of television programmes in English translated into Italian by a professional category which, as we have illustrated in the preceding chapters, has enjoyed great authorial freedom while, at the same time, having to tackle several technical constraints.

The main idea to be stressed in this conclusive section is that cultural specificity is a relative term that can be best assessed in situations where two (or more) cultures meet each other; cultures that are not a stable and clear-cut set of practices but rather continuously altering and subject to change. This relativity has been taken into account by some scholars, but it has seldom been reflected in their classifications of CSRs, which have shown a tendency to classify these elements according to lexical units that cannot always account for their dynamism in terms of geographic and temporal collocation. By taking fully into consideration their relative nature, a more objective categorisation can be made possible, one which looks at the relationship between the two (or more) cultures involved as a point of reference.

In spite of the efforts made so far, their very dynamism renders even the definition of cultural elements a theoretical challenge as the notion of what is culture specific or not is in itself debatable.

The remaining chapters will present the results drawn from the analysis of the corpus in an attempt to combine a quantitative evaluation—in terms of the different strategies implemented by translators—and a qualitative one by reflecting on the nature of cultural references as it has been conceived in this chapter.

NOTES

1. The concept of 'context' is familiar to Translation Studies at least since the polysystem theory (see Chapter 2) developed in the 1970s. In the late 1980s and 1990s, it became essential thanks to the work of culturalist scholars who stressed how there is always a context in which a translation occurs, always

a history from which a text emerges and into which a text is transposed (Bassnett and Lefevere 1990: 11).
2. As the rest of the discussion will clarify, although theoretically valid for both macro categories, the category of asynchronous references applies more logically to the real-world rather than the intertextual references.
3. I am borrowing here Genette's (1982) influential definition of what he terms 'hypotext': an ST giving origin to other texts (the 'hypertexts') which use material from their sources on different levels and with different styles in an act of intertextual re-creation.
4. The other implications of the Italian adaptation of this dialogue, notably the heterosexual translation of Nate's generic line "I'm all for you getting laid", are discussed in Chapter 7.
5. See for example Hutcheon (2006: 7–8): "an adaptation is an announced and extensive transposition of a particular work or works [. . .]. Transposition can also mean a shift in ontology from the real to the fictional, from a historical account or biography to a fictionalized narrative or drama".
6. I am aware that both these examples do not refer to CSRs, but they may however be useful to illustrate this strategy and the creative way in which it is sometimes used in Italian dubbing.

REFERENCES

Agost Canós, Rosa. 1999. *Traducción y doblaje: palabras, voces e imágenes*. Barcelona: Ariel.
Austen, Jane. 1818/2007. *Persuasion*. London: Penguin.
Austen, Jane. 1813/2012. *Pride and Prejudice*. London: Penguin.
Ballester Casado, Ana. 2001. *Traducción Traducción y nacionalismo: La recepcion del cine americano en España a través del doblaje, 1928–1948* (Colección Interlingua, Volume 19). Granada: Editorial Comares.
Bassnett, Susan and André Lefevere. 1990. *Translation, History and Culture*. London: Pinter.
Ben-Porat, Ziva. 1976. "The poetics of literary allusion". *PTL: A Journal for Descriptive Poetics and Theory of Literature* 1: 105–128.
Bowie, David. 1969. *Space Oddity*. Philips Records. UK.
Bugarski, Ranko. 1985. "Translation across cultures: some problems with terminologies", in Kurt R. Jankowsky (ed.) *Scientific and Humanistic Dimensions of Language: Festschrift for Robert Lado on the Occasion of his 70th Birthday on May 31, 1985*. Amsterdam: John Benjamins, 159–164.
Chaume, Frederic. 2004. "Film studies and translation studies: two disciplines at stake in Audiovisual Translation". *Meta* 49(1): 12–24.
Chesterman, Andrew. 1997. *Memes of Translation*. Amsterdam: John Benjamins.
Chiaro, Delia. 2009. "Issues in audiovisual translation", in Jeremy Munday (ed.) *The Routledge Companion to Translation Studies*. London: Routledge, 141–165.
Cuddon, J. A. (ed.). 1999. *Dictionary of Literary Terms and Literary Theory*. London: Penguin.
Díaz Cintas, Jorge. 2001. *La traducción audiovisual: el subtitulado*. Salamanca: Ediciones Almar.
Díaz Cintas, Jorge. 2003. *Teoría y práctica de la subtitulación: inglés-español*. Barcelona: Ariel.
Díaz Cintas, Jorge and Aline Remael. 2007. *Audiovisual Translation: Subtitling*. Manchester: St Jerome.

Dickens, Charles. 1861/2012. *Great Expectations*. London: Penguin.
Dylan, Bob. 1965. *Mr. Tambourine Man*. Columbia, USA: Tom Wilson.
Fawcett, Peter. 1998. "Presupposition and translation", in Leo Hickey (ed.) *The Pragmatics of Translation*. Clevedon: Multilingual Matters, 114–123.
Finkel, A. M. 1962. "Ob avtoperevode". *TKP* 1: 104–125.
Forster, E. M. 1908/2006. *A Room with a View*. London: Penguin.
Franco Aixelá, Javier. 1996. "Culture-specific items in translation", in Román Álvarez and M. Carmen-África Vidal (eds.) *Translation Power Subversion*. Clevedon: Multilingual Matters, 52–78.
Gambier, Yves. 2001. "Traduire le sous-texte", in Hans Kronning, Coco Norén, Bengt Novén, Gunilla Ransbo, Lars Göran Sundell and Brynja Svane (eds.) *Langage et référence. Mélanges offerts à Kerstin Jonasson à l'occasion de ses soixante ans*. Uppsala: Uppsala Universitët, 223–235.
Genette, Gérard. 1982. *Palimpsestes. La littérature au second degré*. Paris: Editions du Seuil.
Gottlieb, Henrik. 1994. "Subtitling: diagonal translation". *Perspectives: Studies in Translatology* 1(2): 101–121.
Gottlieb, Henrik. 2009. "Subtitling against the current: Danish concepts, English minds", in Jorge Díaz Cintas (ed.) *New Trends in Audiovisual Translation*. Bristol: Multilingual Matters, 21–43.
Hermans, Theo. 1988. "On translating proper names, with reference to De Witte and Max Havelaar", in Michael J. Wintle (ed.) *Modern Dutch Studies. Essays in Honour of Professor Peter King on the Occasion of his Retirement*. London: The Athlone Press, 11–24.
Homer. 2003. *The Odyssey*. London: Penguin.
Hutcheon, Linda. 2006. *A Theory of Adaptation*. New York: Routledge.
Irwin, William. 2001. "What is an allusion?". *The Journal of Aesthetics and Art Criticism* 59(3): 287–297.
Irwin, William. 2002. "The aesthetics of allusion". *The Journal of Value Inquiry*, 36: 521–532.
Ivir, Vladimir. 1987. "Procedures and strategies for the translation of culture". *Indian Journal of Applied Linguistics* 13(2): 35–46.
Johnson, Anthony L. 1976. "Allusion in poetry". *PTL: A Journal for Poetics and Theory of Literature* 1: 580–581.
Kaskenviita, Rauni. 1991. "Alluusiot Asterix-sarjan kulttuurisidonnaisena käännösongelmana [Allusions as a culture-bound translation problem in the Asterix series]". *Sananjalka* 33: 77–92.
Katan, David. 2004. *Translating Cultures. An Introduction for Translators, Interpreters and Mediators*. Manchester: St Jerome.
Kosunen, Riina and Susanne Väisänen. 2001. *Kääntämisen opetussanasto*. Turku: Universidad de Turku.
Kwiecinski, Piotr. 2001. *Disturbing Strangeness: Foreignisation and Domestication in Translation Procedures in the Context of Cultural Asymmetry*. Torun: Wydawnictwo.
Leemets, Helle. 1992. "Translating the "untranslatable" words", in Hannu Tommola, Krista Varantola, Tarja Salmi-Tolonen and Jürgen Schopp (eds.) *Papers Submitted to the 5th EURALEX International Congress on Lexicography, in Tampere, Finland*. Part 2. Tampere: University of Tampere, 473–478.
Lefevere, André. 1992. *Translation, Rewriting and the Manipulation of Literary Fame*. London: Routledge.
Leppihalme, Ritva. 1994. *Culture Bumps: On the Translation of Allusions*. Helsinki: Helsinki University.
Leppihalme, Ritva. 1997. *Culture Bumps. An Empirical Approach to the Translation of Allusions*. Clevedon: Multilingual Matters.

Leppihalme, Ritva. 2001. "Translation strategies for realia", in Pirjo Kukkonen and Ritva Hartama-Heinonen (eds.) *Mission, Vision, Strategies, and Values*. Helsinki: Helsinki University Press, 139–148.
Leppihalme, Ritva. 2011. "Realia", in Yves Gambier and Luc van Doorslaer (eds.) *Handbook of Translations Studies*. Amsterdam: John Benjamins, 126–130.
López Rodríguez, Clara Inés. 2003. "Electronic resources and lexical cohesion in the construction of intercultural competence". *Lebende Sprachen* 48(4), 152–156.
Mailhac, Jean-Pierre. 1996. "The formulation of translation strategies for cultural references", in Charlotte Hoffmann (ed.) *Language, Culture and Communication in Contemporary Europe*. Clevedon: Multilingual Matters, 132–151.
Meyer, Herman. 1968. *The Poetics of Quotation in the European Novel*. Princeton, NJ: Princeton University Press.
Nedergaard-Larsen, Birgit. 1993. "Culture-bound problems in subtitling". *Perspectives: Studies in translatology* 2: 207–242.
Newmark, Peter. 1981. *Approaches to Translation*. London: Prentice Hall.
Newmark, Peter. 1988. *A Textbook of Translation*. London: Prentice Hall.
Nida, Eugène A. 1945. "Linguistics and ethnology in translation problems." *Word* 2: 194–208.
Nida, Eugène A. 1964. *Toward a Science of Translating. With Special Reference to Principles and Procedures Involved in Bible Translating*. Leiden: E.J. Brill.
Obama, Barack. 2008. "Obama acceptance speech in full". *The Washington Post*: President Obama's acceptance speech (Full transcript). http://www.washingtonpost.com/politics/decision2012/president-obamas-acceptance-speech-full-transcript/2012/11/07/ae133e44-28a5-11e2-96b6-8e6a7524553f_story.html, last accessed 27th March 2015.
Pedersen, Jan. 2005. "How is culture rendered in subtitles?". *MuTra 2005—Challenges of Multidimensional Translation: Conference Proceedings*, in www.euroconferences.info/proceedings/2005_Proceedings/2005_Pedersen_Jan.pdf, last accessed 27th March 2015.
Pedersen, Jan. 2007. *Scandinavian Subtitles. A Comparative Study of Subtitling Norms in Sweden and Denmark with a Focus on Extralinguistic Cultural References*. PhD thesis. Stockholm: Stockholm University.
Perego, Elisa. 2003. "Evidence of explicitation in subtitling: towards a categorisation". *Across Languages and Cultures* 4(1): 63–88.
Pucci, Joseph Michael. 1998. *The Full-Knowing Reader: Allusion and the Power of the Reader in the Western Literary Tradition*. New Haven, Conn.: Yale University Press.
Pym, Anthony. 2010. *Translation and Text Transfer. An Essay on the Principles of Intercultural Communication*. Tarragona: Intercultural Studies Group.
Ramière, Nathalie. 2006. "Reaching a foreign audience: cultural transfers in audiovisual translation". *The Journal of Specialised Translation* 6: 152–166.
Ramière, Nathalie. 2007. *Strategies of Cultural Transfer in Subtitling and Dubbing*. PhD thesis. Brisbane, Australia: University of Queensland.
Ramière Nathalie. 2010. "Are you 'lost in translation' (when watching a foreign film)? Towards an alternative approach to judging audiovisual translation". *Australian Journal of French Studies* 47(1): 100–115.
Rantanen, Aulis. 1990. "Culturally-bound material and its treatment in literary translation". *International Journal of Translation* 2(2): 49–59.
Ruokonen, Minna. 2010. *Cultural and Textual Properties in the Translation and Interpretation of Allusions: An Analysis of Allusions in Dorothy L. Sayers' Detective Novels Translated into Finnish in the 1940s and the 1980s*. PhD thesis. Turku: University of Turku.
Santamaria Guinot, Laura. 2001. *Subtitulació i referents culturals. La traducció com a mitjà d'adquisició de representacions socials*. PhD thesis. Barcelona: Universitat Autònoma de Barcelona.

Sapir, Edward. 1949/1985. *Selected Writings in Language, Culture, and Personality.* Berkeley: University of California Press.
Shakespeare, William. 2003. *Romeo and Juliet.* London: The Arden Shakespeare.
Shakespeare, William. 2006. *Hamlet.* London: The Arden Shakespeare.
Tolstoy, Leo. 1865–69/2006. *War and Peace.* London: Penguin.
Tomaszczyk, Jerzy. 1983. "The culture-bound element in bilingual dictionaries", in www.euralex.org/elx_proceedings/Euralex1983/042_Jerzy%20Tomaszczyk%20 (Lodz)%20-%20The%20culturebound%20element%20in%20bilingual%20 dictionaries.pdf, last accessed 12th July 2015.
Vinay, Jean-Paul and Jean Darbelnet. 1958. *Stylistique comparée du français et de l'anglais.* Paris: Didier.
Vinay, Jean-Paul and Jean Darbelnet. 2002. "A methodology for translation", in Lawrence Venuti (ed.) *The Translation Studies Reader.* London: Routledge, 128–137.
Vlahov, Sergej and Sider Florin. 1969. "Neperovodimoe v perevode. Realii". *Masterstvo perevoda* 6: 432–456.
Zabalbeascoa, Patrick. 1996. "Translating jokes for dubbed television situation comedies". *The Translator* 2(2): 235–257.

Filmography

American Beauty, Sam Mendes, 1999, USA.
The Bridges of Madison County (I ponti di Madison County), Clint Eastwood, 1995, USA.
Bridget Jones's Diary (Il diario di Bridget Jones), Sharon Maguire, 2001, UK/France/USA.
Bridget Jones: The Edge of Reason (Che pasticcio, Bridget Jones!), Beeban Kidron, 2004, UK.
Buffy the Vampire Slayer (Buffy l'ammazzavampiri), Joss Whedon, 1997–2003, USA.
Dawson's Creek, Kevin Williamson, 1998–2003, USA.
Desperate Housewives, Marc Cherry, 2004–2012, USA.
Don't Look Now (A Venezia . . . un dicembre rosso shocking), Nicolas Roeg, 1973, UK/Italy.
Friends, Marta Kauffman and David Crane, 1994–2004, USA.
Grease, Randal Kleiser, 1978, USA.
Life on Mars, Matthew Graham, Tony Jordan and Ashley Pharoah, 2008–2009, USA.
Manhattan Murder Mystery (Misterioso omicidio a Manhattan), Woody Allen, 1993, USA.
A Room with a View (Camera con vista), James Ivory, 1985, UK.
The Shining, Stanley Kubrick, 1980, USA/UK.
Six Feet Under, Alan Ball, 2001–2005, USA.
Skins, Jamie Brittain and Bryan Elsley, 2007–2013, UK.
Some Like It Hot (A qualcuno piace caldo), Billy Wilder, 1959, USA.
South Park, Trey Parker and Matt Stone, 1997–in production, USA.
The Sweeney, I. K. Martin, 1975–1978, UK.
2001: A Space Odyssey (2001: Odissea nello spazio), Stanley Kubrick, 1968, UK/USA.
The Wizard of Oz (Il mago di Oz), Victor Fleming, 1939, USA.

5 "The Lesser-Known *I Don't Have a Dream* Speech"
Cultural Humour in *Friends*

INTRODUCTION

Following the aim of collecting a sufficiently varied corpus in terms of genres and target audiences, the reason for choosing *Friends*, one of the most successful US sitcoms of all time, was to have an intelligent but definitely mainstream audiovisual programme to work on. The international success that this sitcom enjoyed with audiences all over the world has brought up translation issues that the other programmes of the corpus, conceived for more selected audiences, could not raise.

From a preliminary viewing of the series, it was evident that it presented a considerable number of elements specific to US culture. This is not unusual among even the most internationally diffused TV programmes, and one of my aims was to try to find out how much bearing culture specificity had on the original writing and how much of it was transferred to the Italian dubbing.

Not all audiovisual programmes use CSRs for the same purposes or to attain the same effects. *Friends* often uses culturally embedded references to make jokes which can be at times quite erudite and sophisticated for a programme that is not conceived for an elite but for a very wide audience. One of the most interesting reasons for analysis was then to investigate the apparent clash between the cultural specificity of some references and the declared international spectatorship that *Friends* aimed at from the very early seasons.

Another reason for the interest in *Friends* lay in its longevity: 10 years provide enough scope to measure any possible evolution of both the original dialogue and their adaptations into Italian. That meant that a substantial number of episodes had to be taken into account for a diachronic analysis, and special focus is laid on ascertaining if any meaningful statistical conclusions can be drawn from the investigation.

The analysis covers Seasons 1, 2, 3, 5, 8 and 10 of the 10 seasons of *Friends*, which totals 145 episodes of about 22 minutes per episode. This is a total of about 3,190 minutes of programme. The first three seasons have been chosen because the preliminary assumption—based on previous analyses of other television products—was that a programme needs some time to find its ideal TA and its ideal collocation (i.e., broadcasting time and possibly channel). Thus, it is very likely that in the very first seasons, some crucial adjustments in terms of script writing and of TL adaptation may have taken place. The other, later seasons allow us to evaluate if indeed any changes in translation policies have taken place, both in the original production and in the Italian version.

Friends has been the object of several studies from a linguistic perspective, notably the ones by Quaglio (2009a, 2009b), who uses this sitcom as a means to investigate fictional versus natural conversation, and by Tagliamonte and Roberts (2005), who analyse the high occurrence of some intensifiers in the dialogue and the influence of this way of speaking on American vernacular. From a translational angle, Baños-Piñero (2005, 2009, 2010) and Baños-Piñero and Chaume (2009) have investigated the Spanish dubbing of this sitcom as a form of prefabricated orality, whilst Romero Fresco (2006, 2008, 2009) has analysed discourse markers in the Spanish dubbing to investigate its degree of naturalness. Nevertheless, this programme has never been researched for its high incidence of CSRs in dubbing (though Pedersen 2007 includes some of its episodes in his subtitled corpus). The material gathered in the pages that follow is thus analysed through the lenses of the classification of strategies for the translation of CSRs discussed in Chapter 4, adding the qualitative insight that a reflection on the nature of some of the references has to offer, with the specific purpose of finding out if there are any regularities in the translation of each category, if any of these strategies is more relevant than the others and why, and of verifying if the translation into Italian may affect the style and general impact of the series on its new audience, with a particular focus on humour and jokes.

Friends

Friends is an American sitcom created by David Crane and Marta Kauffman, which originally ran on NBC from 22 September 1994 to 6 May 2004.

The main plot of the series is very simple. In a nutshell, it revolves around a group of friends in their 20s (early 30s at the end of the series) living in New York City, and tells us about their (humorous) way of coping with reality and with growing up. As Quaglio (2009b: 77) notes, the sitcom's humour is not created in a "social vacuum", but it is set against the backdrop of sometimes controversial moral and social issues pervading US culture in the 1990s and 2000s, such as "same-sex marriage, artificial insemination, surrogate mothers, and age difference in romantic relationships".

Friends was broadcast on NBC at 8.30 p.m. (first season) and at 9.30 p.m. (after the first season, with an exception of the sixth season which was broadcast at 8 p.m.). It received positive reviews throughout most of its

Table 5.1 Friends's viewers

Season	Viewers in millions
1	14.88
2	17.93
3	16.30
4	15.78
5	15.61
6	20.95
7	19.7
8	24.5
9	21.14
10	20.84

run and became one of the most popular sitcoms of all time, translated into numerous languages. Ratings in the USA were consistently high through all the 10 seasons, as shown in Table 5.1[1]:

In Italy, *Friends* was broadcast by Rai, the national TV channel, from 1997 to 2005 (Rai 3 for Seasons 1 to 4 and then Rai 2 for Seasons 5 to 10). It is often repeated both on satellite and cable TV channels. The length of the episodes varies slightly in the Italian version as they were consistently reduced to 22 minutes, while in the original their length varied from 22 to 24 minutes.

Officially, the authors of the Italian version remained the same throughout: Luigi Brunamonti, Anna Teresa Eugeni and Donatella Laureati as adapters and authors of the dialogue exchanges and Sergio Di Stefano as dubbing director.

One of the fundamental keys required to understand *Friends's* construction of humour is its good portrayal of the idiolects of the main characters. This is an aspect that is never highlighted by the relevant literature, which tends to analyse the characters' dialogues as if they were uniform in their style and form. In the following section, a brief description of the main features of the friends' different idiolects is presented.

Idiolects: Their Own Kind of Humour[2]

The main characters of *Friends* are six young people from the New York area: Monica, Phoebe, Rachel, Chandler, Joey and Ross. They each have a distinctive voice and a distinctive kind of humour punctuated by distinctive linguistic nuances. The characters make people laugh, both friends and audience, through different humorous mechanisms.

From a non-diegetic perspective, Rachel is perhaps the star of this group of friends, due most probably to the fact that the actress who played her role, Jennifer Aniston, has managed for years to monopolise the public's attention on her private life. However, there is also a diegetic reason for her centrality: her arrival in the circle of friends in the pilot episode of the series was construed as to create sensation. Dressed as a bride in white dress and veil, she walks into the café where the others are gathered for a drink, having just fled from her own wedding ceremony.

Rachel's fictional role evolved over the years: from a spoilt although charming girl from a middle-class upbringing, who never did a stroke of work in her life and did not have much else to do other than shopping and flirting with boys, to an independent professional in a top fashion company and (more or less) single mother of a baby girl. Her peculiar linguistic aura has a touch of surrealism to it—thanks especially to her use of metaphors—which marks many of her humorous expressions, as in the instance below:

EXAMPLE 5.1: SEASON 1 EPISODE 1 (PILOT)

CONTEXT: Rachel is talking on the phone to her dad, trying to explain why she fled her own wedding ceremony and left her husband-to-be at the altar.

ORIGINAL FILM DIALOGUE

RACHEL: C'mon Daddy, listen to me! It's like, it's like, all of my life, everyone has always told me, 'You're a shoe! You're a shoe, you're a shoe, you're a shoe!'. And today I just stopped and I said, 'What if I don't wanna be a shoe? What if I wanna be a—a purse, y'know? Or a—or a hat! No, I'm not saying I want you to buy me a hat. I'm saying I am a ha– It's a metaphor, Daddy!

ROSS: You can see where he'd have trouble.

ITALIAN ADAPTATION	BACK-TRANSLATION
RACHEL: Papà il fatto è che per tutta la vita gli altri mi hanno detto **sei una ciabatta, una ciabatta, una scarpaccia**... così oggi mi sono bloccata e ho detto: e se non volessi essere una ciabatta se volessi essere una borsa o magari un cappello... non devi comprarmi un cappello, sto dicendo che SONO un cappello, è una metafora papà...	RACHEL: Dad, the fact is that all of my life the others have told me, 'You're a slipper, you're a slipper, you're an old shoe'... so today I stopped and I said, 'And if I didn't want to be a slipper? And if I wanted to be a purse or maybe a hat... **You don't have to buy me a hat. I'm saying I AM a hat. It's a metaphor, Daddy**...
ROSS: Ecco l'origine dei tuoi problemi...	ROSS: That's the root of your problems...

In this excerpt, the repetition of the term 'shoe' and its banality as an unmarked, everyday object mostly contribute to create the humour of the joke by preparing more suitably the punchline which occurs two lines later, when she tells her father that she *is* a hat. This construction was partly manipulated in Italian, which uses the marked terms *ciabatta* [slipper] twice and *scarpaccia* [old, ugly shoe] once to replace the unmarked word 'shoe'. The humour of the joke, playing on subtle nuances, is not lost but sensibly diminished, and this effect is aggravated by the manipulation of Ross's funny conclusion, 'You can see where he'd have trouble', which refers ironically to the trouble Rachel's father might have in understanding Rachel's joke. Its replacement in the dubbed version with a generic remark on *her* troubles is somehow an anticlimax, whereas Ross's comment served in fact as the climax of the exchange.

In the next example, Rachel makes use of the possibilities of word formation in English—in this case the possibility to adjectivise a whole sentence—to create her humorous repartee:

EXAMPLE 5.2: SEASON 1 EPISODE 1 (PILOT)

CONTEXT: Rachel has indulged in the activity she most enjoys: shopping.

ORIGINAL FILM DIALOGUE

CHANDLER: And yet you're surprisingly upbeat.
RACHEL: You would be too if you found John and David boots on sale, 50 percent off!
CHANDLER: Oh, how well you know me . . .
RACHEL: They're my new 'I don't need a job, I don't need my parents, I've got great boots' boots!

ITALIAN ADAPTATION	BACK-TRANSLATION
CHANDLER: Eppure sei incredibilmente gasata.	CHANDLER: And yet you're incredibly upbeat.
RACHEL: Be', lo saresti anche tu se avessi trovato questi stivali al saldo del 50%!	RACHEL: Well, you would be too if you had found these boots on sale, 50 percent off!
RACHEL: Alla faccia di tutti. Non mi serve un lavoro, non mi servono i genitori, ma ho due magnifici stivali!	RACHEL: Eat your heart out. I don't need a job. I don't need my parents, but I've got great boots!

The Italian simplification of Rachel's last line, with the loss of the long adjective ('I-don't-need-a-job-I-don't-need-my-parents-I've-got-great-boots' boots), reduces the impact of the joke, which in the original could also count on the CSR (John and David) to create an in-joke effect. CSRs can give the audience the fulfilling feeling that they have some insider information and are, therefore, sharing private jokes with the characters.

"The Lesser-Known I Don't Have a Dream *Speech*"

If Rachel's sometimes odd choice of words and themes is matched by her down-to-earth aims and goals, this is not the case with Phoebe, a weird young woman from a dysfunctional family. The insights we get on her childhood and adolescence would be tragic if they were not so funny. Phoebe's way of speaking is unusual, often subtle and even too cultured on occasions to be fully appreciated by part of the audience, even in the original version. The following is a typical example of Phoebe's lines:

EXAMPLE 5.3: SEASON 1 EPISODE 9

CONTEXT: The friends are discussing how they are going to spend the typically American holiday of Thanksgiving.

ORIGINAL FILM DIALOGUE

MONICA: And I assume, Chandler, you are still boycotting all the **Pilgrim holidays**.
CHANDLER: Yes, every single one of them.
MONICA: Phoebe, you're gonna be with your grandma?
PHOEBE: Yes, and her boyfriend. But we're celebrating **Thanksgiving** in December 'cause he is **lunar**.

ITALIAN ADAPTATION	BACK-TRANSLATION
MONICA: E Chandler continuerà a stare alla larga dal **tacchino**, giusto?	MONICA: And Chandler will continue to keep away from the **turkey**, right?
CHANDLER: Sì, e **da tutti gli altri pennuti**.	CHANDLER: Yes, and from **all the other feathered animals**.
MONICA: Phoebe, tu starai con tua nonna?	MONICA: Phoebe, you're going to be with your grandma?
PHOEBE: Sì, e il suo fidanzato. Ma loro festeggiano il **ringraziamento** a dicembre perché lui è un **lunatico**.	PHOEBE: Yes, and her boyfriend. But they celebrate **Thanksgiving** in December because he is **moody**.

The reference to lunar months, whose length is based on the average time between new or full moons, is a quite cultivated remark that, arguably, even some members of the SA may not get. The Italian translation replaces 'lunar' with the calque *lunatico* [moody] and the 'Pilgrim holidays' has been substituted by a general comment on turkeys. Thanksgiving has gradually become a well-known celebration in Italy in more recent years, although it is considered as typically Anglo-Saxon and has not yet been fully absorbed as opposed to, for example, Halloween. However, other Thanksgiving-related terms such as 'Pilgrim' do not enjoy the same recognition, hence the need to change the reference.

One of the main objectives of this analysis is to see if there is any contrast between the American Phoebe and the Italian 'Febe' as her character in particular does seem to be the most difficult to render in translation.[3] Unfortunately, of all the dubbing actors, the one who impersonates Phoebe is the weakest and the blandest in terms of tone, rhythm and prosody.

Less hesitant and generally goofier, Ross's character, too, sounds very different in Italian. Having a PhD and being a lecturer in palaeontology, he is the most educated member of the group. His dialogues often contain highbrow CSRs; he shows a painstaking attention to details that the other friends find boring, and he is prone to fastidious clarifications. The following example illustrates his typical, cultured way of quipping after his friends' comments:

EXAMPLE 5.4: SEASON 1 EPISODE 15

CONTEXT: Ross makes a comment on Chandler's complaints about his own lack of goals and ambitions.

ORIGINAL FILM DIALOGUE

CHANDLER: Hey, you guys in the living room all know what you want to do. You know, you have goals. You have dreams. I don't have a dream.
ROSS: Ah, the lesser-known **"I don't have a dream" speech.**

ITALIAN ADAPTATION	BACK-TRANSLATION
CHANDLER: Dunque, voi che siete sul divano sapete cosa volete. Avete tutti delle mete, avete dei sogni. Io non ce l'ho un sogno. ROSS: Ehi, sembra quasi **il discorso di Martin Luther King.**	CHANDLER: Well, all of you sitting on the sofa know what you want. You all have goals, you have dreams. I don't have a dream. ROSS: Hey, it sounds almost like the **Martin Luther King speech.**

This allusion to a famous episode of American history such as Martin Luther King Jr.'s 'I Have a Dream' speech, would certainly be understood by most of Ross's friends but probably not by Joey who, on the other hand, is blatantly ignorant. Joey is an actor of Italian descent and has a typical New York accent which he accentuates with some Italian American overtones in a few expressions: 'How you doin'' and 'fuggetaboutit'. His humour builds generally on simple, dumb jokes. Most of the times, he inadvertently offers the others the occasion for a punchline as in the following instance, that also shows the other friends' customary reaction to his antics:

EXAMPLE 5.5: SEASON 1 EPISODE 24

CONTEXT: This quick exchange of conversation between Ross, Joey and Chandler is focused on two main themes: Ross's forthcoming and sudden work trip to China and his long-time, as yet undisclosed, love for Rachel, expressed by his jealousy for anyone she dates.

"The Lesser-Known I Don't Have a Dream Speech"   111

ORIGINAL FILM DIALOGUE

ROSS: I have to go to China.
JOEY: The country?
ROSS: No, no, this big pile of dishes in my mom's breakfront. Do you guys know who Carl is?
CHANDLER: Uh, let's see . . . Alvin . . . Simon . . . Theodore . . . no.
ROSS: Well, Rachel's having drinks with him tonight.
JOEY: Oh no! How can she do that when she's never shown any interest in you?
CHANDLER: Forget about her.
JOEY: He's right, man. Move on. Go to China. Eat Chinese food.
CHANDLER: Course there, they just call it food.

ITALIAN ADAPTATION	BACK-TRANSLATION
ROSS: Devo andare in Cina.	ROSS: I have to go to China.
ROSS: No, no, in quella grossa pila di piatti nella credenza di mia madre. Sapete chi è Carl?	ROSS: No, no, to this big pile of dishes in my mom's breakfront. Do you know who Carl is?
CHANDLER: Vediamo . . . Alvin . . . Simon . . . Theodore . . . no.	CHANDLER: Let's see . . . Alvin . . . Simon . . . Theodore . . . no.
ROSS: Be', Rachel esce con lui stasera.	ROSS: Well, Rachel's going out with him tonight.
JOEY: Oh no! Esce con lui e non si degna di uscire con te?	JOEY: Oh no! She goes out with him and doesn't stoop to go out with you?
CHANDLER: Dimenticala.	CHANDLER: Forget her.
JOEY: Giusto. Muoviti. Vai in Cina. Mangia cibo cinese.	JOEY: Right. Move. Go to China. Eat Chinese food.
CHANDLER: Solo là lo possono chiamare cibo.	CHANDLER: Only there, they can call it food.

The official translation of 'China' [*Cina*] in Italian can only be used to refer to the country, and it does not have the second meaning of 'porcelain' which offers the basis for the wordplay in the original dialogue. Arguably, the term *cineserie* [objects of porcelain] could have been used somewhere in the exchange as a compensation to create a more suitable adaptation. Chandler's punchline at the end, 'Course there, they just call it food', is lost in Italian which becomes more negative by resorting to a generic criticism of Chinese food.

Monica's humour is probably the less characterised. Her obsessive tidiness, her obese and bulimic past, and her second child syndrome (her brother, Ross, has always been more brilliant to the eyes of their parents) all contribute to place her on the receiving end of the others' jokes more than

112 *"The Lesser-Known* I Don't Have a Dream *Speech"*

a creator of ones. However, she, too, makes wide use of cultural references to construct her usually intelligent comments:

EXAMPLE 5.6: SEASON 3 EPISODE 6

CONTEXT: Monica's comment when she sees her friend's big engagement ring.

ORIGINAL FILM DIALOGUE	
MONICA: Oh my God, you can't even see **where the Titanic hit it.**	
ITALIAN ADAPTATION	**BACK-TRANSLATION**
MONICA: Accidenti, ma è un iceberg.	MONICA: Oh my, but it's an **iceberg**.

The use of a globally known CSR such as the Titanic is replaced in Italian by a line that is a sort of explicitation of Monica's words as it reduces the number of associations the audience has to make to get the joke. The line achieves its humorous aim by using less sophisticated means.

Probably the funniest character in *Friends* is Chandler, who openly plays the role of the court jester of the group. He has declaredly been using humour, and particularly irony, as a defence mechanism since the early years of his difficult childhood. Regarding his phonetic idiolect, Chandler has a peculiar way of stressing some syllables which, normally, would not be emphasised. This gives his speech a particular prosody, sometimes derided by his friends. He, too, makes extensive use of references taken from popular culture to create his jokes, whether it is a famous fairy-tale, as in Example 5.7, or a cartoon, as in Example 5.8:

EXAMPLE 5.7: SEASON 1 EPISODE 15

CONTEXT: Monica is describing the restaurant where she is going to start work. Her description prompts Chandler's reference to the fairy-tale of "Goldilocks and the Three Bears".

ORIGINAL FILM DIALOGUE	
MONICA: It's this cute little place on 10th Street. Not too big, not too small. Just right. CHANDLER: **Was it formerly owned by a blonde woman and some bears?**	
ITALIAN ADAPTATION	**BACK-TRANSLATION**
MONICA: E' un posticino nella 10° strada. Non è troppo grande, né troppo piccolo. Proprio la misura ideale. CHANDLER: **Avevi il centimetro per misurare tutto così bene?**	MONICA: It's a cute little place on 10th Street. It is not too big, nor too small. Exactly the ideal measure. CHANDLER: **Did you have a meter to measure everything so well?**

The story of "Goldilocks and the Three Bears", a fairy-tale first recorded in writing by Robert Southey in 1837, is well-known in most parts of Europe. Monica's description of the restaurant she has just seen reminds Chandler of Goldilocks's often repeated words in the fable: "This chair is too big ... This chair is just right!". This clever reference has been eliminated in the version for Italy, where the story is also known but perhaps not as popular as in the English-speaking countries, and the solution opts for a nondescript comment by Chandler on Monica's line.

In the next example, Chandler also typically uses a popular reference in an elaborate way:

EXAMPLE 5.8: SEASON 1 EPISODE 18

CONTEXT: Chandler wonders why Ross is not seeing Linda, an ex-girlfriend, anymore.

ORIGINAL FILM DIALOGUE

CHANDLER: You know, I can't believe you. Linda is so great! Why won't you go out with her again?
ROSS: I don't know.
CHANDLER: Is this still about her whole '*The Flintstones* could've really happened' thing?

ITALIAN ADAPTATION	BACK-TRANSLATION
CHANDLER: Non posso crederci, Linda è magnifica. Perché non ci esci un'altra volta? ROSS: Non lo so. CHANDLER: E' ancora perché ti ha detto che le piacciono soltanto i cartoni animati?	CHANDLER: I can't believe it. Linda is great. Why won't you go out with her again? ROSS: I don't know. CHANDLER: Is this still because she told you she only likes cartoons?

This joke, completely lost in the Italian translation, makes reference to the *Flintstones* cartoon (William Hanna 1960–1966), whose characters and stories are set in a primitive age, as an association to Ross's profession as a researcher in palaeontology. His friends often find Ross pedantic in his scientific explanations of the facts of life and in his consequent condescending attitude towards other people's more 'ignorant' views and opinions, and in this case Chandler skilfully exaggerates this trait to make a joke about a girl who apparently believed that the stories in *The Flintstones* could actually be true.

Apart from their individual speech traits, the group of friends is characterised by some linguistic features—notably their frequent use of the intensifier 'so' in the place of the standard 'really'—which have been recognised as innovative and influential on American vernacular (Tagliamonte and Roberts 2005). Although these linguistic features are not central to the present analysis, it would be hard not to notice, in most of the examples already quoted and in the ones which follow, the drastic reduction, in the Italian translation, of these discourse markers, features which make a dialogue more similar to natural conversation.[4] The result is that the Italian dialogue exchanges sound more scripted than it is normally the case with fictional conversation.

After this overview of the peculiarities of the various characters' idiolects, the next section discusses the cultural embeddedness of a non-diegetic feature, laugh tracks, one of the essential constituents of the sitcom genre.

The Cultural Specificity of Laughter

In her book on the language of jokes, Chiaro (1996: 85) states that "if it were not for the cues given by canned laughter, many jokes and humorous quips occurring in foreign versions of imported American comedies could easily pass unnoticed". One could paraphrase this quotation by stating that if it were not for the elimination of cues contained in the original laugh tracks, many dubbed jokes and humorous quips would perhaps be noticed by the TA more easily.

Live laugh tracks, such as the ones used in *Friends*, are part of the original production audio. The laugh track, or 'audience', is recorded on dailies masters during telecine or recorded on videotape dailies in a tape shoot. It is a typical feature of many sitcoms, especially North American ones, which are often recorded in front of live audiences, thus making these types of programmes interesting hybrids between television and stage productions. Laughs, however, can be filled in, if the audience did not provide enough, or inserted altogether if no live laughter exists (Clark and Spohr 2002: 195). Live laughter has been popular in the USA at least since the 1970s. Before that, canned, prerecorded laughter was common in American TV shows.

My contention is that non-diegetic laughter is in itself a culture specific element as different nations appear to have different traditions in relation to this feature. In the case of Italy, for example, live audiences are never used in sitcoms and similar fiction programmes, and prerecorded laughs are added to the shows during post-production.

Audiovisual texts express meaning by a combination of verbal and non-verbal elements as well as by extratextual factors. Following Delabastita (1989: 199–200), who distinguishes between verbal and non-verbal signs transmitted by both the acoustic and the visual channels, laughs are one of the non-verbal signs transmitted by the acoustic channel together with music and background noises. Neglecting in translation any of the various conveyors of meaning can easily unsettle the whole multilayered act of communication. This is particularly evident in dubbing, where the voice of the actor on screen is substituted by another actor's voice, the original words are substituted by translated words, and ambient sounds and even laugh tracks are sometimes altered, muted or replaced by other sounds deemed more suitable for the TA to comprehend or absorb the message.

The dialogue, the sound effects, and the music in a film each have their own separate tracks (dialogue, sound effects and music), and these are mixed together to make what is called the 'composite track', which is heard in the film. When films are dubbed into another language, a new dubbing track in the TL is created. In countries like Italy, where dubbing is the most diffused form of AVT, an important technical element needed to prepare the local version of a film is the music and effects track (M&E track) also known as the international soundtrack, which joins together the separate tracks of sound effects and music. The M&E track contains all sound elements of the film except the dialogue, which comes in a separate track and is substituted by the local distributors with a dubbed track in the native language. A skillful post-production handling of the mixing of this track containing music and sound effects with the new track containing the dubbed dialogue is of crucial importance for the creation of a good local version. Television follows similar technical procedures.

The impact of poor mixing in the creation of a dubbed version has been undervalued and, in general, neglected by research. The analyses of case studies from films and TV programmes show that much content, but especially finely chiselled humorous and ironic content, is often lost due not only to mistakes and poor translation but also to the unsettling of a balance among the words of the dialogue, voices and gestures of the actors, ambient sounds and—where it is the case—laugh tracks. For a good result, the dubbed dialogue has to be considered as one of the elements of the larger context of an audiovisual product sound environment. According to Chaume (1997: 315), non-verbal information has been neglected or taken for granted in Translation Studies, "as if translation of verbal utterances took into account every single paralinguistic, kinesic or semiotic sign which cohesively complements verbal signs".

It is hardly surprising that sounds are neglected in translation as their importance often remains unnoticed even in the critical discussion on films. As Chion (1994: 93) fascinatingly reminds us:

> The camera, though excluded from the visual field, is nonetheless an active character in films, a character the spectator is aware of; but the mike must remain excluded not only from the visual and auditory field (microphone noises, etc.) but also from the spectator's very *mental representation*. It remains excluded, of course, because everything in movies, including films shot in direct sound, has been designed to this end. This naturalist perspective remains attached to sound, but it is a perspective from which the image—60s and 70s theories on the "transparency" of mise-en-scène notwithstanding—has long been liberated. The naturalist conception of sound continues to infuse real experience and critical discourse so completely that it has remained unnoticed by those who have referred to it and critiqued this same transparency on the level of the image.

Chion (ibid.: 144–145) goes on to state that for a long time natural sound or noises were the forgotten elements, the repressed parts of film not just in practice but also in analysis. There are studies on music, dialogue, even on voice, but noises, "those humble footsoldiers, have remained the outcasts of theory, having been assigned a purely utilitarian and figurative value and consequently neglected" (ibid.).

The laugh track is a sound element but, as mentioned before, it is also a culture-bound element as different countries have different traditions with regard to laughter. Fictional television shows shot in front of live audiences, as it is common in the USA and uncommon in Italy, get live responses from live spectators who not only laugh but may squeal with surprise, may cheer and applaud or may audibly feel sorry for the characters.

The analysis of the *Friends* corpus shows that non-diegetic laughter is one of the cultural specificities of the original text that are lost in translation. In the Italian version, live laughter has been substituted by silences and/or by so-called canned laughter, which is the same pre-recorded laughter played over and over again throughout the whole programme. It is my contention that this is a major manipulation which results in an immediate localisation of the show: this sitcom *sounds* Italian not only because the characters speak Italian but also because, with its muted passages and prerecorded laughs, it has been made more similar to the comedy fiction programmes of this genre produced originally in Italy. Moreover, as laughs and other reactions are used in the original to pinpoint the funniest or most emotional moments of the story, their substitution with silences often jeopardises the result of the joke or, more generally, of the dialogue exchange.

In *Friends*, the suppression and substitution of the laugh track is a substantial loss: a great part of the emotion is lost when, for example, unjustified laughs take the place of cries of wonder and surprise. Good examples of this situation can be found all through the series, but a particularly memorable moment is in Episode 24 at the end of the fourth season. In this episode Ross is getting married to a British girl, Emily, and when the priest asks him to repeat after him the words 'I take thee, Emily', Ross unexpectedly says 'I take thee, Rachel', the name of the girl we all know he really loves. This evinces gasps of surprise and general emotional reactions from the live audience, and although the laughs following the first moments of wonder are evidently manipulated (i.e., increased), the result is still very similar to the atmosphere of a live show. In the Italian version, however, a series of identical prerecorded laughter replaces the original audience's varied response.[5]

A further step in the evaluation of humour reception would be to analyse in which moments of the sitcom laughs have been replaced by silence and in others by canned laughter. Replacing a laugh with silence when, for instance, a joke is being told, might mean that that particular joke is not considered funny for the TC or, on the contrary, that it is perceived as funny with no need to be enhanced by other means, or further still, it may just mean that in the opinion of the broadcasters, Italians are not accustomed to hearing so many laughs during a sitcom. In all cases, the handling of

"*The Lesser-Known* I Don't Have a Dream *Speech*" 117

this feature can be read as an index of either the patronage's or, to a lesser extent, the audience's mentality.

After these introductory notes, the next section illustrates the translation strategies used in the Italian adaptation of culture-bound terms.

ANALYSIS OF THE DATA

The following sections contain an evaluation of the role that CSRs play in the original English dialogue of *Friends* and an in-depth, quantitative analysis of the translation strategies used by the Italian adapters. These strategies are analysed on the basis of the taxonomy of translation strategies discussed in Chapter 4, and they become more meaningful if studied in relation to the classification of the categories of CSRs also discussed in the same chapter.

Culture Specific References in the Original Version

A preliminary viewing of *Friends* shows that CSRs play a substantial role in the texture and composition of its dialogue. The first objective is to assess exactly how important this role is and how evenly, or otherwise, the presence of CSRs is distributed along the many seasons of the series.

The first macroscopic data that can be evinced from the analysis of the six seasons composing the corpus is the high number of CSRs included in the scripts: 1,870 items.[6] Figure 5.1 shows their distribution in the seasons taken into account:

As can be seen in Figure 5.1, the very high number of CSRs is distributed quite evenly over the years, although the number of occurrences is higher in Season 1 than in any of the later seasons, with a constantly decreasing trend over the years. Thus, Season 5 has almost 6 percent fewer cultural references than the first season, whilst Season 8 and Season 10 have even fewer references than Season 1: 7 and 11 percent less, respectively.[7]

One of the hypotheses is that, as the programme rapidly gained an international audience, the authors of the scripts made an (un)conscious decision to switch to a less localised, less American reality. Most of the references across the seasons are in fact embedded in the SC, with the majority being part of the source culture category (631, almost 34 percent), that is, elements which belong exclusively to the local reality of the USA, or being overt and covert allusions to texts which are also mostly referred to the US culture. Their decline in number would make the production more palatable to mainstream, culturally distant audiences. As the examples in the corpus clearly show, to the higher number of references of the earlier seasons corresponds a higher density of the most local ones. In the first season, for example, 165 out of 415 elements (almost 40 percent) are directly related to the US culture (SC references). Most of them could in fact be defined, following Pedersen (2005: 11), as "monocultural", in the sense that they are elements which are highly embedded in the SC and possibly known only to

118   *"The Lesser-Known I Don't Have a Dream Speech"*

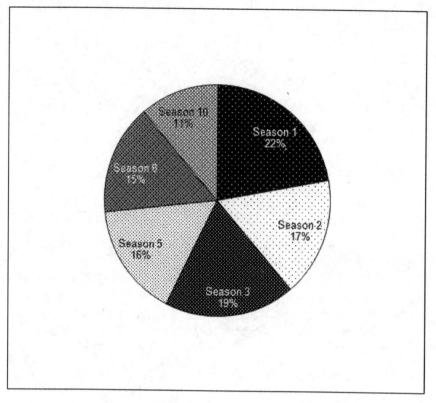

Figure 5.1 Distribution of CSRs in the analysed seasons of *Friends*

a negligible part of the TC.[8] In contrast, in the eighth season only 79 out of 289 (27 percent), and in the tenth season 65 out of 209 (almost 32 percent) of the references, are typical and restricted to US culture. It can be said then that, in keeping with its worldwide success, *Friends* became progressively more global and less local over the years.

Translation Strategies

The following is an analysis of the strategies used by Italian adapters to translate the CSRs contained in the corpus. They are broken down according to the classification set out in Chapter 4. All data are analysed in strict reference to the nature of the cultural reference in question as different strategies acquire different meanings depending on the category into which the cultural elements fall.

Figure 5.2 shows an overall breakdown of the 1,883 instances in which different strategies have been used in the Italian translations:[9]

The feature that stands out from the graph is the overwhelming presence of what could be defined as 'non-creative' strategies. By loan and

"*The Lesser-Known* I Don't Have a Dream *Speech*" 119

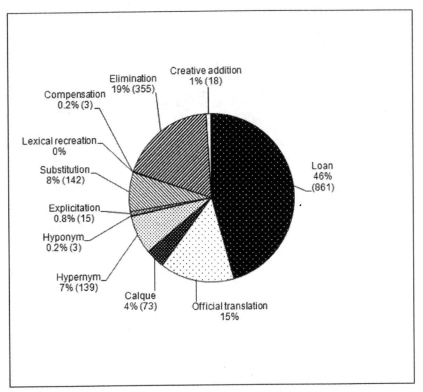

Figure 5.2 Translation strategies in *Friends*

elimination, as defined in Chapter 4, adapters leave the element unaltered, or they eliminate it altogether without replacing it with either an official equivalent or a substitute cultural reference. More elaborate solutions such as compensation, substitution, explicitation, creative addition, official translation, generalisation by hypernym and concretisation by hyponym account, altogether, for only about 35 percent of the total. Calque, which is itself a non-creative strategy as it involves a literal translation which has no actual cultural equivalent in the TC, is the only strategy of this type which accounts for a low percentage (4 percent) of the total. There are no instances of lexical recreation.

Although loan and, as a substantial second, elimination are always the preferred strategies (an exception is in Season 5 where official translation comes second), some discrepancies among the seasons are relevant as the graphs (see Figures 5.3, 5.4, 5.5, 5.6, 5.7 and 5.8) showing the breakdown of the strategies chosen per season illustrate:

The percentage of loans is constant through the seasons, from 43 percent of the third season to 48 percent of the fifth and tenth seasons. The ratio among the three strategies which preserve the original CSRs in the

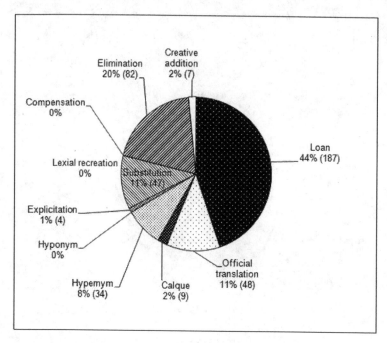

Figure 5.3 Translation strategies in *Friends* Season 1

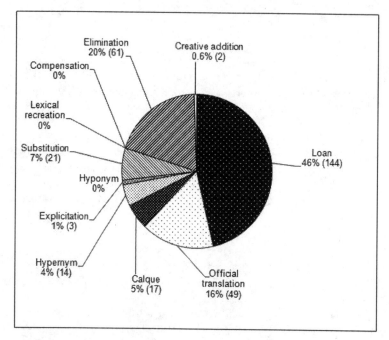

Figure 5.4 Translation strategies in *Friends* Season 2

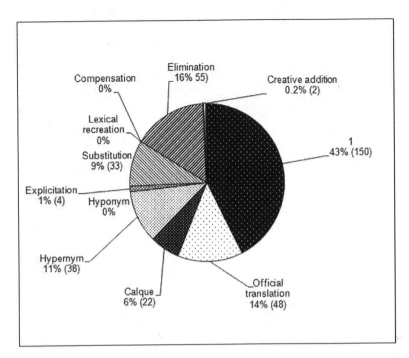

Figure 5.5 Translation strategies in *Friends* Season 3

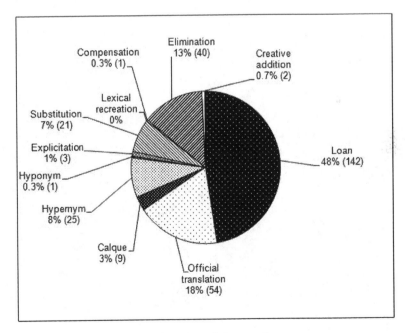

Figure 5.6 Translation strategies in *Friends* Season 5

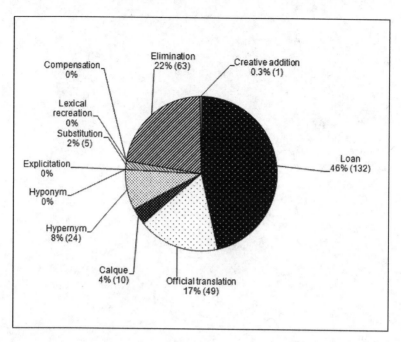

Figure 5.7 Translation strategies in *Friends* Season 8

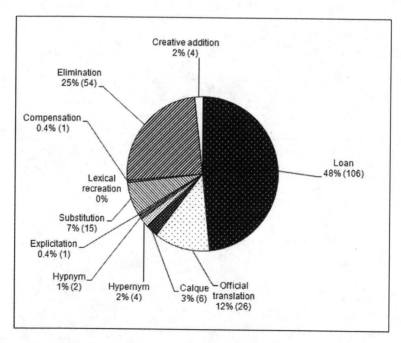

Figure 5.8 Translation strategies in *Friends* Season 10

TT—that is, loans, official translations and explicitations—and the rest of the strategies that can be considered more manipulative of the ST, insofar as they imply a more substantial semantic departure from the ST, is constant on the average, although it gets close to 50/50 in the first season (56 to 44 percent), while in the fifth season the former were used as much as 34 percent more often than the latter. However, it is important to remember that the inclusion in the corpus of currency, measures and the many geographical terms (see discussion in Chapter 4), elements usually translated with loans and official translations, objectively unbalances the statistical figures in favour of the most respectful strategies. In other words, if highly frequent CSRs such as 'New York', for example, had been excluded from the corpus, the percentage of loans would be much lower.

The following subsections discuss the various translation strategies used, illustrating them with some meaningful examples from the corpus.

Loan

According to the findings of this study, the strategy used most by Italian adapters in the translation of *Friends* is loan, chosen in 46 percent of cases. Although lexical loan, as it has been mentioned, is often considered by scholars an exoticising translation strategy, the fact is that its implementation in the case of *Friends* sensibly reduces the actual bearing of its supposed exoticism. Indeed, in the majority of occurrences it has been used to translate intercultural references—that is, elements which are not only widely known but which, to a certain extent, have also been absorbed by the TC—as well as overt allusions to fictional works to which the TC can easily relate. Loan, in fact, is not the preferred strategy for most SC references, that is references to things, places, people and events which are highly embedded in the SC and which, whether unknown, little known or widely known by the TC, are elements which have not taken root or created associations in the TC other than those linked to the SC itself. A truly exoticising translation would have chosen to translate this category also with a loan.

Other categories of references which have been widely translated with a loan are third culture references, which are also known to the TC viewers, as well as TC references, for which the loan was the most obvious solution, although not always the most suitable.[10]

One more piece of evidence that exoticising was not one of the goals of the adapters is shown by the fact that some intercultural elements, such as 'Annie Leibovitz', were not translated with a loan as they were not considered as widely popular and as diffused in the TC as others. Example 5.9 illustrates this point:

EXAMPLE 5.9: SEASON 8 EPISODE 18

CONTEXT: Rachel is describing her imaginary marriage with Ross to her parents' friends.

124   *"The Lesser-Known* I Don't Have a Dream *Speech"*

ORIGINAL FILM DIALOGUE	
RACHEL: At sunset. And **Stevie Wonder** sang *Isn't She Lovely* as I walked down the aisle. LADY: Really? RACHEL: Yeah, **Stevie** is an old family friend. LADY: Oh my God, that sounds amazing. I'd love to see pictures. RACHEL: Yeah, so would I. You wouldn't think that **Annie Leibovitz** would forget to put film in the camera. ROSS: Would you excuse us for a second? (Pulls Rachel off to the side) Umm . . . what are you doing? RACHEL: What? I'm not you. This may be the only wedding I ever have. I want it to be amazing. ROSS: Okay, okay. Ooooh, ooh maybe I rode in on a **Harley**. RACHEL: Okay, Ross, it has to be realistic.	
ITALIAN ADAPTATION	BACK-TRANSLATION
RACHEL: Era il tramonto. E **Stevie Wonder** cantava *Isn't She Lovely* mentre io andavo all'altare.	RACHEL: It was sunset. And **Stevie Wonder** sang *Isn't She Lovely* while I walked to the altar.
SIGNORA: Davvero?	LADY: Really?
RACHEL: Sì, **Stevie** è un vecchio amico di famiglia.	RACHEL: Yes, **Stevie** is an old family friend.
SIGNORA: Che cosa stupenda. Spero di vedere le foto.	LADY: What a wonderful thing. I hope to see the photos.
RACHEL: Sì, anch'io. Ti immagini il **fotografo dei VIP** che dimentica di mettere il rullino nella macchina?	RACHEL: Yes, me too. Can you imagine the **photographer of VIPs** who forgets to put film in the camera?!
ROSS: Volete, volete scusarci un secondo? Ma che stai facendo?	ROSS: Would, would you excuse us for a second? Well, what are you doing?
RACHEL: Che vuoi, questo potrebbe essere l'unico matrimonio della mia vita. E voglio che sia strepitoso.	RACHEL: What do you want? This could be the only wedding of my life. And I want it to be amazing.
ROSS: D'accordo. Uh, io potrei essere arrivato su una **Harley**.	ROSS: All right. Ooh, I could have arrived on a **Harley**.
RACHEL: Senti Ross, deve essere realistico.	RACHEL: Listen, Ross, it has to be realistic.

This example contains a few CSRs which have been translated as loans. They are immediately recognisable names of people (Stevie Wonder), titles of songs (*Isn't She Lovely*) and objects (the motorcycle Harley Davidson). The one proper name which has not been translated with a loan is that of Annie Leibovitz, an intercultural reference to a celebrity photographer whose name has been assumed to be less well-known than the others to the TA. This kind of example, containing a cluster of references, shows that the Italian translations assume a hierarchy of popularity among the cited names, which is then used as a deciding parameter when choosing the translation strategy to be implemented. The following example also illustrates this point:

EXAMPLE 5.10: SEASON 10 EPISODE 11

CONTEXT: Joey is participating in a television contest game in which he and another contestant, Gene, have to enumerate as many top models as possible.

ORIGINAL FILM DIALOGUE 23.36–23.44

GENE: Cindy Crawford, Christie Brinkley, Heidi Klum, Claudia Schiffer . . .
JOEY: Oh, oh, oh . . . *(5 seconds left)*
GENE: Christie Turlington, Kate Moss . . .

ITALIAN ADAPTATION	BACK-TRANSLATION
GENE: Allora Cindy Crawford, Naomi Campbell, Claudia Schiffer . . . vediamo . . . JOEY: Oh, oh, oh . . . GENE: Christie Turlington, Kate Moss . . .	GENE: So Cindy Crawford, Naomi Campbell, Claudia Schiffer . . . let's see . . . JOEY: Oh, oh, oh . . . GENE: Christie Turlington, Kate Moss . . .

In this case, all of the popular top model names have been kept as loans in the target version, except for two which were at the time considered to be slightly less popular in Italy: Christie Brinkley and Heidi Klum. Although their names could still be said to be part and parcel of the "encyclopedic knowledge" of the TC, to quote Pedersen (2005), the assumed low popularity of these two proper names inclined the adapters to opt for substitution and elimination, respectively, rather than loan.

Far from being an exoticising strategy, as it is customarily conceived (Vinay and Darbelnet 2004: 129), loan in *Friends* is used mostly in the case of household names that are not perceived as exotic and are assumed to be easily recognised and understood by the Italian viewer. Exotic names included in the corpus, such as Annie Leibovitz or Christie Brinkley, seldom make it to the TT.

Apart from these considerations, the high presence of this strategy is of course also due to the fact that the loan word is normally the official translation used in the TC. Names of singers, actors, politicians and other celebrities (from Barbra Streisand to Russell Crowe to Bill Clinton), names of typically Anglo-Saxon festivities which have become popular in Italy in recent years (Halloween), international brands (from Chanel to Mentos), titles of songs (from *New York, New York* to *Ebony and Ivory*), titles of novels and plays (from *The Shining* to *Macbeth*) and films (from *Mrs Doubtfire* to *Ghost*) are normally left in English in the TC because they have in fact already been fully absorbed by the Italian culture. In this sense, they can be said to have become part of the TL, leaving translators little choice but to use them.

In other words, the loan strategy in *Friends* is not used to bridge the divide between SC and TC but to reassure the TA in what they already know. This is also evident in the next interesting case of a loan which underwent a semantic change:

EXAMPLE 5.11: SEASON 1 EPISODE 3

CONTEXT: Rachel is very proud of her skills at her new waitressing job.

ORIGINAL FILM DIALOGUE 4.09–4.26

RACHEL: *(bringing drinks)* Alright, don't tell me; don't tell me! *(handing them out)* Decaf **cappuccino** for Joey. Coffee black. **Latte**. And an iced tea. I'm getting pretty good at this!

ITALIAN ADAPTATION	BACK-TRANSLATION
RACHEL: Okay ragazzi non me lo dite. **Cappuccino** decaffeinato per Joey … caffè nero … **latte** … e un tè freddo. Sto diventando brava!	RACHEL: Okay boys, don't tell me. Decaffeinated **cappuccino** for Joey … black coffee … **milk** … and one iced tea. I'm getting good!

Apart from the lexical loan in English of the Italian word *cappuccino*, one can notice the presence of another loan word which underwent a semantic change. 'Latte', shortening of 'caffellatte' is a beverage that has become quite popular in the English-speaking world, especially since the spread of chain coffee stores. The original Italian word literally means 'milk', but the British and American 'latte' is actually a drink of foamed milk with coffee. The drink which is then associated with the word is different in the SC and in the TC as 'latte' is also different from the actual Italian *caffellatte*, which is mostly considered a homemade drink, rarely ordered in bars by Italians but rather prepared at home and enjoyed with biscuits or soaked bread. To keep the word 'latte' in the translation is then only apparently a re-appropriation of an Italian word through a loan, while it is actually the elimination of a CSR which is simply lost in translation and not replaced by an equivalent CSR of the TC. 'Latte' is a North American and British, not Italian, culture specific term. Once again, the use of loans in the dubbed version of *Friends*, whether real or apparent, proves to be a non-creative strategy which somehow fails to acknowledge true cultural specificity. What it does acknowledge is the internationalisation of foreign but already firmly globalised elements. It is the sign of the globalisation of certain references and, especially, of the pervasiveness of US culture, whose influence in Italy, from the historical roots traced in Chapter 3, can now be followed in its impact on the dubbed text.

It can be noted that terms referring to TC foods common in the USA (*pizza, mozzarella, lasagne, cappuccino, espresso*, etc.) are always translated by means of a loan. There are, however, a few exceptions: the word *grappa*, a very strong Italian liquor, was eliminated; a generic reference to 'Tuscan-style finger food'—which does not mean much in Italian as its mention only shows how fashionable the Tuscany region is abroad—has been replaced by the reference to a third culture food (*cibo esotico, magari messicano* [exotic food, possibly Mexican]), and the (in Italy) quite uncommon '*mozzarella* steaks' have been replaced by the Italian dish *lasagne al ragù* [lasagne with tomato and meat sauce].

Terms referring to third culture food widely spread in the multicultural USA (falafel, Kung Pow chicken, noodles, bagels, etc.) are seldom rendered with a loan in the more culinarily conservative Italy, and they are either eliminated or substituted. The few exceptions in the whole corpus, in which a loan has been chosen for the translation of this category, are the following, mostly of Hispanic origin: 'taco' shells; the popular 'Earl Grey' and 'English Breakfast' teas; 'margarita' cocktails; 'Cajun' catfish; 'tequila'; 'paté'; and 'fajitas'. This transfer approach shows how Italians perceive Hispanic items and words as being familiar and not too exotic and how translators tend to use loans in these cases even when the objects they refer to are not very popular in Italy. One clear reason for their use is because their sound will be perceived as familiar and they will facilitate the task of lip-synching.

As a conclusion of this section, the point can be stressed once again that the loan strategy in *Friends* is quite the opposite of the exoticising strategy which it is normally considered to be. In this sense, loan is the preferred strategy in *Friends* for the reasons already stated, including the fact that it helps in lip-synching.

Official Translation

Official translation, a strategy involving some research work by the translator to find the established equivalent of an element in the TC, has been used in 15 percent of the cases, especially to translate a number of film and book titles, names of festivities such as Christmas and Easter, and of international organisations and institutions such as the United Nations (UN).

Little consistency has been found in the few recurring terms rendered with an official translation, but the single most recurring one of all—Thanksgiving—reveals the translators' attitudes over the years towards this once exotic, now not too exotic, typical US festivity. It also offers an insight on the importance of a diachronic analysis in the case of long-running series such as *Friends*. Thanksgiving is mentioned 48 times in the corpus, with a higher number of occurrences in two Thanksgiving episodes (Season 1 Episode 9 and Season 5 Episode 8). In the first one, Thanksgiving was officially translated with the word *Ringraziamento* only 4 out of 13 times (30 percent), whereas in the later episode, the term *Ringraziamento* was used 7 times out of 16 (44 percent). In more than half of the 21 occurrences

"The Lesser-Known I Don't Have a Dream *Speech"*

in the first three series of *Friends* (57 percent), the chosen strategy was *not* the official translation.

The following example, in which the word was translated twice with the official equivalent and twice without, shows an interesting incongruity:

EXAMPLE 5.12: SEASON 1 EPISODE 9

CONTEXT: Chandler tells his friends why Thanksgiving stirs up sad memories for him.

ORIGINAL FILM DIALOGUE

MONICA: *(hands Chandler a bag)* Chandler, here you go. Got your traditional **Thanksgiving** feast; you got your tomato soup, your grilled cheese fixin's, and your family size bag of **Funyuns**.

RACHEL: Wait, wait, Chandler, this is what you're havin' for **Thanksgiving** dinner? What, what, what is it with you and this holiday?

CHANDLER: All right, I'm nine years old.

ROSS: Oh, I hate this story.

CHANDLER: We just finished this magnificent **Thanksgiving** dinner. I have—and I remember this part vividly—a mouthful of pumpkin pie, and this is the moment my parents choose to tell me they're getting divorced.

RACHEL: Oh my God.

CHANDLER: Yes. It's very difficult to appreciate a **Thanksgiving** dinner once you've seen it in reverse.

ITALIAN ADAPTATION	BACK-TRANSLATION
MONICA: Chandler, ecco il tuo tradizionale **pasto controcorrente**: crema di pomodoro, patatine al formaggio e un **hamburger da riscaldare**.	MONICA: Chandler, here is your traditional **maverick meal**: tomato soup, cheese chips and a **hamburger to be heated up**.
RACHEL: Aspetta, e questa sarebbe la tua cena del **Ringraziamento**? Insomma che cos'hai contro questa giornata?	RACHEL: Wait, and that would be your **Thanksgiving** dinner? In short, what do you have against this day?
CHANDLER: E va bene, avevo nove anni. Avevamo appena finito il **cenone**, me lo ricordo come se fosse ieri, avevo ancora la bocca piena di torta di zucca. E i miei hanno scelto proprio quel momento per dirmi che stavano per divorziare.	CHANDLER: Alright, I was nine years old. We had just finished the **big dinner**. I remember as if it were yesterday. I had still my mouth full of pumpkin pie. And my parents chose just that moment to tell me they were about to divorce.
RACHEL: Ah davvero?	RACHEL: Ah really?
CHANDLER: Sì, sì, ed è difficile godersi la cena del **Ringraziamento** quando la si è vista al contrario.	CHANDLER: Yes, yes, and it is difficult to enjoy **Thanksgiving** dinner when you've seen it in reverse.

After the elimination of the reference to 'Thanksgiving' in the first line,[11] the official term *Ringraziamento* is used twice in this excerpt. In the last occurrence of the word, 'Thanksgiving' has been replaced by a reference which is specific to the TC: *cenone* [big dinner], which is the Christmas Eve traditional dinner in Italy. This incongruity, in an episode first aired in Italy in 1997, reflects the (low) degree of popularity of this festivity in Italy. Although Italian audiences have long been used to watching Thanksgiving dinners on cinema and TV screens, the notion was in the past somewhat confusedly associated with Christmas. The situation has gradually changed over the years, and today Thanksgiving is a fairly well known festive occasion, even celebrated by some Italian families prone to exoticisms. Nowadays, most people are aware that it occurs on a different date from Christmas and that it is quite distinct from it. The evidence of this change of mentality can be found in the later seasons (8 and 10, first aired in Italy in 2003 and 2005), in which Thanksgiving was always translated with the official equivalent, apart from a few negligible eliminations implemented to avoid repetition.[12] The example of the word 'Thanksgiving' shows the benefits of a diachronic analysis to get further insights on the changing mentality of a culture in its contacts with another one.

Calque

Calque, or literal translation, has been the chosen strategy in 4 percent of the cases, mainly to translate film and book titles and to give account of song lyrics. Calques in *Friends* are never justified by lip-synch, and they generally give the impression that a cultural element has not been acknowledged or maybe even recognised. The application of this translation strategy does not seem to be systematic and, for example, the soap opera *All My Children* (Agnes Nixon, 1970–2011, USA), popular in Italy under the title *La valle dei pini* [The valley of pines] has been translated with the calque *Tutti i miei figli* in one of the examples and with a substitution reflecting an evident mistake in another instance in which the chosen translation, *Erano tutti miei figli* [(they) were all my sons], is the official Italian title of Arthur Miller's classic play *All My Sons* (1947/2009).

In the next dialogue, calque was more purposely used to keep in the TT an adapted version of wordplay contained in the original:

EXAMPLE 5.13: SEASON 8 EPISODE 19

CONTEXT: Nice but ignorant as always, Joey, who is being interviewed about his acting role in a soap opera, would like to use a cultivated word but cannot quite do it.

ORIGINAL FILM DIALOGUE

JOEY: In my spare time I read to the blind. And I'm also a mento for kids.
INTERVIEWER: A mento?

JOY: You know, a mento, a role model.
INTERVIEWER: A mento.
JOEY: Right.
INTERVIEWER: Like the candy?
JOEY: As a matter of fact I do.

ITALIAN ADAPTATION	BACK-TRANSLATION
JOEY: Nel tempo libero leggo racconti ai ciechi. E sono anche un mento per i ragazzi.	JOEY: In my spare time I read stories to the blind. And I'm also a chin (= *mento* in Italian) for kids.
INTERVISTATRICE: Hai detto mento?	INTERVIEWER: Did you say chin?
JOEY: Una specie di punto di riferimento.	JOY: A kind of reference point.
ROSS: Calma, state calmi.	ROSS: Calm, keep calm.
INTERVISTATRICE: Un mento?	INTERVIEWER: A chin?
JOEY: Certo.	JOEY: Sure.
INTERVISTATRICE: Vuoi dire, mentore?	INTERVIEWER: Do you mean mentor?
JOEY: Se preferisci così.	JOEY: If you like it better that way.

The wordplay is not easy to translate as in Italian *un mentore* is masculine and *una [caramella] mentos* is feminine. It would have been possible to transfer it, though, by avoiding the article before the noun. The real obstacle here was trying to avoid the explicit mention of the brand of Mentos candies, so the adapters resorted to the homophone *mento* [chin], which is also the ending of the substantive *riferimento* [reference]. Brand names are generally omitted in Italian AVT, sometimes because some products are not distributed in Italy but more often than not because the law prohibited quite strictly, until 2004, the mentioning of brand names on television outside commercials. After 2004 the law was partly revised, but brand names are still handled carefully by adapters. The adaptation is not as funny as the original, not so much because of the *mento*/Mentos semantic shift but because the last line from the interviewer ('Like the candy?'), which plays on the double meaning of 'like' as both adverb and verb, could not be kept in the adapted version.

In general, calques in *Friends* give the impression of awkward translations and missed opportunities for more suitable adaptations.

Hypernym
Generalisation by a hypernym accounts for 7 percent of the chosen strategies, and it is always used to avoid brand names and references to cultural

items which are not so well-known in the TC. This strategy, together with explicitation (see following section), provides the best evidence that lip-synch constraints are not the main reason for major departures from the original as generalisations can be quite elaborate or involve, in any case, different consonants and vowels for which a perfect lip-synch and sometimes even isochrony can be achieved with difficulty, as the next example clearly shows:

EXAMPLE 5.14: SEASON 8 EPISODE 20

CONTEXT: Rachel and Ross are reviewing the presents they received for their daughter Emma.

ORIGINAL FILM DIALOGUE

ROSS: Wow, looks like we got a lot of good stuff.
RACHEL: Oh, we did. But my mum got us the greatest gift of all.
ROSS: **A Play-Doh Barber Shop?**
RACHEL: No. She's going to live with us for eight weeks.

ITALIAN ADAPTATION	BACK-TRANSLATION
ROSS: Wow, abbiamo ricevuto un sacco di belle cose.	ROSS: Wow, we got a lot of good things.
RACHEL: Sì, ma la mia mamma ci ha fatto il regalo più bello.	RACHEL: Yes, but my mum got us the greatest gift of all.
ROSS: **Il negozio di barbiere giocattolo?**	ROSS: **The toy barber shop?**
RACHEL: No, ma lei verrà a vivere con noi per otto settimane.	RACHEL: No, but she's going to live with us for eight weeks.

Play-Doh toys are also distributed in Italy, but as noted previously, adapters tend to restrain from mentioning brands. The generalisation, however, makes the line longer in Italian, as it contains a third more syllables and no consonants or vowels—except for the ones present in the word *barbiere/* barber—appear to have played any role in the adaptation. The fact that the camera is not focussed on the face of the actor allows for this latitude in the translation.

Hyponym
Concretisations or specifications by the use of a hyponym have been used three times in *Friends* (and in the whole corpus), that is, a percentage in this series of 0.2 percent. All of the occurrences are relative to the established habit among Italians of referring to British people and objects

132 *"The Lesser-Known* I Don't Have a Dream *Speech"*

by the term *Inglese* (English). See Example 4.11 in Chapter 4 for an exemplification.

Explicitation

Explicitation has been used in *Friends* only 15 times, amounting to a mere 0.8 percent of the total. As in the case of official translation, this strategy involves some effort of research on the part of the translators. In addition, explicitation often calls for the introduction of information, and as with generalisation by hypernym, it involves a shift in the qualitative and quantitative features of the phrase. These alterations do not seem to worry the dubbing adapters when they have to depart substantially from the source text, as is evident from the following examples in which the camera is focussing on the speaker:

EXAMPLE 5.15: SEASON 1 EPISODE 2

CONTEXT: Ross and his first wife Carol are choosing names for the baby she is expecting.

ORIGINAL FILM DIALOGUE 16.11–16.32

CAROL: Marlon.
ROSS: Marlon?
CAROL: If it's a boy, Minnie if it's a girl.
ROSS: As in **Mouse**?
CAROL: As in my grandmother.
ROSS: Still, you– you say **Minnie**; you hear **Mouse**. Um, how about, um . . . how about Julia?

ITALIAN ADAPTATION	BACK-TRANSLATION
CAROL: Marly.	CAROL: Marly.
ROSS: Marly?!	ROSS: Marly?
CAROL: Se è un maschio e Minnie se è una femmina.	CAROL: . . . if it's a boy and Minnie if it's a girl.
ROSS: Come la **fidanzata di Topolino**?	ROSS: As **the fiancée of Mikey Mouse**?
CAROL: Come si chiamava mia nonna.	CAROL: As my grandmother was called.
ROSS: Ma se dici Minnie pensi **alla fidanzata di Topolino**. Che ne pensi . . . che pensi di Julia?	ROSS: But if you say Minnie, you think of **the fiancée of Mikey Mouse**. What do you think . . . what do you think of Julia?

The phrase *la fidanzata di Topolino* [the fiancée of Mikey Mouse], which explains in more words who Minnie Mouse is, is evidently much longer than the single word 'mouse', and it implies different articulation movements for the lip-synch. This is also the case with the next reference:

EXAMPLE 5.16: SEASON 1 EPISODE 3

CONTEXT: Chandler makes a comment on one of Monica's boyfriends.

ORIGINAL FILM DIALOGUE

CHANDLER: I'd marry him just for his David Hasselhof impression alone.

ITALIAN ADAPTATION	BACK-TRANSLATION
CHANDLER: Lo sposerei solo per la sua imitazione di **David Hasselhof**, quello di *Baywatch*.	CHANDLER: I'd marry him just for his impression of **David Hasselhof**, the guy from *Baywatch*.

In this case, the explicitation by the introduction of more information was deemed necessary as *Baywatch* (M. Berk, D. Schwartz and G. J. Bonann, 1989–2001) was in fact a very popular television series in the TC, but the names of its actors were not, as is often the case with many foreign TV personalities when their fame is restricted to the small screen.

The extremely low percentage of explicitation can thus be explained more than by lip-synch considerations but by the general trend detected so far in this adaptation: that of privileging strategies which do not involve extensive efforts of research and problem solving.

Substitution

Substitution adds up to 8 percent of the total of strategies. As defined in Chapter 4, it is the replacement of a cultural element by another cultural element which may or may not have something to do with the original and may be part of the TC, of the SC itself, or of any third culture. Especially when the target reference belongs to the TC, substitution can be one of the most revealing translation strategies as it can shed light on the mores and habits of the TC, its degree of knowledge of a given CSR and its attitude towards foreign elements. Typical North American traditions relative to open-casket funeral viewings and ball dropping on New Year's Eve, shown in Season 1 Episode 10, were both replaced by examples which the Italian audience could more easily associate with, namely *bara di vetro* [glass coffin, such as Snow White's] and *quando tutti stappano lo champagne* [when everybody uncorks the champagne]. The following example also shows a typical substitution of a US reference by an Italian one:

EXAMPLE 5.17: SEASON 1 EPISODE 9

CONTEXT: All the friends had planned to spend Thanksgiving somewhere else, but in the end all plans collapse, and they gather to have dinner together.

134 *"The Lesser-Known* I Don't Have a Dream *Speech"*

ORIGINAL FILM DIALOGUE	
JOEY: Set another place for **Thanksgiving**. My entire family thinks I have VD. CHANDLER: Tonight, on a very special **Blossom**.	
ITALIAN ADAPTATION	BACK-TRANSLATION
JOEY: **Aggiungi un posto a tavola.** Anche la mia famiglia pensa che abbia la sifilide. CHANDLER: Va bene, d'accordo, ma ti sei fatto visitare?	JOEY: **Add one more place at the table.** Even my family thinks I have syphilis. CHANDLER: Alright, okay, **but did someone visit you?**

Aggiungi un posto a tavola [Add one more place at the table], the CSR which in the target version replaces the original 'Thanksgiving', is the name of a classic Italian musical play written by Garinei and Giovannini in 1973. Since then, it has become a common catchphrase in Italian, uttered when somebody turns up unexpectedly for dinner or lunch. Incidentally, the allusion to the TV series *Blossom* (Don Reo 1990–1995), centred on a dysfunctional family, has been eliminated from Chandler's line. Substitutions are resorted to when CSRs are considered to be outside the encyclopaedic knowledge of most of the TA.

In the next excerpt, it is not Thanksgiving itself but associated concepts related to this festivity which did not come across:

EXAMPLE 5.18: SEASON 2 EPISODE 8

CONTEXT: Monica is proposing some new dishes for Thanksgiving, made with a new ingredient she is testing.

ORIGINAL FILM DIALOGUE	
MONICA: How about Mockolate mousse? PHOEBE: It's not, it's not very **Thanksgiving**-y. MONICA: Okay, how about **Pilgrim** Mockolate mousse? PHOEBE: What makes it **Pilgrim**? MONICA: We'll put **buckles** on it.	
ITALIAN ADAPTATION	BACK-TRANSLATION
MONICA: Mousse di Mocholata?	MONICA: Mockolate mousse?
PHOEBE: Non è da festa del **Ringraziamento**.	PHOEBE: It's not **Thanksgiving**-y.
MONICA: E allora mousse di **Carnevale**.	MONICA: **Carnival** mousse, then?
PHOEBE: Perché **Carnevale**?	PHOEBE: Why **Carnival**?
MONICA: Per i **coriandoli**.	MONICA: For the **confetti**.

It is the images which historically relate to this American festivity that have not travelled as much as the name itself: the story of the Pilgrims and the buckles they wore on their shoes are all details which the adapters have turned into rather incoherent Carnival images: paper *coriandoli* are thrown by children and adults during the Carnival period.

However incongruous it may be on occasion, substitution appears to be, from the analysis of this corpus, a more elaborate strategy than the ones illustrated in the former sections as the loss of cultural references is always intentionally compensated by the introduction of new ones which bring into the text their own web of related associations.

Compensation
Compensation has only been used three times in the whole corpus (0.2 percent), somewhat remarkable data considering that authors like Díaz Cintas and Remael (2007: 206) have referred to it as a popular strategy in subtitling. In fact, the problem that compensation, understood as the "making up for a translational loss in one exchange by overtranslating or adding something in another" (ibid.), might create in dubbing is a technical one to do with lip synchronisation. However, as illustrated in previous pages, the nature and quantity of syllables have often been bypassed by the adapters of this show, indicating that the explanation for such a low use of compensation may lie elsewhere. The scarce use of compensation is striking only if one does not consider the general translational trend of this dubbing which, as seen above, seems to shy away from the use of the more elaborate translation strategies, that is, the strategies which involve efforts of research and creativity.

Elimination
The elimination of CSRs was used in 19 percent of the cases, a considerable loss since this strategy, as defined in Chapter 4, involves the deletion of a CSR which is not replaced by any other cultural reference. Eliminations generally lead to the greatest departures from the ST, and the original dialogue exchanges are adapted in such a way as to change the meaning of the sentences substantially.

Cultural elements are fundamental in the construction of humour in *Friends*, and the implementation of this strategy takes its toll in the translated text. Lost cultural references are often replaced by generic comments which do not convey the same humorous load to the TT as the associations triggered by the original elements—responsible for the humour of the joke—are deleted.

The following excerpts, both based on the same CSR, are a good illustration of this procedure:

EXAMPLE 5.19: SEASON 1 EPISODE 19

CONTEXT: Monica is looking everywhere for a pair of her shoes which Rachel seems to despise.

ORIGINAL FILM DIALOGUE	
RACHEL: Oh, those little clunky **Amish things** you think go with everything.	
ITALIAN ADAPTATION	**BACK-TRANSLATION**
RACHEL: Quelle **scarpettine insignificanti** che dici che vanno su tutto.	RACHEL: Those **dull little shoes** you say go with everything.

EXAMPLE 5.20: SEASON 2 EPISODE 8

CONTEXT: Ross and Chandler are compiling a list of Rachel's qualities, which Ross would like to write by pen while Chandler prefers to use a computer.

ORIGINAL FILM DIALOGUE	
ROSS: Can't we just use a pen? CHANDLER: No, **Amish boy**.	
ITALIAN ADAPTATION	**BACK-TRANSLATION**
ROSS: Non potremmo usare una penna? CHANDLER: Perché, **esistono ancora?**	ROSS: Couldn't we use a pen? CHANDLER: Why? **Do they still exist?**

The group of Christian, Anabaptist, Amish churches are mostly found in some parts of the United States. Thanks to some TV series and cinematographic films—*Witness* by Peter Weir (1985) in particular—their culture, characterised by a frugal way of living, plain clothes and no technology, became more widely known across the globe. Nevertheless, the Italian adapters opted for the elimination of the term 'Amish' and decided instead to use an allusion to the essentiality and to some characteristics perceived as primitive of these communities' style of life. The price paid, especially in Example 5.20, is that of a considerable loss of the humorous load.

As mentioned previously, brand names are generally omitted in audiovisual translations into Italian, irrespective of how well-known they are in Italy. The following is a list of the brand names eliminated from the first season alone, amounting to 92 percent of their total: Sweet'n'Lo, Pop Tart, Dairy Queen, Visa, Snuggles, Band-Aid, Raggedy Ann, Bactine, Funyuns, Obsession, Etch-a-Sketch, Hitachi, Cheese Nip, KerPlunk, Weebles, Fresca, Sugar-O, Crabtree & Evelyn, Tic Tac, Ikea, Lysol, Wonder mop, Jell-O and Chunky. The only other two brand names—John and Davies boots and Chanel perfume (two occurrences)—were translated with generalisations, thus resulting in the virtual disappearance of the brand name, and with just one loan (Chanel).

The elimination of brand names is the only case of manipulation of cultural references which in *Friends* does not appear to be detrimental to the humorous impact of most of the jokes. This is due to the fact that commercial products, even when they are eliminated, can be replaced by other objects more easily recognisable than certain other cultural elements. The following example illustrates this point:

EXAMPLE 5.21: SEASON 8 EPISODE 18

CONTEXT: After the initial enthusiasm, Phoebe is getting quite fed up with her new boyfriend's optimistic-at-all-costs zest for life.

ORIGINAL FILM DIALOGUE

PHOEBE: You don't have to put a good spin on everything.
PARKER: I'm sorry. That's who I am. I'm a positive person.
PHOEBE: No. *I'm* a positive person. You're like **Santa Claus** on **Prozac**. At **Disneyland**. Getting laid!

ITALIAN ADAPTATION	BACK-TRANSLATION
PHOEBE: No, aspetta, non puoi interpretare positivamente tutto. PARKER: Scusa. Sono fatto così, sono una persona positiva. PHOEBE: No, *io* sono una persona positiva. Tu sei come **Babbo Natale** sotto **cocaina**. A **Disneyland**. Che fa sesso!	PHOEBE: No, wait, you can't interpret everything positively. PARKER: I'm sorry. That's how I am. I'm a positive person. PHOEBE: No. *I'm* a positive person. You're like **Santa Claus** on **cocaine**. At **Disneyland**. Having sex!

While the two cultural references to Santa Claus and to Disneyland have been rendered with an official translation and with a loan, respectively, the psychotropic drug Prozac, a prescribed antidepressant, has been replaced by the more generic and illegal drug 'cocaine'. The substitution can be considered innocuous, and the joke is still funny.

More elaborate chains of associations, as the ones which are triggered by the names of well-known personalities, are never eliminated without creating a more substantial translational loss. The following dialogue exemplifies this type of situation:

EXAMPLE 5.22: SEASON 3 EPISODE 3

CONTEXT: Monica intends to have a child by resorting to a sperm bank and is now reading the anonymous files of the donors.

ORIGINAL FILM DIALOGUE

MONICA: Okay, he's 6'2", 170 pounds, and he describes himself as a male **Geena Davis**.
CHANDLER: You mean there's more than one of us.

ITALIAN ADAPTATION	BACK-TRANSLATION
MONICA: Allora, il nostro eroe è alto 1 metro e 90, pesa 85 Kg e **si è laureato a 18 anni.**	MONICA: Okay, our hero is 1.90 meters tall, he weighs 85 kg, and **graduated when he was 18 years old.**
CHANDLER: Vuol dire che è anche intelligente?	CHANDLER: Does it mean he's also intelligent?

Geena Davis is a famous actress even if her celebrity status has been waning over the years in Italy, though not in the USA. Nonetheless, details of her personal life such as her unusual height and her self-boasted high intelligence quotient are mostly known only to people of her own country, and the adapters probably considered that they would not trigger any association among the TA. Hence, the decision to manipulate the joke completely, resulting in an Italian version free of any joke: in this adaptation, Monica refers to the donor's precocious graduation, and Chandler infers that the prospective father must be very intelligent. These are the only pallid remains of the original covert allusion to Geena Davis's physical strength and intelligence, which the SA would get without further explanation.

Another way to look at CSRs, no matter how internationally popular the person or thing in question are, is to see them as a culture's own private joke, or in-joke. Admittedly, only a small sector of the TA may get the meaning and the implications of some of these jokes in the short time an actor delivers the line. A good example is found in the following excerpt:

EXAMPLE 5.23: SEASON 2 EPISODE 4

CONTEXT: Phoebe is dismayed because she has just discovered that someone she always thought was gay turned out to be heterosexual.

ORIGINAL FILM DIALOGUE

PHOEBE: I, I don't, I don't understand. How can you be straight? I mean, you're, you're so smart and funny, and you throw such great **Academy Award parties**.

ITALIAN ADAPTATION	BACK-TRANSLATION
PHOEBE: Ma, non capisco, come eterosessuale? Sei così in gamba e divertente e fai delle **feste** che sono strepitose.	PHOEBE: But, I don't understand. How can you be heterosexual? You're so smart and funny, and you throw such extraordinary **parties**.

The cluster of images that Phoebe evokes at the end of her line with the words 'Academy Awards parties' can be rapidly comprehended by the SA. This annual event is in fact the occasion for many people in the USA to hold reunions of friends, who avidly watch the show while eating junk food and making comments on the actors' outfits. The example above is the case of an SC reference which has only partly become intercultural as Academy Awards have indeed become part of the TC, but Academy Awards parties have not and are still firmly embedded in the SC.

The measure of 19 percent eliminations is outstanding data, making this one of the strategies in which the process of translation as rewriting is most evident. The Italian dubbed versions contain 355 fewer CSRs than the original, thus resulting in a substantial departure from the ST.

Creative Addition

In the analysed seasons, there was also a total of 18 additions of cultural references (1 percent) included in the Italian dialogues when there were none in the original script.

Creative additions are part of the tradition of dubbing adaptation in Italy (Ranzato 2009 and 2011a), and especially in cinema, there are many examples of this usually very interesting type of text rewriting. *Friends* does not offer examples of such creative re-elaborations, and the term 'creative', as explained in Chapter 4, is mainly meant to stress the action of introducing a new CSR into a sentence which had none. However, the goal of the adapters appears to be in most cases that of making the Italian joke funnier than the original, as the next example may illustrate:

EXAMPLE 5.24: SEASON 10 EPISODE 8

CONTEXT: Phoebe finds a way to express her revolt against the killing of turkeys at Thanksgiving.

ORIGINAL FILM DIALOGUE

RACHEL: Happy Thanksgiving.
PHOEBE: Hey. **Happy Meatless Turkey-Murder Day.**

ITALIAN ADAPTATION	BACK-TRANSLATION
RACHEL: Auguri tesoro.	RACHEL: Best wishes, darling.
PHOEBE: Sì, oggi è **il giorno del tacchino ignoto**.	PHOEBE: Yes, today is **the day of the Unknown Turkey**.

While Rachel's mention of Thanksgiving has been eliminated, the introduction of a new cultural reference in Phoebe's line is particularly funny in this example, in which Phoebe's protest against the murder of innocent turkeys at Thanksgiving assumes a gloomy aura by the allusion to the tomb of the Unknown Soldier, which after World War I started to be commemorated in many countries in memory of dead soldiers. Phoebe's original line did not actually contain a CSR, although it can be argued that it did contain an invented one: a 'Meatless Turkey-Murder Day'. However, the few made-up elements present in *Friends*, that is elements which were invented by the authors and do not have a corresponding referent in reality, have not been taken into account as they are not considered to be representative of a culture.

The creative addition of a reference can be triggered by phonetic associations, as in this case:

EXAMPLE 5.25: SEASON 5 EPISODE 12

CONTEXT: Chandler is talking to his boss, Doug.

ORIGINAL FILM DIALOGUE

DOUG: Say uh, Bing, did you hear about the law firm we got working for us?
CHANDLER: No, sir.
DOUG: Yeah, **Dewey, Cheatum, and Howe.**

ITALIAN ADAPTATION	BACK-TRANSLATION
DOUG: Eh, sai che abbiamo nuovi clienti? Degli avvocati . . .	DOUG: Hey, do you know we have new clients? Some lawyers . . .
CHANDLER: Davvero?	CHANDLER: Really?
DOUG: **Qui Quo Qua.**	DOUG: **Huey, Dewey, Louie.**

The names of Dewey and possibly Howe stimulated the association with Disney's characters, Huey, Dewey and Louie, Donald Duck's nephews (*Qui, Quo, Qua* in Italian). The incongruity of the quotation and the funny sound of their names add a humorous quip in a line which contained none in the ST.

An allusion to a classical text replaces wordplay in the next example:

EXAMPLE 5.26: SEASON 1 EPISODE 12

CONTEXT: Ross is jealous of Rachel's Italian boyfriend, Paolo, and was hoping for the affair to be over soon.

ORIGINAL FILM DIALOGUE

ROSS: Wasn't this supposed to be just a fling, huh? **Shouldn't it be** *(makes flinging motions with hands)* **flung by now?**
RACHEL: I mean, we are way past the fling thing. I mean, I am feeling things that I've only read in **Danielle Steele books**, y'know?

ITALIAN ADAPTATION	BACK-TRANSLATION
ROSS: Non doveva essere solo un'avventura? **A me sembra già un'Odissea.**	ROSS: Wasn't this supposed to be just and adventure? **It sounds like an Odyssey to me.**
RACHEL: Ormai è passata la fase dell'avventura, sto provando delle sensazioni che pensavo esistessero soltanto nei **romanzi rosa**.	RACHEL: We are past the fling thing by now. I am feeling things that I thought existed only in **sentimental books.**

The reference to Homer's text has become a fixed metaphor in Italian, meaning that a story or an experience is very long and adventurous. Although the addition plays with the word *avventura* [adventure, fling], the overused *Odissea* metaphor loses the impact of Ross's wordplay on a fling that should have long been flung.[13]

Additions in the rest of the corpus show that a few of them enhance the humorous load of the original, but the majority follows the same fate as the excerpt above, in which humour is actually diminished. Given that additions tend to have a profound impact on the original dialogue, they can be considered, together with elimination, as one of the strategies which most manipulate the form and content of the ST.

CONCLUSIONS

This case study has highlighted the presence of a rather uniform trend in the strategies used by Italian adapters to translate CSRs. When considering the whole corpus, the breakdown of strategies shows the steady preference for loan (46 percent) followed by elimination (19 percent). Nevertheless, as we have seen, some discrepancies among the series are relevant. If the cumulative percentage of the strategies which preserve the original text in the TT (loans, official translation, explicitation) is always higher than that of the other, more manipulative strategies, the ratio between the two groups shows considerable variations, and while it gets close to 50/50 in the first season (56 to 44 percent), the divide between the two figures increases in the other seasons, with a peak on the fifth, as we can see in Table 5.2.

The table shows that in the first season, loans, official translations and explicitations were used only 12 percent more often than the more manipulative strategies, as opposed to other seasons, most notably the fifth, in which the former were implemented much more frequently. If the CSRs which usually have an established form of translation (currency, measures

Table 5.2 'Respectful' vs. 'manipulative' strategies

Season	Loans, official translations and explicitations	Rest of the strategies
1	56%	44%
2	63%	37%
3	58%	42%
5	67%	33%
8	63%	37%
10	60%	40%

and geographical terms) had not been included, the importance of the manipulative strategies would be even clearer: in this case the first season, for example, would add up to less than 48 percent in the first column, as opposed to 62 percent in the second, thus reverting the balance in favour of manipulation. It can be clearly concluded from this data that the first season of *Friends* was subjected to more manipulation forces than the other seasons. Arguably, a programme which has not yet defined its ideal audience, which has not yet established itself in terms of successful viewership rates, can incur in less respectful adaptations, ones which try to attract the audience by means of more localising, comforting strategies.

As previously stressed, the frequent use of loans in this series does not imply, not even in the later seasons, a tendency to exoticism since, in most cases, the words borrowed are the ones already known by the TC, that is to say, the least exotic, which have been labelled as 'intercultural'.

The elimination of CSRs has been used in an average 19 percent of the cases, with a peak of 25 percent in the tenth season—a considerable loss since this strategy involves the elimination of a CSR which is not replaced by any other one. Eliminations tend to lead to the greatest departures from the ST, and the original dialogue exchanges are adapted in such a way that they usually change substantially the meaning of the sentences.

As highlighted, this strategy demonstrates the importance played by CSRs in the construction of humour in *Friends* since their elimination and replacement by generic comments jeopardise the humorous effect of the message. Since the associations triggered by these elements are responsible for the humour of the joke, their disappearance in the TT makes the text not as funny in Italian as it was in the original.

Reading the graphs from another perspective, it can also be confirmed that what has been defined as 'non-creative' strategies in these pages, that is, loan and elimination, are always and steadily the ones most preferred by the adapters, with a peak in Seasons 8 and 10, where these two strategies amount to 68 and 73 percent respectively.

The only strategy present in the classification proposed in Chapter 4, which has not been used by the adapters, is lexical recreation. This strategy is usually chosen by translators when a neologism has been coined in the ST, so the lack of occurrences of this strategy is not particularly revealing as there was only one case of neologism in the *Friends* corpus ('Spudnik', derived from the words 'spud' and 'Sputnik') which was translated with a loan.

As we have seen, the raw statistical figures can be given more substance and further clarification when the *type* of reference as well as the *number* of them is taken into account in the analysis. As this work focuses on the translational strategies, the conceptual categories of cultural references proposed in Chapter 4 cannot be explored in all their implications, but it is worth stressing how the analysis of the present corpus can be approached from several points of view.

In other words, I would like to point out how, from a qualitative point of view, there is room for further reflections that an analysis of the data from other perspectives would facilitate, pointing at new research avenues. Although the frequent overlappings among categories on the nature of the references (i.e., allusions can belong to the SC, to a third culture, etc.) prevent drawing clear-cut statistical conclusions, as it is possible with an analysis by strategy, nonetheless, these categories are crucial when choosing a strategy.

Friends contains the following numbers of references divided by type in Table 5.3.

For each of these figures, important considerations could be made also in connection to their being either verbal or non-verbal, synchronous or asynchronous. Being impossible for reasons of space to delve deeper into an analysis of this type, I would just like to make a few comments to show how this kind of qualitative analysis may be further and successfully developed.

We can see from the table, for example, the substantial number of references (320) to a third culture. These may be problematic for the translator because their connection with the SC may be closer or more distant than their connection with the TC. This state of affairs can be safely exemplified by the Jewish culture with which North Americans, and especially New Yorkers, are more familiarised than Italians. The Jewish expression *mazel tov*, literally meaning 'good luck' and often used to express congratulations, is used twice in the *Friends* corpus and is never rendered with a loan but with two eliminations. The Italian version prefers to eliminate these references as the knowledge of Jewish traditions is very different in Italy than it is in the United States. This is due to historical and social reasons that have created a web of associations that it would be impossible to explore here in all their implications but that, to sum up, conjure up a world which, to the eyes of an Italian, is graver and more serious, certainly not as colourful, noisy and cheerful as the one portrayed in some American films set in New York (e.g., Woody Allen's films). One of the reasons is that the memory of World War II is still a burden for many Italians, even of younger generations. Additionally, in spite of an important presence of Jewish people in Italy, Jewish culture has

Table 5.3 Types of references in *Friends*[14]

Type of CSR	Number of occurrences
Source Culture	633
Intercultural	397
Third Culture	320
Target Culture	70
Overt Allusion	402
Covert Allusion	28

not integrated with the Italian culture as successfully as it has in many parts of the USA, and many customs, expressions, foods and traditions are still exotic for the non-Jewish Italians. This explains why *mazel tov* would sound alien and even incomprehensible to the ears of many Italians as expressions of this nature have not been absorbed by the mainstream culture.

As emphasised in Chapter 4, one of the most interesting categories in terms of culture bumps for the translator is that of the references to the actual TC. This can be explained by the fact that this particular category is one of the most sensitive in terms of ideological- or censorship-related issues but also, more simply, because the familiarity of the elements compels the translator to find means to achieve a similar effect on the TA as the original element had on the SA. The impact that these particular elements may have on the TC is of course very different from the one it had on the SC, where the element will have been felt as exotic. The adapter should ideally make the effort to find an equally exotic equivalent which would not disrupt the balance of the whole text and produce a similar impact as the original. In *Friends* there are 70 occurrences of this type, including the following example which is particularly telling:

EXAMPLE 5.27: SEASON 3 EPISODE 11

CONTEXT: Joey warns Chandler—who just had a fling with one of Joey's sisters—about the violent reactions of his grandmother.

ORIGINAL FILM DIALOGUE

JOEY: Now look, listen, listen, you got to be cool, 'cause my grandma doesn't know about you two yet, and you do not want to tick her off. **She was like the sixth person to spit on Mussolini's hanging body.** Yeah.

ITALIAN ADAPTATION	BACK-TRANSLATION
JOEY: Chandler, aspetta un secondo, sta' a sentire: devi mantenere un certo contegno perché mia nonna non sa ancora di voi due e non è il caso di farglielo sapere così perché **potrebbe ricorrere al suo vecchio fucile a pallettoni.**	JOEY: Chandler, wait a second, listen: you should keep a certain composure because my grandmother doesn't know about you two yet, and it is better not to let her know this way because **she could grab her old gun loaded with large shots.**

This example risks having, even today, a shocking impact on an Italian audience, if left unaltered, because of the symbolism played by the head of the Italian Fascist government, in power from 1922 until 1943, even in the present Italian political arena, with some politicians still declaring they are inspired by him. On the other hand, Benito Mussolini in the USA is history and has no or little bearing on today's politics. This unusually graphic line for a mainstream series like *Friends* would simply have a different effect in a country where the historical events linked to Mussolini's dictatorship are not felt yet as remote. The perception of the historical past is always very different when the past is some other nation's and not one's own. The Italian version has opted for the elimination of the CSR, which has been replaced by a generic comment on the grandmother's possible violent reaction. However, the object chosen to replace it, *un vecchio fucile a pallettoni* [an old gun loaded with large shots] conjures up the image of a weapon usually associated with mafia and brigandry, thus keeping a generic link with Italian reality.

This brief conclusive overview is meant to show the importance of an analysis which takes into account not only the strategies adopted by the translators but also these same strategies in relation to the nature of the CSRs. Elimination, substitution, loan, and so on, assume different values whether they are applied to a SC element or a TC element or to the other categories present in the classification. More importantly, as in the last example I have shown, the analysis of some categories may reveal important ideological aspects implied by the translator's options.

One of the goals of the analysis was to find out how much bearing culture specificity had on the original writing and how much of it was transferred to the Italian dubbing. For this purpose, it is worth repeating that the Italian texts contain 355 fewer CSRs (19 percent) than the original 1,870, thus resulting in a substantial departure from the ST, that is, in a TT that is less culture specific. The preliminary assumption was that a programme needs some time to find its ideal target audience and, consequently, to stabilise and/or prioritise the use of certain translation strategies. The analysis of the *Friends* corpus partly confirms this trend because, although elimination is steadily an important strategy, the general increase of loans and the overall decrease of substitutions (which also imply great departures from the ST)—at their lowest in the eighth season (2 percent)—would show that, after the first season, a more literal transfer of the ST was certainly given priority.

However, the general impression drawn from the first season onwards, especially from the recurrent and persistent use of the strategies of loan and elimination, and from the low percentages reached by more creative strategies, is that of an overall flat adaptation. Although considerations related to broadcasting strategies and reception and viewership data are outside the scope of the present research, one would be encouraged to infer, from the analysis of this series adaptation, that the target audiences the authors aimed at were different in the USA and in Italy. If the original *Friends* aimed at an audience of late teenagers and young to not-so-young adults, the audience for the Italian *Friends* seems to be composed of people in their early teens, people who would find it harder to grasp all of the associations rendered necessary by the dense presence of CSRs in the original text. In other words, *Friends* in Italian has been simplified; it has become more accessible to younger generations and perhaps a little less palatable for the older ones.

NOTES

1. See http://www.classictvhits.com/tvratings/index.htm; *Variety:* http://www.variety.com/index.asp?layout=chart_pass&charttype=chart_topshows99&dept=TV; "The Bitter End": 2001. *EW.Com.* http://www.ew.com/ew/article/0,,256435,00.html; "How Did Your Favorite Show Rate?": 2001. *USA Today.* http://www.usatoday.com/life/ television/2002/2002–05–28-year-end-chart.htm; http://groups.google.com/group/rec.arts.tv/browse_thread/thread/ee82c0640bcaeb06/82c78e0fe7710443?lnk=st&q=nielsen+top+156&rnum=1#82c78e0fe7710443; http://web.archive.org/web/20070208132303; http://www.abcmedianet.com/pressrel/dispDNR.html?id=060204_11.
2. A condensed version of this and the following section is included in Ranzato (2011b).
3. The character's name is still Phoebe in all Italian synopses, character descriptions, press reviews and so on, but it is actually pronounced by the actors as Febe [febə], the Italian corresponding name.
4. For a collection of essays on dialogue in audiovisual programmes versus natural conversation, see Freddi and Pavesi (2009). See also Mattson (2006, 2009) for a study on the subtitling of discourse particles in Swedish.
5. Incidentally, as evidence that the handling of laugh tracks is indeed culture specific, the Spanish and French tracks were also manipulated by adding canned laughter, although in both of them the original reactions can still be heard faintly in the background.
6. Although figures are as accurate as possible, one must allow for a low percentage of overlooked items.
7. Season 10, however, includes a smaller number of episodes (18) when compared to the other seasons, which consist of 24 episodes each.
8. As noted in Chapter 4, the evaluation of the nature of a cultural reference is, to a certain extent, subjective. In a limited number of cases, to judge what is monocultural rather than transcultural is left to the researcher and depends on their subjective evaluation of the recipient's culture and on the moment in time a text is translated into another language. The character of the children's book *The Grinch* (1957/2007), for instance, a title present in one of the dialogues of the corpus, can be considered a monocultural reference because at the time that season of *Friends* was first broadcast, this fairy-tale was virtually unknown in Italy. The situation changed when the film *Dr Seuss' How the Grinch Stole Christmas* by Ron Howard was released in 2000.
9. The number of cultural elements and the number of strategies, in this and in the following case studies, do not coincide because strategies such as addition and compensation involve an introduction of new cultural elements.
10. As explained in Chapter 4, the impact on the TC of an (Italian) object or word present in the original English dialogue is very different from the impact it has on the SA, to which the same element or word may sound truly exotic.
11. Incidentally, another CSR, 'Funyans', is also eliminated from the same line because this snack brand is unknown in Italy.
12. Italian does not tolerate the repetition of words as much as English does. Repetition in Italian is normally used for effect, such as to add emphasis, and various strategies are used in English–Italian translations to overcome this stylistic challenge.
13. Incidentally, a reference to the author of sentimental books, Danielle Steele, has been replaced by a hypernym that spells out her literary incline.

14. Tables on the number of references by type do not include the categories which are more difficult to count, that is, intertextual macroallusions and asynchronous references as well as non-verbal references which were included in the corpus only when they were directly related to the dialogues.

REFERENCES

Baños-Piñero, Rocío. 2005. "La oralidad prefabricada en los textos audiovisuales: estudio descriptivo-contrastivo de *Friends y Siete vidas*". *Forum de Recerca*. www.uji.es/bin/publ/edicions/jfi10/trad/6.pdf, last accessed 27th February 2015.

Baños-Piñero, Rocío. 2009. "Estudio descriptivo-contrastivo del discurso oral prefabricado en un corpus audiovisual comparable en español: oralidad prefabricada de producción propia y de producción ajena", in Pascual Cantos Gómez and Aquilino Sánchez Pérez (eds.) *Panorama de investigaciones basadas en corpus*. Murcia: Asociación Española de Lingüística del Corpus, University of Murcia, 399–413.

Baños-Piñero, Rocío. 2010. "El diálogo audiovisual en la traducción para el doblaje y en producciones domésticas: parecidos y diferencias", in Rafael López-Campos Bodineau, Carmen Balbuena Torezano and Manuela Álvarez Jurado (eds.) *Traducción y modernidad: textos científicos, jurídicos, económicos y audiovisuales*. Córdoba: Universidad de Córdoba, 199–210.

Baños-Piñero, Rocío and Frederic Chaume. 2009. "Prefabricated orality. A challenge in audiovisual translation". *Intralinea* Special Issue—The translation of dialects in multimedia. www. intralinea.org/specials/article/Prefabricated_Orality, last accessed 31st March 2015.

"The Bitter End": 2001. *EW.Com*. http://www.ew.com/ew/article/0,,256435,00.html, no longer available.

Chaume Varela, Frederic. 1997. "Translating non-verbal information in dubbing", in Fernando Poyatos (ed.) *Nonverbal Communication in Translation*. Amsterdam: John Benjamins, 313–326.

Chiaro, Delia. 1996. *The Language of Jokes—Analysing Verbal Plays*. London: Routledge.

Chion, Michel. 1994. *Audio-vision. Sound on Screen*. New York: Columbia University Press.

Clark, Barbara and Susan J. Spohr. 2002. *Guide to Postproduction for TV and Film*. Charlotte, North Carolina: Baker &Taylor.

Delabastita, Dirk. 1989. "Translation and mass-communication". *Babel* 35(4): 193–218.

Díaz Cintas, Jorge and Aline Remael. 2007. *Audiovisual Translation: Subtitling*. Manchester: St Jerome.

Freddi, Maria and Maria Pavesi (eds.). 2009. *Analysing Audiovisual Dialogue. Linguistic and Translation Insights*. Bologna: Clueb.

Homer. 2003. *The Odyssey*. London: Penguin. (Italian edition: 2014. *Odissea. Testo greco a fronte*. Torino: Einaudi, translated by R. Calzecchi Onesti).

"How did your favorite show rate?". 2001. *USA Today*. www.usatoday.com/life/television/2002/2002-05-28-year-end-chart.htm, 31st March 2015. http://groups.google.com/group/rec.arts.tv/browse_thread/thread/ee82c0640bcaeb06/82c78e0fe7710443?lnk=st&q=nielsen+top+156&rnum=1#82c78e0fe7710443, last accessed 31st March 2015. http://web.archive.org/web/20070208132303, no longer available.

Kander, John and Fred Ebb. 1980. *Theme from New York New York*. Reprise Records. USA.

King, Martin Luther Jr. 1963. "I have a dream" speech. www.americanrhetoric.com/speeches/mlkihaveadream.htm, last accessed 27th February 2015.

King, Stephen. 2011. *The Shining*. New York: Doubleday.

Mattson, Jenny. 2006. "Linguistic variation in subtitling. The subtitling of swearwords and discourse markers on public television, commercial television and DVD". *MuTra 2006—Audiovisual Translation Scenarios: Conference Proceedings*, in www.euroconferences.info/proceedings/2006_Proceedings/2006_Mattsson_Jenny.pdf, last accessed 27th February 2015.

McCartney, Paul and Stevie Wonder. 1982. *Ebony and Ivory*. Parlophone/EMI. UK.

Miller, Arthur. 1947/2009. *All My Sons*. London: Penguin.

Pedersen, Jan. 2005. "How is culture rendered in subtitles?". *MuTra 2005—Challenges of Multidimensional Translation: Conference Proceedings*, in www.euroconferences.info/proceedings/2005_Proceedings/2005_Pedersen_Jan.pdf, last accessed 27th February 2015.

Pedersen, Jan. 2007. *Scandinavian Subtitles: A Comparative Study of Subtitling Norms in Sweden and Denmark with a Focus on Extralinguistic Cultural References*. PhD thesis. Stockholm: Stockholm University.

Quaglio, Paulo. 2009a. *Television Dialogue. The Sitcom Friends vs. Natural Conversation*. Amsterdam: John Benjamins.

Quaglio, Paulo. 2009b. "Vague language in the situation comedy Friends versus natural conversation", in Maria Pavesi and Maria Freddi (eds.) *Analyising Audiovisual Language: Linguistic and Translational Insights*. Bologna: Clueb, 75–91.

Ranzato, Irene. 2009. "Censorship or creative translation?: the Italian experience from Tennessee Williams to Woody Allen to *Six Feet Under*", in Federico Federici (ed.) *Translating Regionalised Voices in Audiovisuals*. Roma: Aracne, 43–69.

Ranzato, Irene. 2011a. "Translating Woody Allen into Italian. Creativity in dubbing". *The Journal of Specialized Translation* 15: 121–141.

Ranzato, Irene. 2011b. "Culturespecific humour, sounds and laughter: strategies in audiovisual translation". *Testo a fronte* 45: 7–27.

Romero Fresco, Pablo. 2006. "The Spanish dubbese: A case of (un)idiomatic *Friends*". *The Journal of Specialized Translation* 6: 134–151.

Romero Fresco, Pablo. 2008. *A Corpus-based Study on the Naturalness of the Spanish Dubbing Language*. PhD thesis. Edinburgh: Heriot-Watt University.

Romero Fresco, Pablo. 2009. "Naturalness in the Spanish dubbing language: A case of not-so-close *Friends*". *Meta* 54(1): 49–72.

Seuss, Dr. 1957/2007. *How the Grinch Stole Christmas! And Other Stories*. New York: Harper Collins Children's Books.

Shakespeare, William. 1997. *Macbeth*. London: The Arden Shakespeare.

Southey, Robert. 1837/2011. *Goldilocks and the Three Bears*. Newbury: Classics Illustrated Junior.

Tagliamonte, Sali A. and Chris Roberts. 2005. "So weird; so cool; so innovative: the use of intensifiers in the television series *Friends*". *American Speech* 80(3): 280–300. *Variety*: www.variety.com/index.asp?layout=chart_pass&charttype=chart_topshows99&dept=TV, last accessed 26th February 2015.

Vinay, Jean-Paul and Jean Darbelnet. 2004. "A methodology for translation", in Lawrence Venuti (ed.) *The Translation Studies Reader*. London: Routledge, 128–137.

Wonder, Stevie. 1976. *Isn't She Lovely*. Motown. USA. www.abcmedianet.com/pressrel/dispDNR.html?id=060204_11, no longer available. www.classictvhits.com/tvratings/index.htm, last accessed 26th February 2015.

Filmography

All My Children (La valle dei pini), Agnes Nixon, 1970–2011, USA.
Baywatch, Michael Berk, Douglas Schwartz and Gregory J. Bonann, 1989–2001, USA.
Blossom (Blossom—Le avventure di una teenager), Don Reo, 1990–1995, USA.
Dr. Seuss' How the Grinch Stole Christmas (Il Grinch), Ron Howard, 2000, USA.
The Flintstones (Gli Antenati/I Flintstones), William Hanna, 1960–1966, USA.
Friends, Marta Kauffman and David Crane, 1994–2004, USA.
Ghost (Ghost—Fantasma), Jerry Zucker, 1990, USA.
Mrs. Doubtfire (Mrs. Doubtfire—Mammo per sempre), Chris Columbus, 1993, USA.
Witness (Il testimone), Peter Weir, 1985, USA.

6 "Follow the Yellow Brick Road"
Cultural Time and Place in *Life on Mars*

INTRODUCTION: THE PLEASURES OF TIME TRAVEL[1]

The most immediate pleasures that period cinema and television give the viewer may be perhaps summed up by a scene in Woody Allen's *Midnight in Paris* (2011). The main character (from our times), with his new girlfriend whom he has met during a lapse into the 1920s, time travels further back to the Belle Époque and listens with disbelief to Gauguin and Toulouse-Lautrec discussing the dullness of their times compared to the exciting Renaissance Age. The golden age is never our age.

At the same time, and more subtly, other, perhaps more poignant recognitions add to the nostalgic feeling stimulated by the contemplation of the past: our predecessors were perhaps more exciting, but they were certainly more sexist, more racist, ecologically unaware, technologically backwards, and they did use a weird vocabulary!

Finally, fictional stories set in past times are, of course, appealing to our senses for their retro visual style. However, the more substantial programmes of this genre add to the aesthetic pleasure the profound insights they have to offer on the way we are today as opposed to the way we were before. The following extract from an essay on *Mad Men* (Matthew Weiner, 2007–2015), a period drama set in the 1960s and probably the artistic peak of this particular kind of television, best conveys the substance and meaning of this and other series set in a time which is distant but still relatively close to us, although it certainly does look remote:

> In a second-season episode of *Mad Men* Don Draper takes his wife Betty and children Sally and Billy on a picnic. After the frolic they leave their garbage on the green field. On that the camera lingers for several silent seconds. [This scene] reveals the drama's essential strategy. From our twenty-first-century perspective the family's litter despoils the landscape, but that was of no concern in the mid-twentieth-century setting. [. . .] In *Mad Men* whatever says 'This was them then' connotes 'This is us now', mutatis mutandis. The characters' smugness is undermined by our knowing more than they do, but that targets our certainty. Those foolish mortals are us, fifty years ago but us. Fifty

years hence our present values and conventions may prove as foolish to the next enlightened age as these are to ours. (Yacowar 2011: 86–87)

Although the term 'period drama' may refer to any past age, what "captures and attracts the zeitgeist" of the present times (Edgerton 2011: xxi) are those shows set in the near past of the last century: the cited *Mad Men*, *The Hour* (Abi Morgan 2011–2012, UK) and *Masters of Sex* (Michelle Ashford 2013–present), set in the 1950s and 1960s; *That 70s Show* (Mark Brazil, Bonnie Turner & Terry Turner 1998–2006, USA) and *Life on Mars* (Matthew Graham, Tony Jordan and Ashley Pharoah 2006–2007, UK and 2008–2009, USA) in the 1970s; and *Ashes to Ashes* (Matthew Graham and Ashley Pharoah 2008–2010, UK), in the 1980s to name some of the best-known television shows belonging to this macro-genre.

Given the density of cultural elements and linguistic conundrums that these programmes include, it is rather surprising that, so far, they have not attracted much attention from translation scholars. Their authors made an evident effort to characterise the mood of the period by rendering the dialogues realistic from linguistic and cultural points of view. One of the main devices they use to this purpose is the introduction of a great number of culture specific references that, firmly rooted in that period, become asynchronous when translation is called for. The category of asynchronous references, as explained in Chapter 4, has been introduced in this work because it is useful to analyse the translation of audiovisual programmes (and theoretically other types of texts) which are temporally displaced with respect to our times.

The fascination that period programmes exert is due to their inherent and universal exoticism—an exoticism which is conveyed not only by costumes and settings but also by the linguistic antics chosen by the authors to define characters:

> This raises issues about national versus international audiences [. . .]. Comprehensibility of language is one of the issues, even when the trade is between one Anglophone country and another, as with American imports to the United Kingdom and vice versa [. . .]. Of course, [cultural references] can contribute an exotic flavor for international audiences (or British viewers too young to access their substantive content). (Richardson 2010: 224–225)

The linguistic and cultural markedness of this kind of series is usefully exemplified by one of these shows, *Life on Mars*.

LIFE ON MARS

Life on Mars is a British television series which inserts elements of science fiction into a traditional detective story. The attraction of this show lies not only in the unusual, gripping plot which develops over two seasons but also in its visual style and its retro and local feel. *Life on Mars* is set in 1970s Manchester and depicts very accurately the atmosphere and social mores of Britain at the time. Created by Matthew Graham, Tony Jordan and Ashley Pharoah and broadcast by BBC One between January 2006 and April 2007, *Life on Mars* inspired an American version of the series, which after an initial interest, suffered from declining viewership, probably due to the major and improbable changes made to the basic plot line as the story went along.[2] The UK show also spawned a spin-off and sequel in the series *Ashes to Ashes* (2008–2010), set in the 1980s, which included many members of the original cast.

The story of the original British version, with which this research is concerned, is best introduced by the short monologue that, after the pilot, the leading character, Sam Tyler, repeats in voice-over at the beginning of each episode as part of the moving imagery of the title sequence:

> My name is Sam Tyler. I had an accident, and I woke up in 1973. Am I mad, in a coma, or back in time? Whatever's happened, it's like I've landed on a different planet. Now, maybe if I can work out the reason, I can get home.

In the pilot episode, detective inspector of Manchester police, Sam Tyler, has a terrible car accident in 2006. When he wakes up, he finds himself inexplicably in 1973, having just been moved from another division in Hyde to the same Manchester police station where he used to work, only to find himself among very different colleagues in a completely alien environment. He also has to deal with a crude boss, DCI Gene Hunt, the other major character of the series with whom Sam, at first reluctantly, ends up forming an inseparable partnership. Although the plots developed in each episode are typical police procedural stories, the basic storyline of the whole series revolves around two major themes. First, Sam experiences continual culture shock in finding himself virtually on another planet as he constantly has to clash against the reality of the 1970s: workplaces full of cigarette smoke, women being constantly abused and taken for granted, racist and sexist jokes, limited and primitive technology and so on. Secondly, Sam is questing all the time for the real meaning of his situation: hints of his being in a state of coma are constant throughout the series, with Sam hearing voices and having hallucinations, although the suspense is kept till the very last episode that the truth might in fact be different.

The setting, the costumes and the dialogue are all very accurate and realistic. A distinctive feature of the show is the culture specific, or rather period specific, use of songs, starting from the title track, *Life on Mars* by David Bowie, that perfectly encapsulates the time, the atmosphere and the ambiguous state of Sam's reality.

Considered by scholars and reviewers as a brilliant example of quality TV, *Life on Mars* gives importance to period detail but "with a grainier, harder, more downbeat take on the period in question" (Richardson 2010: 154) when compared to other, more 'polished' series. *Life on Mars* is a police story with a twist, "but an original twist which opens up potential for it to be much more than a mere reworking of the ingredients in a formula" (Nelson 2007: 179). According to the same author:

> A vehicle is thus created which on one level follows a police procedural trajectory but on another makes comparisons between the ethics of today and those of another age, an era in the living memory of a considerable number of viewers. (ibid.: 177–178)

Richardson (2010: 151–168) has studied this series's dialogues from a sociolinguistic perspective, detecting the features that mark its qualitative high standard. Basing her analysis on Thompson's (1996) much-cited list of characteristics of quality TV,[3] the scholar concludes that *Life on Mars* satisfies a number of the *desiderata* for quality programming. And, she adds, "it is also arguably a valuable series because of its engagement with social issues, especially those that relate to policing" (Richardson 2010: 155).

This complex formula found a very good reception in the UK. The first series achieved an average audience figure of 6.8 million viewers, and despite figures for the second series being initially lower, they rapidly picked up, and the series finale gained an average of 7 million viewers ("Almost 6m experience Life on Mars" 2007; Holmwood 2007).

In Italy the show was broadcast for the first time on the satellite channel Jimmy in 2007 and then later on the national public channel RAI 2 in 2009, which showed it at 10:40 p.m. The audience figures in Italy were much poorer than in Britain: on 6 July 2009, the viewers were 995,000, the following week they were down to 749,000, and the numbers followed this downwards trend for the entire duration of its run (http://www.telesimo.it/news/2009/ascolti-13-19-luglio-2009.html).

The author of the Italian dialogue is Tiziana Bagatella, and the dubbing director was Antonello Ponzio.

In this study, both Seasons 1 and 2 of *Life on Mars* are analysed, consisting of a total of 16 episodes of 60 minutes per episode, that is, 960 minutes of programming.

ANALYSIS OF THE DATA

The following sections contain an evaluation of the nature and the role that CSRs play in the original English dialogue of *Life on Mars* and discuss the translation strategies used by the Italian adapters, including what could be defined as the 'extreme' strategy of cutting scenes containing CSRs. As CSRs are instrumental in understanding the nature of this particular show, more crucially than is the case with the other series of the corpus, a section dealing with the categories in which some of the CSRs fall into will precede in this chapter the analysis of the actual translation strategies.

Culture Specific References in the Original Version

Life on Mars includes a total number of 431 CSRs, 237 of which were found in the first season and 194 in the second. The graphic in Figure 6.1 shows the respective percentages:

As with the former case study, the number of occurrences is higher in Season 1 (55 percent), exceeding the second by 10 percent. In this case, however, it would be hard to apply the same consideration we made for *Friends* (a possible, conscious move towards a less culture specific narrative as the show acquired a global audience). *Life on Mars* is a quintessentially and proudly British programme whose CSRs are used to describe a realistic geographical and temporal landscape. Cultural elements are thus used here in a different way than in *Friends*, whose plots, like in most sitcoms, take place in a less connoted environment. CSRs are here even more fundamental than in other shows as the theme of the series is culture shock. As evidence of this, it should be considered that the show's Britishness required its authors to localise the format when it was exported to the USA (and Spain).

Most Relevant CSR Categories in *Life on Mars*

Life on Mars contains the following numbers of references divided by type in Table 6.1:

As with the former case study, a reflection on the nature of the references would open up interesting research scenarios that cannot be explored in this book, which is based on a quantitative analysis of translation strategies. Thus categories are used here to shed further light on the analysis offered in the following sections. However, as mentioned earlier, the nature of some of the

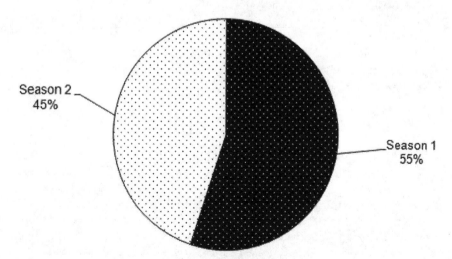

Figure 6.1 Distribution of CSRs in the two seasons of *Life on Mars*

Table 6.1 Types of references in *Life on Mars*

Type of CSR	Number of occurrences
Source Culture	139
Intercultural	93
Third Culture	101
Target Culture	2
Overt Allusion	79
Covert Allusion	10

CSRs contained in this show are instrumental in understanding its peculiarity, thus the following paragraphs in this section include some qualitative insights on the cultural makeup of this programme.

The CSRs present in *Life on Mars* broadly belong to two macro-categories which revolve around the concept of time: (1) names, objects and allusions to the contemporary world, that is, Sam's life in the 21st century, whether they are strictly and exclusively British (SC references) or well-known to the TC (intercultural), and (2) elements belonging to the past, the 1970s world in which Sam has been living since his accident. In this sense, this series is set apart from all the other period TV shows we have mentioned, except of course for its spin-off and sequel, *Ashes to Ashes*, as this story, being set both in our contemporary society and in an earlier time, virtually doubles up the mental connections, echoes and reverberations that CSRs stimulate in the audience. Sam is in fact dealing not only with one but with two different cultures—Britain and the world having changed so much in 30 years. Unlike Don Draper in *Mad Men* or Freddie Lyon in *The Hour*, Sam is in a special position—both diegetic and, in a way, extra-diegetic—in relation to the world surrounding him. The characters of the other shows are only the objects, never the subjects, of our entomological viewing, while Sam is a critical spectator of the past as well as we are.

One of the main consequences of this premise is that this analysis has to take into account not only the possible reaction of the TA but also that of the first and foremost target of the various cultural stimuli: Sam Tyler. Another consequence is that, in this particular case, we have to speak of asynchronous references as well as culture specific references. The potentially alien elements, which *Life on Mars* is full of, are mostly embedded in British culture, but they are also bound to a specific moment in time which is remote for Sam and remote for part of the British audience too. The TA finds itself in new, fascinating, but doubly estranging territory. Although *Life on Mars* contains examples from most of the categories of CSRs listed in Chapter 4,[4] the following subsections survey the most relevant of these categories in that they connote this text, contributing to shape its originality.

156 *"Follow the Yellow Brick Road"*

Non-verbal References

Cultural references are one of the main means by which the writers of the show create the atmosphere of the story and Sam's feeling of alienation. The pilot episode in particular makes it evident how the new world Sam finds himself experiencing is virtually another planet. Many of the references used in this and other episodes are, visually speaking, highly evocative images for a British audience. This is the case of the following instance, which also introduces one of the leitmotifs of *Life on Mars*: as well as hearing sounds and voices in his head, Sam is often directly addressed by people who suddenly start talking to him from the TV screen:

EXAMPLE 6.1: SEASON 1 EPISODE 1 (PILOT)

CONTEXT: The lecturer of an Open University programme suddenly starts speaking about Sam's coma and, turning directly to the TV screen, seems to address Sam himself.

ORIGINAL FILM DIALOGUE

LECTURER: Sam?
SAM: I can hear you. I can hear you!
LECTURER: Sam Tyler?
SAM: Yeah, yeah! (*Now the lecturer is so close to the camera that he's gone out of focus. SAM pats at the screen, but the man inside it can't hear him*)
SAM: Wait! No! Wait, don't leave me, I'm in **BUPA**! Please don't leave me! (*The screen goes dark then lights up again with nothing but the **test card**.*)

ITALIAN ADAPTATION	BACK-TRANSLATION
PROFESSORE: Sam?	LECTURER: Sam?
SAM: Riesco a sentirti, sì.	SAM: I can hear you, yes!
PROFESSORE: Sam Tyler?	LECTURER: Sam Tyler?
SAM: Sì sì.	SAM: Yes, yes!
SAM: Aspetta! No! Aspetta, non lasciarmi, **ehi, sono qua!** Per favore non lasciarmi.	SAM: Wait! No! Wait, don't leave me. **Hey, I'm here!** Please don't leave me!

Open University programmes were an educational service for degree students broadcast by BBC since the 1960s (and removed in 2006). They constitute a visual cultural element which is immediately recognisable by British audiences but not by Italian ones. The same can be said of another recurring visual theme: the girl on Test Card F, a test card used by the BBC when no programme was being broadcast, which featured a young girl playing noughts and crosses with a clown doll. This test card can often be seen on Sam's TV screen, and the girl in the photo appears recurrently in Sam's dreams and hallucinations. The image of this young girl can only represent an ominous presence for Italian viewers, who cannot associate it with anything from their own past.[5] In this sense, it is important to stress how the reception experience of the show is sensibly different in the two countries. The pleasure derived from the series by most parts of the British audience is one of recognition as the exotic elements are stored in the memory as part of the viewers' own pasts. The TA, on the other hand, derives its pleasure, if any, given the scarce success of the show in Italy, from the unsettling sense of complete estrangement from these same elements.

It was probably to reduce the level of exoticism that the adapters chose to eliminate altogether an element such as 'BUPA' (British United Provident Association), a private healthcare scheme which Sam mentions in desperation to stop the doctors from disconnecting his life-supporting machine. It has to be remembered that the ongoing premise of the series is that what is happening to the leading character might be either Sam's hallucination (he really does live in the 1970s, and thinks he comes from the future because he has turned mad) or the truth (he is in a coma and lives in the 1970s inside his brain or in a kind of limbo). In the first case the person speaking inside the television screen would really be a lecturer, whereas in the other case he would actually be one of the doctors who are treating Sam after his accident.

Overt and Covert Allusions

Cultural elements in *Life on Mars* (431 in total) are mainly related to popular culture or to topical and current events and people of the past and present ages. More highbrow allusions are extremely rare, especially from the lips of the intelligent but decidedly unrefined Gene, Sam's boss. It is useful to note that Gene's crude way of speaking, full of slang words, idiomatic phrases, wordplay and swear words, was sensibly simplified in Italian with regard to all these linguistic features, but his idiolect has been partly maintained with the transfer of most of the original CSRs, which give colour to his way of speaking, either by loans, substitutions or official translations. The following is one of the few instances in the series which contains what can be considered a highbrow allusion to a literary character, and it shows how most of the original dialogue of *Life on Mars* achieves a quality standard which is higher than that of the average police story, especially due to the skilful handling of both highbrow and lowbrow cultural references:

EXAMPLE 6.2: SEASON 2 EPISODE 2

CONTEXT: After sending away two twin boys who were asking Sam for information, Gene is puzzled by Sam's perturbed expression when he reads the front page of a newspaper.

ORIGINAL FILM DIALOGUE

GENE: Oi! **Bill and Ben**, sod off. We're working here.
GENE *(noticing SAM's face)*: What's up with you? You're as white as a pint of gold-top.

SAM: The bloke who looked after me when I joined the force. He's dead.
GENE: Oh. Close, were you?
SAM: You could say he was my mentor. I used to go to him for advice on everything, even when they promoted him upstairs. I learnt the job from him, really.
GENE: I think I knew him. It was **DI Frankenstein**, weren't it? He's certainly lumbered me with **a monster**.

ITALIAN ADAPTATION	BACK-TRANSLATION
GENE: Fuori dai piedi, **Cip e Ciop**. Stiamo lavorando.	GENE: Off you go, **Chip 'n' Dale**. We're working.
GENE: Che ti succede? Sei bianco come la schiuma della birra.	GENE: What's up with you? You're as white as beer foam.
SAM: Il comandante in carica quando sono entrato in polizia è morto.	SAM: The chief in charge when I joined the police is dead.
GENE: Oh. Eravate legati?	GENE: Oh. Were you close?
SAM: E' stato il mio mentore. Andavo da lui per chiedergli consiglio su tutto, anche quando l'hanno promosso a cariche importanti. Ho imparato il mestiere da lui.	SAM: He was my mentor. I used to go to him to ask for advice on everything, even when they promoted him to important positions. I learnt the job from him.
GENE: Lo conoscevo anch'io. Si chiamava **Frankenstein**. Mi ha lasciato in eredità **un mostro**.	GENE: I knew him too. His name was **Frankenstein**. I inherited **a monster** from him.

It can be argued that the character Gene is referring to is the Frankenstein of the more popular and lowbrow world of horror cinema, but it is also true that his use of this allusion, his referring correctly to Frankenstein as the creator of the monster (instead of Frankenstein as the monster itself, as in more popular usage), and the fact that this association was triggered by Sam's reference to a mentor, renders Gene's last line one of those fairly sophisticated remarks which are interspersed in this story of raw policemen and criminals.

The name of Frankenstein, certainly an intercultural allusion, given the high degree of popularity of this character in the TC, has been kept as a loan. The example also contains a more popular allusion to the twin characters Bill and Ben from a British children TV show, *Flower Pot Men* (Freda Lingstrom and Maria Bird 1952–1954). In Italian, they have been transposed into the more internationally popular Disney chipmunk characters. In addition to Chip 'n' Dale looking like twins and belonging to the world of childhood as well as Bill and Ben, the adapters have also tried not to lose the alliteration created by the two names, *Cip e Ciop*, pronounced as Chip and Chop.

Allusions play an important part in *Life on Mars* (89 occurrences). This particular type of CSR, creating a special bond between audience and audiovisual text, belongs, as emphasised in Chapter 4, to a category which is substantially different from real-world elements and which appeals, by playing on intertextuality, directly to the audience's cultural knowledge.

An important sub-category in this show is represented by a particular kind of allusion: pop songs. The centrality of popular songs in this programme is evident from the title of the series itself, *Life on Mars*, based on the homonymous 1971 song by David Bowie. Symbolically, the song is playing on Sam's i-Pod just before he has the car accident in 2006 and on an 8-track tape just after he wakes up in the same spot in 1973 as a metaphor of the new planet on which Sam has landed.

Original songs from bands and singers of the 1970s—by the likes of The Who, Roxy Music, Thin Lizzy, Uriah Heep, David Bowie and many others—can be heard throughout the two seasons. The main objective of the soundtrack is to create a period atmosphere, as the lyrics do not necessarily relate to the story. However, even when they do relate to the story—as Uriah Heep's *Traveller in Time* (Season 2 Episode 6)—the songs are never subtitled into Italian and thus can be appreciated by the TA mainly as pieces of good filler music.[6] In this way the TA loses diegetic information that could help capture the spirit of the show. Even the surreal lyrics of Bowie's *Life on Mars* add atmosphere to the climactic moment of Sam's accident, and the TA would have certainly benefited from a translation.

Besides listening to the actual songs, lyrics and titles of songs are often quoted or alluded to as when Gene Hunt refers to himself in several episodes as 'Gene Genie' in reference to another Bowie song, *The Jean Genie*. As mentioned, titles and lyrics are mainly used as references to create the atmosphere of the period, but the allusions are subtler than simple quotations and appeal to the audience's collective memory, as in the following example:

EXAMPLE 6.3: SEASON 1 EPISODE 4

CONTEXT: Sam was drugged and handcuffed to the bed, and that's the way Gene finds him the morning after. Things are not what they seem, but what they do seem is that he has had a night of sex and drugs, the ideal target for his colleague's jokes.

ORIGINAL FILM DIALOGUE

GENE: Bad dreams, were they?
SAM: I've had better.
GENE: Was **Lucy** there? **Did she have her diamond with her?**

SAM: What?
GENE: Lysergic acid diethylamide. LSD to you.
CHRIS: Better be careful boss. That stuff lasts for hours.

ITALIAN ADAPTATION	BACK-TRANSLATION
GENE: Brutti sogni, non è vero?	GENE: Bad dreams, weren't they?
SAM: Ne ho fatti di migliori.	SAM: I've had better.
GENE: **Hai usato il prezioso diamante?**	GENE: **Did you use the precious diamond?**
SAM: Cioè?	SAM: That is?
GENE: Acido lisergico dietilammidico. LSD.	GENE: Lysergic acid diethylamide. LSD.
CHRIS: Meglio andarci piano capo. Quella roba dura parecchie ore.	CHRIS: Better be careful boss. That stuff lasts several hours.

The allusion to The Beatles' 1967 song *Lucy in the Sky With Diamonds*, whose title, according to popular belief, is supposedly an acronym for LSD—although John Lennon, who wrote the song, always denied it—disappears in the Italian adaptation. The translation makes the allusion much more diffuse and cryptic by referring to the drug as a *prezioso diamante* [precious diamond], a metaphor which has never been used, either in Italian or in English, to refer to LSD.

The next dialogue between Gene and Sam also concerns the same adventure described in the context above, which is summed up in Gene's customarily crude words:

EXAMPLE 6.4: SEASON 1 EPISODE 4

CONTEXT: Following the handcuffs episode in which Sam fell into the trap of a beautiful girl who had asked him for help, Gene is explaining to Sam why he did a very stupid thing when he tried to challenge a dangerous criminal.

ORIGINAL FILM DIALOGUE

GENE: You challenged his authority, so he stitched you up like a **kipper**. Pretty girl appealed to your vanity as the only decent sheriff in **Dodge City**. Slipped you a mickey, tied you up, and bounced on your **ding-a-ling**.
SAM: Why?
GENE: Well, I suspect the answer will lie in the post. Photos, you idiot. So, next time he asks you a little favour, I suggest you do it. Otherwise your pictures will be landing on the desk of the **Chief Constable**. And **he gets**

a Christmas card from Mary Whitehouse. And believe you me, you'll be out of here in the time it takes to say **Red bloody Rum**.

SAM: She was a honey trap.

ITALIAN ADAPTATION	BACK-TRANSLATION
GENE: Tu l'hai sfidato e lui ti ha appeso come un'**aringa affumicata**. La ragazza ha approfittato del fatto che ti senti lo sceriffo più corretto di **Dodge City**. Ti ha dato un sonnifero e ha cavalcavato il tuo bel **pivellino**.	GENE: You challenged him, and he hung you up like a **smoked herring**. The girl took advantage of the fact that you feel like the most correct sheriff of **Dodge City**. She gave you a sleeping pill and rode your nice little **willy**.
SAM: Perché?	SAM: Why?
GENE: La risposta non tarderà ad arrivare. Ti ha fatto delle foto, idiota. La prossima volta che ti chiederà un favore ti suggerisco di farglielo se non vuoi che le tue foto finiscano dal **comandante**. E quando avrà visto **che razza di pervertito sei** sarai fuori di qui nel tempo che ci vuole per dire: **Cosa ho fatto di male**?	GENE: The answer will not take long to arrive. She took photos of you, you idiot. Next time he asks you for a favour, I suggest you do it if you don't want your photos ending up in the **chief's** office. And when he sees **what kind of pervert you are**, you'll be out of here in the time it takes to say: **What did I do wrong?**
SAM: Era una trappola.	SAM: She was a trap.

This excerpt contains a cluster of CSRs, as is often the case with Gene's colourful way of speaking. The allusion to a song is represented by the ambiguous word 'ding-a-ling'. This onomatopoeic word was first recorded in the late 19th century in its imitative meaning of "ringing sound of a bell" (*New Oxford American Dictionaries*) and in 1935 is recorded as meaning "mad or foolish person", from the notion of hearing bells in the head (*Online Etymology Dictionary*). Gene's allusion, however, refers to Chuck Berry's 1972 hit song *My Ding-a-Ling*, whose lyrics are all based on the double entendre of an object which is described as a toy with silver bells but actually stands in for 'penis'. Since then, the word 'ding-a-ling' has also been used in English in this sense, and this is the sexual innuendo encountered in this example too. The allusion to the song is confirmed by the mention of Mary Whitehouse, made by Gene a few lines later, a British morality campaigner who tried unsuccessfully to get the song banned. The potential culture bump constituted by the mention of Mary Whitehouse was avoided by the elimination of the reference, which was not replaced by another CSR but by one among the categories of people she claimed to stand against: perverts.

Among the other CSRs, only 'Dodge City' was kept in the dialogue as a loan, probably because it sounds as a generic allusion to Western movies more than specifically to the film of the same name, known in Italy under a different title (*Gli avventurieri*, Michael Curtiz 1939). 'Kipper', on the other hand, a CSR that refers to a way of preparing herrings which is a typical British dish, has been translated with a hypernym, *aringa affumicata* [smoked herring]. Finally, the reference to the horse Red Rum, featuring frequently in this episode, has been systematically eliminated from the dubbed version and replaced here by a nondescript phrase which does not do justice to Gene's imaginative speech, often full of incongruous quotations. In the example above, the original rests part of its creativity in the use of the funny alliteration at the end of the sentence: 'in the time it takes to say Red bloody Rum', which gets translated with a rather flat *nel tempo che ci vuole per dire: cosa ho fatto di male?* [in the time it takes to say: what did I do wrong?].

In conclusion, popular music plays a substantial part in all the episodes of *Life on Mars* and it is used—both as part of the soundtrack and as quotations and allusions in the dialogue—as a powerful means to characterise a culture and a moment in time. The members of the TA would recognise only the most popular (i.e., intercultural) songs, but even then they would not have access to the text as the non-diegetic songs are never subtitled, and the allusions to songs in the original dialogues were often eliminated (by a percentage of 38 percent).

Intertextual Macroallusions

Life on Mars as a whole plays on at least three macroallusions to other audiovisual and literary texts. The first one is a nod to another television series, a cult British programme titled *The Sweeney* (Ian Kennedy Martin 1975–1978). It has been considered by some as the first modern police series on British television, in the sense that it is realistic in its dialogue and settings and graphic in its depiction of violence (Clark n.d.). The writers of *Life on Mars* repeatedly declared to have been influenced by *The Sweeney*:

> None of us fancied littering the airwaves with yet more cop shows, and yet we knew that's what people love watching. So, we came up with a police show that we would want to watch: a cop falls back in time and tries to solve crimes in the midst of *The Sweeney*. ("Life on Mars. A sign of the times: how the Seventies were brought back to life" 2008)

The style of *The Sweeney* is continuously evoked in *Life on Mars*, not only in the gritty aesthetics of the show but also in the dialogue, especially that of Sam's boss, Gene Hunt:

> **EXAMPLE 6.5: SEASON 1 EPISODE 1 (PILOT)**
>
> **ORIGINAL FILM DIALOGUE**
>
> SAM: Alright. Surprise me. What year is it supposed to be? [...] Who the hell are you?
>
> GENE: Gene Hunt, your DCI, and it's 1973. Almost dinner time. **I'm havin' 'oops.**
>
> | ITALIAN ADAPTATION | BACK-TRANSLATION |
> |---|---|
> | SAM: Va bene, sentiamo. Chi sei tu? | SAM: Alright, let's hear. Who are you? |
> | GENE: Gene Hunt, il tuo ispettore capo. E' il 1973, ora di cena. E muoio dalla fame. | GENE: Gene Hunt, your chief inspector. It's 1973, time for dinner. **And I'm starving.** |

This phrase is a hint to one of *The Sweeney*'s most quoted replies, made, as this one from *Life on Mars*, in the middle of a quite violent altercation: "We're the Sweeney, son, and we haven't had any dinner" (*The Sweeney*, Series 1 Episode 1). Incidentally, the CSR in the *Life on Mars* dialogue, a reference to the Heinz spaghetti hoops that Gene is planning to have for dinner, was omitted in the Italian dialogue, which translated the sentence with a more general *E muoio dalla fame* [And I'm starving].

Life on Mars's high standard of script writing is testified by the fact that the authors managed to convey the most far-fetched influences into the apparently simple storylines. In this respect, another intertextual macroallusion is represented by the frequent echoes from the *Wizard of Oz* (L. Frank Baum 1900/2008 and Victor Fleming's celebrated 1939 film) as illustrated in the following examples:

> **EXAMPLE 6.6: SEASON 1 EPISODE 2**
>
> **ORIGINAL FILM DIALOGUE**
>
> GENE: Hello, is that the **Wizard of Oz**? The **Wizard**'ll sort it out. It's because of the wonderful things he does.
>
> | ITALIAN ADAPTATION | BACK-TRANSLATION |
> |---|---|
> | GENE: Pronto, è il **Mago di Oz**? Il **Mago di Oz** è uscito. Sai, ha un sacco di cose da fare. | GENE: Hello, is that the **Wizard of Oz**? The **Wizard of Oz** has gone out. You know, he has a lot of things to do. |

> **EXAMPLE 6.7: SEASON 1 EPISODE 1 (PILOT)**
>
> **ORIGINAL FILM DIALOGUE**
>
> SAM: **Follow the yellow brick road.**
> ANNIE: And what will you find? Mist? A big cliff? White door?
> SAM: I don't know.
>
> | ITALIAN ADAPTATION | BACK-TRANSLATION |
> |---|---|
> | SAM: **Segui la strada di mattoni gialli.**
ANNIE: E che cosa troverai? Nebbia? Una grande scogliera? Una porta bianca?
SAM: Non lo so. | SAM: **Follow the yellow brick road.**
ANNIE: And what will you find? Mist? A big cliff? A white door?
SAM: I don't know. |

> **EXAMPLE 6.8: SEASON 1 EPISODE 4[7]**
>
> **ORIGINAL FILM DIALOGUE**
>
> PHYLLIS: I don't recall asking you to sneak her out through the back door, take her home and sleep with her.
> SAM: It wasn't like that.
> GENE: Hey, go easy on him, Phyllis. He's just taken a stroll down **the yellow brick road!**

In addition to these direct quotations, Gene Hunt sometimes calls Sam 'Dorothy' in reference to his supposed effeminate manners, as 'friends of Dorothy' is a slang expression meaning 'gay'. Dorothy is the name of the main character in *The Wizard of Oz*, a gay cult character (Harvey & Ravano 1999: 305) played by Judy Garland in Fleming's 1939 film. Although this slang term has not been included in the corpus as it is not properly a CSR, it is worth mentioning that the four references to Dorothy were eliminated on one occasion and kept as loan in the other three occurrences, one ironically uttered by Sam. However, even in the latter cases, the TA would only be alerted to Gene's hints by the use of a feminine name and by the context: all instances are in fact related to Sam's getting emotional or too panicky, thus the perfect butt for Gene's sarcasm. Dorothy is not linked to the gay imaginary in Italy, and in general, *The Wizard of Oz*, although very popular, is far from being a nation's cautionary tale as it is in the USA and, to a lesser degree, in Britain.

The pivotal character of Frank Morgan in the series is also the artistic name of one of the actors in *The Wizard of Oz*, who played the dual roles of Professor Marvel in the Kansas sequences and of the wizard in the Oz sequences. The Frank Morgan of *Life on Mars*, too, has a dual role: he is both Gene's nemesis in 1973 and Sam's surgeon in 2006.

Finally, one of the songs from the soundtrack of the film, *Over the Rainbow*, sung by Judy Garland, features prominently in the last episode of the series in which, when Sam and Annie finally kiss, a rainbow can be seen at a distance.

These intertextual allusions to *The Wizard of Oz* work as a macroallusion in the sense that their significance permeates the whole concept of the show: Sam is in fact like a Dorothy in a strange, magic world which, just like in the fable, may be just a hallucination, the result of a concussion or maybe not.

The third intertextual reference prominent in *Life on Mars* and functioning as a macroallusion is represented by the East Manchester town of Hyde, Sam's former police division in 1973, very often quoted in various episodes. The name of Dr Jekyll's alter ego is probably a clue to the fact that Sam's self in 1973 may in fact be a double of the real one lying in a coma on a hospital bed.

These literary references, in the form of covert and overt allusions to other works of fiction, add new and sophisticated layers of meaning to a storyline resembling, on the surface, the typical detective and crime stories of which *The Sweeney* can be considered a prototype.

Doing Away With Culture Bumps

The first macroscopic difference between the original show and the Italian version of *Life and Mars* is a difference in length. All the episodes broadcast in Italy were an average of seven to eight minutes shorter than the ones shown in the UK. The fact that the cuts are constant all through the series, and of approximately the same length, shows that this choice was probably due to broadcasting strategies. Nevertheless, an analysis of the deleted scenes could shed some light on the adapters' strategies.

The deleted scenes, or parts of scenes, contain one or more CSRs, and tellingly, the first season has been submitted to heavier pruning than the second season. As would be expected, most of the CSRs used in the sitcom are deeply embedded in British culture (SC references) and, more specifically, in the British culture of the 1970s: titles of TV shows, songs titles and lyrics, references to popular actors and sportsmen, and so on. Some of the deleted excerpts contain a high number of these elements which are strongly bound to a local reality and are specific of that time, thus asynchronous in relation to the time we are watching and even to the eyes of Sam, a 21st-century man looking at things which are not in synchronicity with his time. Tables 6.2 and 6.3 show a breakdown of the number of suppressed excerpts per episode, indicating the ones that contained CSRs and the respective number of CSRs included in them:

The reason why there is a fluctuation in the number of deleted excerpts can be accounted for by their different lengths; sometimes they are in fact whole

Table 6.2 Deleted excerpts in *Life on Mars* Season 1

Season 1	N° of deleted excerpts	N° of deleted excerpts containing CSRs	Total number of deleted CSRs
Episode 1	7	4	4
Episode 2	5	3	4
Episode 3	5	2	2
Episode 4	12	10	30
Episode 5	7	6	14
Episode 6	11	3	6
Episode 7	4	2	2
Episode 8	3	2	4

Table 6.3 Deleted excerpts in *Life on Mars* Season 2

Season 2	N° of deleted excerpts	N° of deleted excerpts containing CSRs	Total number of deleted CSRs
Episode 1	17	5	11
Episode 2	10	3	11
Episode 3	7	3	4
Episode 4	8	5	19
Episode 5	12	4	7
Episode 6	4	3	8
Episode 7	8	3	5
Episode 8	7	3	8

scenes, sometimes only fragments, and always amounting to a total of seven to eight minutes of the original episode. Except for a very limited number of cases, all the excerpts which were cut out, even the ones not containing any CSRs, included potentially problematic elements for the translator: slang expressions, idiomatic phrases, swear words or disturbing content. Some of the messages Sam gets from the future have also been deleted. A particularly long scene of this kind, in Season 1 Episode 7, consists of a lecturer from the BBC Open University programme directly addressing Sam from the TV set. Thus a long scene containing an SC visual reference—the British Open University programme mentioned earlier—disappeared from the Italian version of the show. One of the reasons may be that the reference is too 'monocultural' (in Pedersen's terms), too linked to the British reality, and thus difficult to be appreciated by the TA. However, another reason is that the Italian version shows a tendency to simplify the storyline by means of deleting the parts which make it less of a police story and more of a programme which subtly plays with different genres.

It is worth noticing that the deleted excerpts, especially in some of the episodes, are marked by a strong presence of culture-bound elements. The dialogue contained in these scenes is often meant to describe Sam's alienation from the new world that surrounds him, describing the effect of the repeated culture shocks he suffers on this 1970s new planet. The deleted scenes, even the ones which do not use CSRs, frequently deprive the episodes of sociologically relevant information on the kind of atmosphere one could experience in a police station of the 1970s. The next quite long and partly reported example shows how the translation strategy of deletion has a serious impact on the possibilities of the TA of understanding this show's atmosphere while marring its general concept:

EXAMPLE 6.9: SEASON 1 EPISODE 1 (PILOT)

CONTEXT: Sam stands in front of a blackboard in the office. He makes a point of involving actively the agent Annie Cartwright, who being a woman, has so far never been taken seriously by the other policemen.

ORIGINAL FILM DIALOGUE

SAM: To predict what this killer might do next, we have to understand what he's thinking and feeling. Annie? You're familiar with this case, aren't you? (*Annie, at the back of the room, looks surprised and nervous at being addressed in front of the entire room full of CID officers.*)
ANNIE: Er . . . yes, sir.
SAM: Could you help us out here, please?
SAM: WPC Cartwright has a **BA in psychology.** (*There's a mocking murmur around the room and then laughter.*)
SAM: Now the victim wasn't gagged. Why didn't he gag her, Annie?
RAY: Forget the mind reading act. Let's get down to the striptease. (*There's an approving laugh.*)
ANNIE: Because he needed to . . . He needed to see a mouth. The lips. We have to see the things that we value.
[. . .]
SAM: And then one day, you just snap. Strangle her, using bootlace, and then the cycle starts all over again, with a different girl. And this time, you're positive you're gonna be brave enough to kiss her.
ANNIE: Only you won't be.
CHRIS: I look at your lips all the time, Cartwright. D'you think I should turn myself in? (*The men laugh. GENE strolls forward.*)
GENE: I think you'd better trot along now, sweetheart, before I have to hose this lot down.

168   *"Follow the Yellow Brick Road"*

> ANNIE: Yes, sir.
> SAM: Thank you.
> GENE: How would he keep her quiet without gagging her?
> SAM: I don't know.
> GENE: Alright. Maybe this nutter moved to the area recently. Maybe he's on day release from the loony bin. Maybe there's a new face in the local boozers, let's find out. Let's not wait for another skirt to wind up dead. And let's just hope we haven't been led up a blind alley.

Apart from the only CSR present in this excerpt—a BA in psychology—which usually does not create a problem and is often translated with the hypernym *laurea* [degree], the scene shows the stifling sexist environment most working women had to put up with at that time. The rude jokes of Annie's colleagues are matched by the paternalistic—but just as sexist—tone of her boss, Gene Hunt. His typically brisk and crude way of speaking is best exemplified in his last line, full of slang words and idioms, of which he makes ample use, either in their common forms or in his personally altered recreations. The deletion of this scene from the pilot episode represents a considerable loss as it limits the viewers' understanding of the social interactions depicted quite vividly in the original episode.

The data also show that Episode 4 of the first season suffered 12 cuts, 10 of which contain CSRs, altogether a number of 30 deleted CSRs. It is one of those episodes which makes ample use of CSRs which are both entertaining and alienating if seen through Sam's eyes and which thus best exemplify the loss caused by the omissions. Some references have multiple resonances, as in this deleted excerpt, in which famous British racing horses are mentioned:

EXAMPLE 6.10: SEASON 1 EPISODE 4

CONTEXT: Chris, one of the policemen, is handing out slips of paper he has drawn from a glass. They have the names of racing horses written on them, on which they all intend to bet.

ORIGINAL FILM DIALOGUE

GENE *(reading from the slip of paper he has just taken)*: **Red Rum**.
CHRIS: Never heard of him.
SAM: I'll swap you **Red Rum** for **Proud Percy**.
GENE: Why?
SAM *(wiggling a finger in front of his face)*: **Redrum, Redrum**. *(They stare at him as if he's crazy.)*
SAM *(attempting to explain and holding out his "Proud Percy" slip)*: I just like his name.
GENE *(suspicious)*: You got inside information?

The excerpt contains a reference to two famous British racing horses, Proud Percy and Red Rum, none of which would be known to the TA. More importantly, this scene also contains a visual allusion: Sam's wiggling finger reminds the contemporary audiences of the young boy who has the shining in Stanley Kubrick's 1980 film of the same name. The boy in the film often holds conversations with his finger which acts as an oracle for usually dreadful events; in one of the most momentous scenes of the film, the boy repeats obsessively and ominously the word 'redrum', 'murder' read backwards. In *The Shining*, the word 'redrum' also appears painted in red blood on a door, so it has visually stuck in people's minds all over the world. Sam's wiggling finger in the dialogue excerpt above implies that, as the boy in *The Shining*, he has a premonition on which horse will win the race. Of course, Sam's 1973 colleagues do not have a clue of what Sam is talking about and think that the reason he wants to exchange the horses' names is that he has some insider information on which one will actually win. This example shows the sophisticated play on synchronous and asynchronous references, from the non-diegetic points of view of the audience and Sam, which the writers so skilfully devised and which are often lost to the TA.

Other references which can be interpreted differently from the 1970s and 2000s perspectives and which are part of the fun of the show never made it to the Italian audience, like this amusing allusion to the *Star Wars* film saga (G. Lucas, 1977–present) for which a literal, and official, translation of the joke would have been perfectly understandable:

EXAMPLE 6.11: SEASON 1 EPISODE 8

CONTEXT: After a car chase of some suspects, Sam's subordinate, Chris, makes a comment which elicits Sam's contemporary response.

ORIGINAL FILM DIALOGUE

CHRIS: They've gotta give it up. What else they gonna do? We're **the Force**.
SAM: **And may the Force be with you.**

Episode 4, which as mentioned, is one of the most culturally marked episodes of the series, contains a particularly entertaining scene also deleted in the Italian version:

EXAMPLE 6.12: SEASON 1 EPISODE 4

CONTEXT: Sam and Gene are making their way in a crowded bar full of famous people.

ORIGINAL FILM DIALOGUE

SAM stops and stares.
SAM: **Bobby Charlton.**

> GENE: Yeah, and **Francis Lee**.
> SAM: **Denis Law?**
> GENE: Half a million pounds wouldn't buy you that lot. (*SAM catches sight of a young man with curly hair.*)
> SAM: Oh my God.
> GENE: What?
> SAM: **Marc Bolan.**
> GENE: Who?
> SAM: Lead singer with **T. Rex**.
> GENE: Yeah, yeah, whatever. I'll go and tell Warren we're here. (*He walks off, leaving SAM to stare at Bolan, talking to some girls.*)
> MARC BOLAN: If God were to appear in my room, obviously I'd be in awe, but I don't think I'd be humble.
> SAM: Excuse me, Mr **Bolan**?
> MARC BOLAN: **What happened to your hair**, man? (*The girls giggle. Slightly taken aback, SAM manages to grin.*)
> SAM: Er . . . I . . . I just wanted to say I'm a big fan.
> GENE: Sam! (*SAM starts to walk off but can't resist saying one last word.*)
> SAM: Listen. Drive carefully, okay? Especially in **Minis**. (*He gives MARC a significant look, which he doesn't understand at all.*)

Footballers Bobby Charlton, Francis Lee and Denis Law; singer Marc Bolan and his quotation ("If God were to appear in my room, obviously I'd be in awe, but I don't think I'd be humble"); the Mini car, an icon of the British 1960s; and the allusion to Sam's unusually short hair for those years are all CSRs gathered to conjure up a precise, if rather blatant, portrayal of a determinate place in a determinate time which probably would have required extra effort of major adaptations to work properly in Italian.

To sum up, the analysis of deleted scenes shows that the excerpts which were cut from the original episodes are never neutral. They are all either linguistically or culturally marked, falling into these three general categories:

1. Cultural: Scenes marked by one or more CSRs
2. Linguistic: Scenes marked by linguistic variation that deviates from standard usage and plays on the use of idiomatic and slang terms
3. Diegetic: Scenes which contain clues as to Sam's possible state of coma—voices of doctors and relatives, sounds from his hospital chamber, 1970s TV programmes speaking to him directly about his condition, telephone calls from the future, and so on.

The first point testifies to a strategy of dilution of all CSRs which are originally used to give substance and colour to this show. Deletions in the second category tend to a standardisation of the language. Indeed, a neutral standard Italian characterises the whole target version, and that is probably why some of the most difficult parts containing slang terms and idiomatic expressions were cut. Finally, the cuts belonging to the third category seem to point in the direction of a concerted effort to give less emphasis to the science-fiction theme of the plot, thus rendering *Life on Mars* more of a normal police drama, keeping the elements which might be perceived as weird and confusing by the TA to a minimum.

This is the only series in the corpus to have suffered such major cuts (some *Friends* episodes were sometimes cut by one or two minutes, but the deleted excerpts were not marked in any way, and cuts were clearly dictated by broadcasting requirements). This free handling and the way in which it has been carried out, by eliminating some vital points of the storyline and jeopardising characters' construction to some extent, demonstrate that this show's potential was not fully grasped by the Italian broadcasters and authors of the Italian version.

Translation Strategies

The following is an analysis of the strategies used by Italian adapters to translate the CSRs contained in *Life on Mars*. They are broken down according to the classification set out in Chapter 4.

Figure 6.2 shows an overall breakdown of the 424 instances in which translation strategies have been implemented in the Italian version in relation to CSRs in the two seasons of the series:

The first data that stand out from the graph is that—as in the former case of *Friends*—there is an overwhelming presence of the strategies of loan and elimination, which together, account for a notable 70 percent (52 and 18 percent respectively) of the total strategies used. However, the strategy of official translation was chosen in a substantial 17 percent of cases. Calque accounts for 4 percent of the instances, while more elaborate solutions—substitution, generalisation by hypernym, explicitation and creative addition—do not even reach 10 percent of occurrences. In *Life on Mars* there is only one instance of addition (0.2 percent) and two of explicitation (0.5 percent). There are no instances of lexical recreation or concretisation by hyponym, and no occurrences of compensation have been detected at any point in any of the two seasons. This general overview testifies how a very limited range of translation options has been implemented by the Italian adapters.

The following subsections discuss the various translation strategies which have been used, with an emphasis on elimination, as this particular strategy, although second to loan in the number of occurrences, characterises the Italian version of *Life on Mars*.

Loan

Loans are used in this series when handling objects, people and concepts which are considered to be immediately recognisable by the TA. Institutions

172 "Follow the Yellow Brick Road"

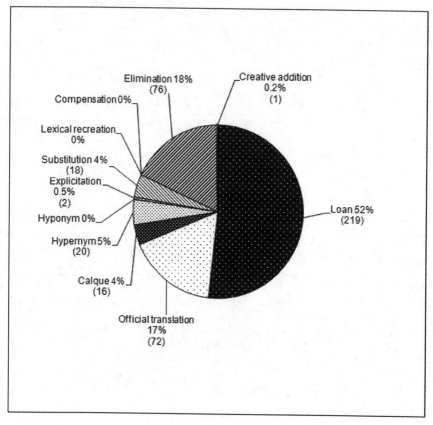

Figure 6.2 Translation strategies used in *Life on Mars*

like Scotland Yard, globally spread TC references such as Pinocchio (often used as a metaphor for liars in both English and Italian), famous actors like Gary Cooper, places like Heathrow airport, brands like Ajax and popular football teams such as Manchester United find their way into Italian in their original forms. Virtually all of the elements included as loans in the TT are thus intercultural references or internationally known third culture or TC references, except for a negligible figure (one occurrence) of a loan word belonging exclusively to the SC: the British newspaper *Sporting Life* being the only example of an element not diffused in the TC and probably largely unknown to its audience. These data testify to a non-creative use of the loan strategy, as it has already been discussed in Chapter 5: loan is not used in the text as means to foregnise the text itself but to comfort and reassure the TA on what they already know because the elements which are transferred to the Italian text as loans are CSRs that have long been assimilated by the TC.

Loans are often resorted to when the contrast between the old world and the new one is emphasised in the dialogue. The pleasure of observing, from our 21st-century perspective, Sam's satisfaction when he feels he knows better than his 1973 peers, derives in many cases from the use of these loan words. Facial expressions and other types of visual reactions would have also made it difficult—in many cases in which the loan strategy was implemented—to use more manipulative strategies. This kind of situation is illustrated by the following dialogue excerpt in which the name of a politician is kept intact in Italian as she is well-known by the TA:

EXAMPLE 6.13: SEASON 2 EPISODE 2

CONTEXT: Sam has just seen Detective Chief Inspector Woolf slouched over a chair with a hip flask on the floor.

ORIGINAL FILM DIALOGUE 17.34–17.45

SAM: Look, half of CID will be alcoholics by the time **Maggie Thatcher** becomes prime minister.
WOOLF: If **Margaret Thatcher** ever becomes prime minister, I'll have been doing something a lot stronger than whisky. (*SAM smiles.*)

ITALIAN ADAPTATION	BACK-TRANSLATION
SAM: Lo sa? Metà degli ispettori saranno alcolisti all'epoca in cui **Maggie Thatcher** sarà primo ministro.	SAM: You know, half the inspectors will be alcoholics at the time **Maggie Thatcher** is prime minister.
WOOLF: Se **Margaret Thatcher** diventerà mai primo ministro, avrò bisogno di qualcosa di più forte del whisky.	WOOLF: If **Margaret Thatcher** ever becomes prime minister, I will need something much stronger than whisky.

Of interest is the arbitrary alteration in the translation of Woolf's line. Whereas the original implies that the appointment of Thatcher as prime minister is so absurd that it can only be the brainchild of an alcoholic, in Italian the implication is that Woolf will need the help of alcohol to overcome the fact that Thatcher has become prime minister. The effect of the sexist joke is thus somehow diminished as in the original the idea of a woman in such an important position was considered inconceivable. All the same, the hint is still entertaining. This is one of those frequent moments in the show in which the audience shares Sam's 21st-century perspective and looks down on the foolish mortals of our recent past.

As with the former case study, the strategy of loan is not used to exoticise the TT but rather to acknowledge the internationalisation of foreign but firmly globalised referents.

Official Translation

Official translation, a strategy that involves some research work by the translator to find the established equivalent of an element in the TC, has been used in 17 percent of the cases. The official translation has been chosen for household names, titles of artistic works and for place names and currency (see Chapter 4 for a discussion on the inclusion of these elements in the corpus). Fictional characters such as Uncle Tom [*zio Tom*], traditional games like hopscotch [*campana*], lyrics like 'For he's a jolly good fellow' [*Perché è un bravo ragazzo*], institutions like the White House [*Casa Bianca*], film titles like *The Mutiny on the Bounty* (*Gli ammutinati del Bounty*, Lewis Milestone 1962) and places like Spain [*Spagna*] have all made their way in the TT in the official manner. The popular duo of Laurel and Hardy has been translated with the fictional names by which they are best known in Italy, *Stanlio e Ollio*. From the analysis, it can be evinced that when a reference is considered to be slightly less popular, at least in contemporary terms, maybe because it is asynchronous, and even when an official translation does exist, the adapters have decided to opt for another solution. Such is the case, for example, of the TV series *The Avengers* (Sydney Newman 1961–1969, UK), popular in the 1970s, which has been translated with the fictional title *Gli invincibili* [The unconquerable] rather than with the official title the series had when it was first broadcast in Italy, *Agente speciale* [Special agent].

Calque

Calque, or literal translation, has been chosen in 4 percent of the cases. Of the 16 occurrences, 15 are included in the first season, and only 1 instance has been found in the second season. Despite the numerical difference, this data is not particularly significant as the figure relative to the first season is mostly due to the repetitions of terms like *Gazzetta di Manchester* [*Manchester Gazette*] or *Rosso* [Red], to indicate a Manchester United supporter. Two cases, however, are more noteworthy than the rest. The first one involves an institutional name:

EXAMPLE 6.14: SEASON 1 EPISODE 1 (PILOT)

CONTEXT: Sam meets Annie, a nice, intelligent policewoman who is conscious of the way she is looked down on by his male colleagues but takes it for granted. She will soon become Sam's best friend and possible romance.

ORIGINAL FILM DIALOGUE

SAM: Are you a doctor?
ANNIE (*laughs*): I'm about as qualified as **Doctor Kildare**. I'm part of **the Women's Department**.
SAM: The what?
ANNIE: Don't you have plonks in Hyde? Go on, sir. Off you jolly well trot.

ITALIAN ADAPTATION	BACK-TRANSLATION
SAM: Lei è un dottore?	SAM: Are you a doctor?
ANNIE: Sono qualificata quasi quanto il **Dottor Kildare**. Faccio parte del **dipartimento femminile**.	ANNIE: I am almost as qualified as Doctor Kildare. I'm part of the female department.
SAM: Cosa?	SAM: What?
ANNIE: Ha bevuto del pessimo vino. Vada, signore, faccia una bella passeggiata.	ANNIE: You have drunk some very bad wine. Go, sir, take a nice walk.

Annie has been asked to pay a health visit to Sam, who looks somewhat lost and confused to the rest of his colleagues in the police department. When Sam asks her about her professional qualifications, Annie confesses that she is as qualified to visit him as Doctor Kildare, the fictional character of a widely known series by the same name (*Doctor Kildare*, directed by Robert Sagal *et al.* 1961–1966, USA), transferred with an official translation because it is also well-known in Italy. The other CSR which is relevant in this exchange is the reference to the 'Women's Department' of police, which was formally integrated into the main police corps the very same year, 1973, in which the story is set. The element has been transferred to the TT by using a literal translation that, of course, conveys the meaning but not the socio-historical relevance of a department which signified women's different professional status compared to men's within the same police force.[8]

Literal translation is often resorted to when there is no equivalent institution or title or concept in the TC, but the meaning is sufficiently transparent to travel across cultures without much alteration. As in the case of the 'Women's Department' mentioned earlier, the literal translation may inform the TA of the general issues, but it usually does not and cannot convey the fine nuances of the British reality that lie behind most of these elements. As mentioned earlier, this show appeals to the recent past memory of the SA. As such, one of the tasks of those who tackle the process of rewriting is to give careful consideration to the entertaining points that will affect the overall reception of a work. If the same points cannot be activated in the TT and others are not found to counterbalance the loss, the obvious risk is that the target dialogue can end up being severely impoverished.

Hypernym
Generalisation by hypernym has been chosen in 5 percent of the cases (20 times). This strategy was equally implemented to translate brand names (50 percent of the cases) and institutional names such as police departments and positions (50 percent). Among the latter I have also included a reference to a law, the 1967 Obscene Publications Act, translated into Italian with the

more generic *decreto legge del 1967* [1967 law decree]. In the case of brand names, the strategy has been used to avoid mentioning them, either because they are remote in time and thus asynchronous or simply because popular brands do not easily make it to the TT for the same reasons explained in Chapter 5. One such case occurs with the 'Garibaldis', a brand of biscuits very popular at the time in Britain but that in the translation has been transposed into more general *biscotti* [biscuits]. In the case highlighted below, the end solution may have been prompted by the zeal to avoid mentioning a brand name that is unknown as such in Italy but which contains a word, 'virgin', which might elicit misunderstandings:

EXAMPLE 6.15: SEASON 1 EPISODE 1 (PILOT)

CONTEXT: At the beginning of the pilot episode, Sam is desperately trying to contact the world of 2006 from which he comes.

ORIGINAL FILM DIALOGUE

OPERATOR: Operator.
SAM: No, I want a mobile number.
OPERATOR: What?
SAM: A mobile number. 0770 813–
OPERATOR: Is that an international number?
SAM: No, it . . . I. . . . I need you to connect me to a **Virgin . . . number. Virgin mobile.**
OPERATOR: **Don't you start that sexy business with me,** young man. I can trace this call.

ITALIAN ADAPTATION	BACK-TRANSLATION
CENTRALINISTA: Centralino.	OPERATOR: Operator.
SAM: Senta. Vorrei il numero di un cellulare.	SAM: Listen. I would like to have the number of a mobile.
CENTRALINO: Cosa?	OPERATOR: What?
SAM: Il numero di un cellulare. 0770 813 . . .	SAM: The number of a mobile. 0770 813 . . .
CENTRALINO: E' un numero internazionale forse?	OPERATOR: Is it an international number perhaps?
SAM: No. Io ho bisogno che lei mi metta in contatto con un numero di . . . **un cellulare,** un telefono cellulare.	SAM: No. I need you to connect me to a **mobile . . . number,** a mobile phone.
CENTRALINISTA: **La smetta di importunarmi,** giovanotto, per favore, posso rintracciare la chiamata, lo sa?	OPERATOR: **Stop pestering me,** young man, please, I can trace your call. Do you know that?

In the Italian version, the generalisation triggers the omission of the proper name of the company of mobile phone services, 'Virgin'. The second meaning of this term, in its function as a common name, is also activated in the exchange, provoking the reaction of the operator. The fact that the sexual innuendo has disappeared completely from the TT unbalances this dialogue exchange in Italian and makes the operator's reaction sound excessive as it does not respond to the seemingly sexual line of the original. More importantly, the overall result is that the dialogue loses its ambiguity and, hence, its humour.

Explicitation
The strategy of explicitation has been used only twice in this series (0.5 percent). Given this negligible figure, the conclusion which may be drawn is that, as with the former case study, this extremely low percentage can be explained by the general trend detected in these adaptations: that of privileging strategies which do not involve considerable efforts of research and problem solving, such as loan and, as we will see, elimination.

On the other hand, as we noted in Chapter 4, explicitation in dubbing may unquestionably lead to problems of isochrony and lip-synch, and that can be one of the reasons it has been seldom implemented in this case study.

Substitution
Substitution adds up to 4 percent of the total of strategies, that is, 18 cases. As defined in Chapter 4, this strategy consists in the replacement of a CSR by another CSR which may or may not have something to do with the original and may be part of the TC or of the SC itself or of any third culture. In this corpus, substitutions have always been used to replace a proper name, object or brand which was either tightly embedded into the British culture (SC reference or allusion) and/or was asynchronous. The following example is typical of the way in which this strategy is used in *Life on Mars*:

EXAMPLE 6.16: SEASON 1 EPISODE 7

CONTEXT: A suspect's request prompts Gene's typical repartee.

ORIGINAL FILM DIALOGUE

BILLY: I want a solicitor.
GENE: I want **Fiona Richmond** as a secretary; looks like we'll both have to wait.

ITALIAN ADAPTATION	BACK-TRANSLATION
BILLY: Voglio il mio avvocato.	BILLY: I want my lawyer.
GENE: E io la **Bardot** sotto al mio tavolo. Ma per ora non può venire.	GENE: And I want **Bardot** under my table. But she can't come now.

Fiona Richmond is a British sex symbol of the 1970s. The Italian version resorts to a CS referent from a third culture, in this case the French actress Brigitte Bardot, and is somewhat cruder than the original in that it implies a sexual act which was not in the original dialogue, but it is in line with Gene's bawdy personality and with Fiona Richmond's sexual image, thus it can be considered a case of suitable compensating substitution.

All in all, substitutions in *Life on Mars* are not as revealing as some of the ones detected in *Friends*, as the elements chosen to replace the original ones do not seem to follow a common logic other than that of choosing more popular items that can be easily recognised by the TA. However, they all appear to look for the kind of situational equivalence exemplified in this instance and thus are never incongruous: so Joe Bugner is substituted with Cassius Clay; Van der Valk with Perry Mason; *Mr and Mrs* TV programme with the similar Italian *Il gioco delle coppie* [The game of couples]; Woodbines cigarettes with Philip Morris and so on.

Elimination

The elimination of a CSR is a strategy used in 18 percent of the cases, which means that the Italian version of *Life on Mars* contains 76 fewer CSRs than the total 431 of the original two seasons. As already noted, eliminations lead to the greatest departures from the ST, and often the meaning of the dialogue can change substantially. This strategy shows better than others the role played by cultural elements in creating a culture specific and a time specific atmosphere which tends to be sensibly less specific when these lexical items are eliminated.

The majority of CSRs which have not been transferred to the TT are allusions (34 percent), most of which are relative to British shows, films or fictional characters. This percentage is followed by suppressed place names and nationalities (17 percent), most of which belong to the SC category, and by people names (17 percent), for the most part, too, being SC references; 11 percent of eliminations regard brand names, and 8 percent are relative to companies and institutions mostly included in the SC category; other categories like food (4 percent), festivities (4 percent); games and programmes (4 percent); currency and weight (2 percent) follow in lower percentages.

The resulting Italian dialogue is often too generic, as if it took place in a sociocultural void. Elimination can alter deeply the precise perception of a historical moment in time, as in the following excerpt in which the strategy of substitution has also been used:

EXAMPLE 6.17: SEASON 2 EPISODE 2

CONTEXT: Detective Chief Inspector Glen Fletcher is introduced to Sam and his colleagues and has to suffer the racist jokes of Ray, the coarsest policeman of the team. Glen reacts by using a typical defence mechanism.

ORIGINAL FILM DIALOGUE	
RAY: First women, now a coloured. What's gonna be next, dwarfs? (*GLEN holds out a hand. RAY looks at it then at GLEN.*)	
RAY: You here to do the spadework then? Only it can get a bit cold 'round here. It's not like being back home.	
GLEN (*dropping his hand*): What, **Burnage**? (*He laughs.*)	
SAM: You'll have to excuse DS Carling. He's our resident Neanderthal.	
GLEN: No, good point, though. When that heatwave hit last month, **I thought Enoch Powell had had me deported!**	

ITALIAN ADAPTATION	BACK-TRANSLATION
RAY: Prima le donne, poi un nero. Chi saranno i prossimi, dei nani?	RAY: First women, now a black man. Who will be next, some dwarfs?
RAY: Ti sei coperto bene? Può fare molto freddo qui. Non è come a casa tua.	RAY: Have you covered yourself well? It can get very cold here. It's not like your home.
GLEN: Cosa . . . **badrone**?	GLEN: What . . . **massa**?
SAM: Devi scusare il sergente Carling. E' il nostro uomo di Neanderthal.	SAM: You have to excuse Sergeant Carling. He's our Neanderthal man.
GLEN: No, è una buona osservazione. Quando ci fu quell'ondata di freddo il mese scorso, **pensavo che mi avrebbero deportato.**	GLEN: No, it's a good point. When there was that wave of cold last month, **I thought I would be deported.**

Glen, a black Englishman from Manchester, gives a quick repartee to Ray's rude allusion to the colour of his skin by mentioning the area of Manchester where he lives, Burnage. Bearing in mind the lip-synch dimension, the adapters have decided to eliminate the reference to Burnage and to replace it with the word 'badrone', a deformation of 'padrone' [master], which supposedly should mimic the accent of black people of African descent when they speak Italian. The replacement of the initial /p/ with /b/ was (and, to a certain extent, still is) a typical way to depict black people in comedic impressions and in dubbing[9]: the implication is that they are unable to pronounce the initial /p/ properly. In a way, the Italian deformation 'badrone' can be considered an equivalent of the English deformation 'massa' for 'mister', which was used in the back-translation. This way of speaking is chosen by the Italian Glen to defend himself with humour from Ray's aggressive racism. Thus a CSR was replaced with a linguistic feature, however stereotypical.

The elimination in Italian of the name of 'Enoch Powell' at the end of the exchange turns Glen's last line into a generic comment. Powell was a British Conservative politician famous for his "Rivers of Blood" speech in 1968

180   *"Follow the Yellow Brick Road"*

against the perils of immigration, which *The Times* (editorial comment, 22nd April 1968) defined as "the first time that a serious British politician has appealed to racial hatred in this direct way in our postwar history". As always with this show, references which embed the programme to a specific time in British history are eliminated in the translation and dubbing process as their asynchronous nature is felt as a reception problem. This is also true for actresses like Diana Dors, TV programmes like *Clangers* (Oliver Postgate 1969, 1974) and, as it seems to be customary, certain brand names. Brand names have been almost always eliminated in this show—as has been already noted, mentioning brand names on TV was prohibited in Italy, until the law was partly revised in 2004, but they are still handled with care—giving place to some awkward adaptations, as in the following case:

EXAMPLE 6.18: SEASON 2 EPISODE 3

CONTEXT: Sam's attempt to be nice and tender to Annie results in a misunderstanding.

ORIGINAL FILM DIALOGUE 49:19–49:41

SAM: Listen, I forgot to say thanks. I owe you one.
ANNIE: For what?
SAM: For helping me.
ANNIE: **Kit-Kat**'ll do nicely.
SAM: Tell you what, seeing as it's you, I'll make it **a chunky one**.
ANNIE: "Chunky"? (*Angry, Annie leaves.*)
SAM: No!

ITALIAN ADAPTATION	BACK-TRANSLATION
SAM: Ho dimenticato di ringraziarti. Te lo devo.	SAM: I forgot to thank you. I owe you that.
ANNIE: Per cosa?	ANNIE: For what?
SAM: Per avermi aiutato.	SAM: For helping me.
ANNIE: **Un mazzo di fiori** basterà.	ANNIE: **A bunch of flowers** will be enough.
SAM: Sai una cosa, poiché sei tu, ti darò dei **cioccolatini**.	SAM: You know what? Because it's you, I'll give you some **chocolates**.
ANNIE: Cioccolatini?	ANNIE: Chocolates?
SAM: No!	SAM: No!

The Kit Kat chocolate bar has been popular both in the SC and in the TC for decades, and it offers the authors of the script the occasion to play on a reference which is well-known in both of Sam's worlds, the 1970s and the 2000s. Sam's slip in mentioning the 'chunky' type of Kit Kat, a relatively recent introduction unknown to Annie, provokes the latter's hurtful and irritated reaction as she thinks that Sam has made a rude comment about her being slightly overweight. As a result, the girl stands up and leaves, ignoring Sam's protest. The elimination of this CSR in the Italian version renders Annie's reaction virtually incomprehensible as it is hard to understand why a box of chocolates instead of a bunch of flowers should make her so angry. Again, the strategy of elimination erases some of the temporal coordinates which are the strength and the *raison d'être* of this show.

Creative Addition

The term 'creative' is mainly meant to stress the action of introducing a new cultural element into a TT sentence which contained none in the ST. *Life on Mars* offers only one example (0.2 percent) of this strategy in which the adapters have chosen to overdo Gene's customary way of calling people incongruous nicknames. In Season 2 Episode 2 his 'Cindy', in addressing someone whose name was not Cindy, becomes *Cenerentola* [Cinderella], when there is no indication in the original text that Gene intended to use other than a common name.

CONCLUSIONS

The original *Life on Mars* plays on different levels of understanding which multiply the echoes of its references. The full impact of its quality script writing can be fully appreciated only when one takes into account all the elements skilfully used by the writers to construct the dialogue: idiomatic phrases, word play, slang words from the past and the present, as well as a myriad of fine-tuned cultural elements that contribute to creating a quality TV programme that, in turn, can be appreciated on various levels.

The cuts and linguistic manipulations carried out by the Italian adapters have had two main effects. On one hand, the Italian dialogues have been deprived of a substantial number of the linguistic and cultural specificities of the original to the point that at times the dubbed version seems to take place in a sociocultural void. On the other hand, the dubbing shows a marked tendency towards what could be defined a normalisation of its storyline. The science-fiction element, one of the main ingredients of the show's originality, has been heavily curtailed by the cutting and manipulation of the hallucinatory moments of Sam's experience. This could be seen as one of the reasons accounting for the lukewarm reception of this series in Italy. To an audience which has no easy access to the multiple cultural allusions and to the more profound and at times surreal components of the plot, *Life on Mars* can appear as just another police procedural story. In other words, the window to Sam's subconscious is not so open and not so evident in the Italian version, hence risking losing one of the main dimensions of the series. Judged merely as a police story, *Life on Mars* could come across as overly simplistic, both in terms of the plot construction as well as the stylistic features which are today customarily developed for this particular genre.

The strategies chosen more frequently by the adapters are loan and, as a substantial second, elimination. The strategies of compensation, as well as the generally rarer lexical recreation and concretisation by hyponym, were never used in *Life on Mars*. This finding is in line with the results of the former case study. In relation to compensation, in particular, it may just be reiterated that it is one of the most sophisticated strategies involving a certain degree of effort and creativity by the translator. The problem it might create in dubbing is technical relating to lip synchronisation and also isochrony. However, the lack of compensation is striking only if one does not consider, as in *Friends*, the general translational trend of this dubbing adaptation which seems to shy away from the use of the more elaborate translation strategies, that is, the strategies which involve efforts of research and creativity.

The relatively short span of this series, in comparison with *Friends*, does not allow one to make any relevant diachronic considerations. However,

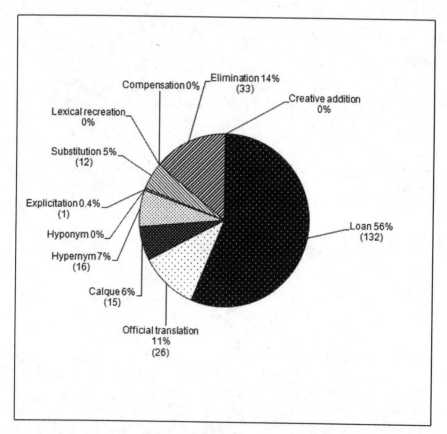

Figure 6.3 Translation strategies used in *Life on Mars* Season 1

it can be noted that the distribution of the translation strategies over the two seasons is not entirely homogenous, as can be seen from the graphs in Figures 6.3 and 6.4.

The data which stand out are the decrease, in the second season, in the use of loans (56 and 46 percent, respectively, in the two seasons), and an increase in the use of elimination and official translation, to the detriment of all the other translation strategies. The sensible increase of eliminations (from 14 to 23 percent) can be noted in particular. The interpretation of these data is not straightforward: if, on the one hand, the increase of official translations would indicate an effort of research by the translators and a more respectful handling of the semantics of the original text, on the other hand the increase of eliminations would point in the opposite direction, that is, to a more manipulative handling of the text. However, after a careful analysis of the corpus, we can establish that loans are used, in the great majority of cases, for items whose knowledge is widely spread in the TC, and official translations are often due to repetitions (the words

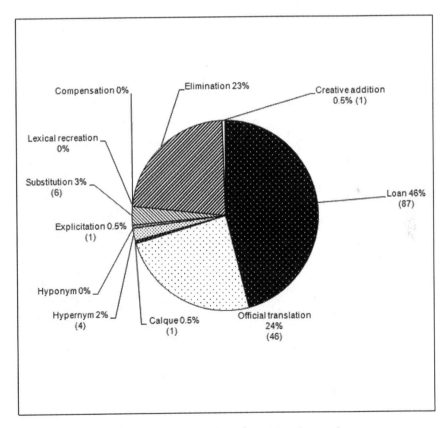

Figure 6.4 Translation strategies used in *Life on Mars* Season 2

'*Fronte Nazionale*' [National Front] are repeated several times in Season 2 Episode 6) and to established translations of currency and weight terms and place names.

It can be concluded that the use of the loan strategy, in this series too, confirms the tendency to comfort the audience by the repetition of firmly globalised items and not to disturb it by introducing exotic elements into the new text. The increase of official translations—which are in many cases, after all, a more elaborate variant of loans—would also seem to corroborate this hypothesis.

In conclusion, it is useful to stress that the highly manipulative handling of CSRs in this series has an impact on the social and sociolinguistic aspects of the series; on the careful mix of genres characterising the show; and to a lesser extent than in *Friends*, in which this was the main consequence of the manipulation, on the humour of the dialogues.

NOTES

1. A condensed version of some of the sections of this chapter are included in Ranzato (2013) where this series's dubbing is contrasted to that of *Mad Men*.
2. The official credits of the US version indicate the same original British authors—Graham, Jordan and Pharoah—as creators of the new version which was in fact criticised by these authors and actually developed by Josh Appelbaum, André Nemec and Scott Rosenberg. Incidentally, there is also another remake, the Spanish *La chica de ayer* (Ignacio Ferrándiz 2009); an Italian one, *29 settembre*, was announced in 2009 but never produced.
3. "A large ensemble cast; a memory; a new genre formed by mixing old ones; a tendency to be literary and writer based; textual self-consciousness; subject matter tending toward the controversial; aspiration toward realism; a quality pedigree; attracting an audience with blue-chip demographics" (Thompson 1996, in Richardson 2010: 155).
4. An exception is the references to the TC. In this sense, 'Garibaldi's biscuits', quoted in some instances, could be defined only an apparent TC reference: although they are named after the famous Italian general Giuseppe Garibaldi and are a testimony to his popularity in Britain in the 1800s, these biscuits have been in fact a typically British snack for 150 years. I would categorise them thus as an SC reference, because they have no intercultural relationship with the TC.
5. The eerie and even devilish aura of children is a common trope in the thriller and horror genres, as numerous films of virtually every age can testify, from *The Bad Seed* (Mervyn LeRoy 1954) to *Kill, Baby . . . Kill!* (Mario Bava 1966), from *It's Alive* (Larry Cohen 1974) to *Pet Sematary* (Mary Lambert 1989) and from *The Good Son* (Joseph Ruben 1993) to *Citadel* (Ciaran Foy 2012), to name but a few.
6. In television shows handled with more care or when lyrics refer consistently to the themes of the series, songs in Italy are usually subtitled, see for example *Glee* (Ryan Murphy, Brad Falchuk and Ian Brennan 2009–2015).
7. This part of scene was cut off the Italian version. See the following section.
8. Annie's last two lines are also interesting from another translational point of view. Although they do not contain any CSRs, they are symptomatic of the

way this series has been generally handled, taking little care of the cultural but also linguistic nuances present in the original text as the section on deletions demonstrates. The word 'plonk' is (or rather was, as it has become dated) a pejorative slang term to refer to policewomen; however, it is more commonly used in contemporary English to define a very bad wine. Considering the solution offered in the TT, the translator probably mistook one for the other as the former meaning is not quoted in general English–Italian dictionaries or monolingual English dictionaries and could only be found in a glossary of slang police terms on the internet ("List of police-related slang terms" n.d.). In addition, Annie's affectionate and motherly expression, 'Off you jolly well trot', which very well expresses Annie's warm, cheerful nature and idiolect, has been turned into the Italian *faccia una bella passeggiata* [take a nice walk], an unmarked standard phrase which sounds very formal, especially since Annie in Italian uses the third-person, distancing form of address (*faccia* instead of the informal *fai*) when talking to Sam.

9. The most famous and quoted example of this kind of speech is the dubbing of the character of Mammy in *Via col vento* (*Gone with the Wind*, Victor Fleming 1939).

REFERENCES

"Almost 6m experience Life on Mars". 2007. http://news.bbc.co.uk/2/hi/entertainment/6361467.stm, last accessed 28th March 2015.

Arlen, Harold and E. Y. Harburg. 1939. *Over the Rainbow*. Decca Records. USA.

Baum, L. Frank. 1900/2008. *The Wizard of Oz*. London: Puffin Classics.

Berry, Chuck. 1972. *My Ding-a-Ling*. Chess Records. USA.

Bowie, David. 1971. *Life on Mars*. RCA Records. USA.

Bowie, David. 1972. *The Jean Genie*. RCA Records. USA.

Box, Mick, David Byron and Lee Kerslake. 1972. *Traveller in Time*, in Uriah Heep. *Demons and Wizards* (album). Bronze. UK.

Clark, Anthony. n.d. "The Sweeney (1975–78)". *BFI Screenonline*, www.screenonline.org.uk/tv/id/473709/.

Edgerton, Gary R. (ed.). 2011. *Mad Men: Dream Come True TV*. London: I. B. Tauris & Co Ltd.

Harvey, Monica and Anna Ravano. 1999. *Wow—The Word on Words*. Bologna: Zanichelli.

Holmwood, Leigh. 2007. "Plenty of Life on Mars". *Guardian Unlimited*, http://www.theguardian.com/media/2007/apr/11/overnights, last accessed 28th March 2015.

Lennon, John and Paul McCartney. 1967. "Lucy in the Sky with Diamonds", in The Beatles. *Sgt. Pepper's Lonely Hearts Club Band*. Parlophone. UK.

"Life on Mars. A sign of the times: how the Seventies were brought back to life". 2008. *BBC Press Office*. www.bbc.co.uk/pressoffice/pressreleases/stories/2005/12_december/08/mars_life.shtml.

"List of police-related slang terms". n.d. http://en.wikipedia.org/wiki/List_of_police-related_slang_terms, last accessed 28th March 2015.

Nelson, Robin. 2007. *State of Play. Contemporary "High-end" TV Drama*. Manchester: Manchester University Press.

Pedersen, Jan. 2005. "How is culture rendered in subtitles?" *MuTra 2005—Challenges of Multidimensional Translation: Conference Proceedings*, in www.euroconferences.info/proceedings/2005_Proceedings/2005_Pedersen_Jan.pdf, last accessed 27th March 2015.

Ranzato, Irene. 2013. "Period television drama: culture specific and time specific references in translation for dubbing", in Pavesi, Maria, Maicol Formentelli and Elisa Ghia (eds.) *The Languages of Dubbing*. Bern: Peter Lang.

Richardson, Kay. 2010. *Television Dramatic Dialogue—A Sociolinguistic Study*. Oxford: Oxford University Press.

Thompson, Robert J. 1996. *Television's Second Golden Age: From Hill Street Blues to ER*. Syracuse, NY: Syracuse University Press.

The Times, editorial comment, 22nd April 1968: www.thetimes.co.uk/tto/archive, requires login. www.telesimo.it/news/2009/ascolti-13-19-luglio-2009.html, last accessed 28th March 2015.

Yacowar, Maurice. 2011. "Suggestive silence in season 1", in Gary R. Edgerton (ed.) *Mad Men: Dream Come True TV*. London: I. B. Tauris & Co Ltd, 86–100.

Filmography

Ashes to Ashes, Matthew Graham and Ashley Pharaoah, 2008–2010, UK.
The Avengers (Agente speciale), Sydney Newman, 1961–1969, UK.
The Bad Seed (Il giglio nero), Mervyn LeRoy, 1954, USA.
La chica de ayer, Ignacio Ferrándiz, 2009, Spain.
Citadel (Rapporto confidenziale), Ciaran Foy, 2012, Ireland.
Clangers, Oliver Postgate, 1969–1974, UK.
Doctor Kildare (Il dottor Kildare), Robert Sagal et al., 1961–1966, USA.
Dodge City (Gli avventurieri), Michael Curtiz, 1939, USA.
Flower Pot Men, Freda Lingstrom and Maria Bird, 1952–1954, UK.
Friends, Marta Kauffman and David Crane, 1994–2004, USA.
Glee, Ryan Murphy, Brad Falchuk and Ian Brennan, 2009–2015, USA.
Gone With the Wind (Via col vento), Victor Fleming, 1939, USA.
The Good Son (L'innocenza del diavolo), Joseph Ruben, 1993, USA.
The Hour, Abi Morgan, 2011–2012, UK.
It's Alive (Baby Killer), Larry Cohen, 1974, USA.
Kill, Baby . . . Kill!, Mario Bava, 1966, Italy.
Life on Mars, Matthew Graham, Tony Jordan and Ashley Pharoah, 2006–2007, UK.
Life on Mars, Matthew Graham, Tony Jordan and Ashley Pharoah, 2008–2009, USA.
Mad Men, Matthew Weiner, 2007–2015, USA.
Masters of Sex, Michelle Ashford, 2013–present, USA.
Midnight in Paris, Woody Allen, 2011, USA/Spain.
The Mutiny on the Bounty (Gli ammutinati del Bounty), Lewis Milestone, 1962, USA.
Pet Sematary (Cimitero vivente), Mary Lambert, 1989, USA.
The Shining, Stanley Kubrick, 1980, USA/UK.
Star Wars (Guerre stellari), George Lucas, 1977–present, USA.
The Sweeney, Ian Kennedy Martin, 1975–1978, UK.
That 70s Show, Mark Brazil, Bonnie Turner and Terry Turner, 1998–2006, USA.
The Wizard of Oz (Il mago di Oz), Victor Fleming, 1939, USA.

7 Coffee Bars in Slumber Rooms
Culture Specific Death in *Six Feet Under*

INTRODUCTION: *SIX FEET UNDER*

From June 2001 to August 2005, the American channel HBO broadcast the five seasons of *Six Feet Under*, a drama series created by Alan Ball, at the time an already-established cinema scriptwriter.[1] The series, which tackles morally compelling themes and is strongly tinged with black humour, has been unanimously considered one of the best TV shows of all time as well as having one of the best final episodes of all time (Bettridge 2009; Cericola 2005; Poniewozik 2007; Wilson 2009). The media impact created by *Six Feet Under* was outstanding. It was the first drama series commissioned by HBO[2] after *The Sopranos* (David Chase 1999–2007), and like its predecessor, it broke new ground in the field of television series. It is—and it was conceived as being[3]—auteur television. Its bonds with the sociocultural context of the period in which it was produced should not be overlooked:

> *Six Feet Under*, premiering only months before the terrorist attacks of September 11, 2001, chimed in with an elegiac cultural zeitgeist obsessed with mortality. Arguably, American culture has long been obsessed with death—with guns, violence, and killing. But September 11 ushered in a period of national introspection, a questioning of the fragility of our lives and how well we live them [. . .]. No television series better captured this cultural mournfulness than *Six Feet Under*—the finality of death and what it means for the living. (Akass and McCabe 2005: 75)

Death is in fact the main theme of the series which centres on the life of a family of undertakers, the Fishers, and on the complex relationships between Ruth, the mother, who in the first episode becomes the widow of Nathaniel senior, and her three children: David, Nate and Claire.

Although killed in an accident in the pilot episode, Nathaniel senior is an important character, making what could be defined as Shakespearean appearances to his children after his death in several episodes in the course of the whole series. His widow, Ruth, is a tormented but affectionate mother; she has grown up to repress her emotions, which sometimes surge out of control in unexpected outbursts. She struggles hard to understand herself, her feelings, her sexuality, and her own relationship with the rest of the family.

The three Fisher children, in spite of being multifaceted, complex characters, each offer their creator the perfect means to delve into contemporary, sensitive social and personal issues. Nate (Nathaniel Junior), the eldest son, has the vocation of a free spirit and struggles hard with his commitment issues, both in his love relationships and in his job at the funeral home, a paternal legacy he has tried in vain to run away from. David is a tormented homosexual who stubbornly soldiers on in a family business he does not particularly like. One of the main themes of the series is how he learns to come out into the open and live his sentimental life with freedom and contentment. Claire, the youngest and only daughter, is an intelligent, aggressive and vulnerable girl who tries to come to terms with her variation of the heavy family burden through sentimental and sexual relationships, experiments with drugs and artistic explorations.

Many other characters join the Fishers along the way. Among these, the most important are Federico and Brenda, who are present in most of the episodes. Federico is a Latin American employee (and later partner) of the Fisher company. A skillful makeup artist with a real passion for his job of making corpses presentable for funeral viewings, Federico is a family man with traditional values. At the same time, his intelligence and sensitivity help him overcome his hesitations and prejudices and open up to the wayward lives of the Fishers. Federico offers an insight into the specificities of a culture within a culture, that of the Latino communities in the United States.

Brenda, Nate's girlfriend and later wife, is the character in *Six Feet Under* who is probably most responsible for the sophisticated register of some of its dialogue: in perennial conflict with her own dysfunctional family, Brenda has inherited an intellectual, sarcastic, detached outlook on life and relationships from her parents (a couple of somewhat irritating psychoanalysts), which is in sharp contrast with her boyfriend's more uncomplicated approach.

The sum of these contrasting personalities living unusual but profoundly realistic lives adds up to a show which is at the same time funny, deep, intelligent, moving and painfully true.

HBO broadcast *Six Feet Under* in its much-vaunted 9 p.m. time slot. It averaged a very good viewership, although numbers decreased steadily after the second season in spite of constantly good reviews. Table 7.1 below shows the figures per year in millions of viewers, although single episodes often reached much higher rates, such as the series finale which peaked at 3.9 million, eclipsing the network's previous best, which was the fourth season debut of *Six Feet Under* in June 2004 (Carter 2002, 2004; Fitzgerald 2003; Pasha 2005; "'Six Feet Under' Finale Draws Viewers" 2005).

In Italy, the national private channel Italia 1 broadcast the first three seasons, after 11 pm, from 2004 to 2008. After a long break of three years, the satellite pay TV channel Cult repeated the first seasons and

Table 7.1 Six Feet Under's viewership

Year	Viewers in millions
2001	5.4
2002	between 7 and 8
2003	4.7
2004	3.7

broadcast the two last, as yet unaired, seasons in 2008. *Six Feet Under* did well for its time slot at the beginning on Italia 1, with 1,274,000 viewers watching the first episode of the first season and 848,000 the second ("Ascolti: Bonolis il più visto in prima serata" 2004). Audience numbers, however, rapidly decreased, and in 2008, the number of people watching *Six Feet Under* on the 21st of November was only 458,000 (www.telesimo.it/news/2008/ascolti-17-23-novembre-2008.html).

Luca Intoppa and Antonella Damigelli were the authors of the Italian dialogues, the latter for Season 3, and Fabrizio Temperini was the dubbing director.

Despite the recent repeats on television and a fair amount of publicity, the series has never become mainstream, and it is unknown to a large portion of the Italian general public. It is, in fact, a cult show, like the name of the pay TV channel which broadcast it.

Seasons 1 and 3 of the five seasons have been analysed, which makes a total of 26 episodes, each of them of 60 minutes (approximately 1,560 minutes of programme).[4]

Given the nature of the problems the Fishers have to cope with and the corpses that they have to sew up and make up on a daily basis to make them presentable at open-casket funeral viewings, I considered this programme a potentially problematic one in terms of translation, not least because of the sexual and gender-related issues which had never before been tackled in this upfront way in any Italian fiction programme, original or translated.

In other words, this show was chosen as a part of the corpus because ideological issues might be expected to come up, issues which would shape the analysis of the data in partly different ways in comparison to the other two cases. In particular, the strong emphasis put on death and the openly gay themes the series deals with have been preliminarily considered sensitive points to be investigated carefully.

ANALYSIS OF THE DATA

In the following sections, the translation strategies used in the Italian dubbed adaptation are discussed on the basis of the taxonomy of strategies discussed in Chapter 4, which become more qualitatively meaningful if studied in relation to the classification of the categories of CSRs also discussed in the same chapter. Further reflections on the nature of the references follow, which include one of the main points of interest in this series, namely the handling of the cultural elements whose transfer into Italian were most at risk: death and death-related subjects.

Culture Specific References in the Original Version

Six Feet Under includes a total number of 688 CSRs, 322 of which were found in the first season and 366 in the third season. The graphic in Figure 7.1 shows the respective percentages.

Unlike the former case studies, the number of occurrences in the later season is higher (53 percent) than in the first (47 percent), exceeding it by 6 percent. However, there is a diegetic reason for this increase: Nate's first wife, Lisa, is reported missing at one point in Season 3, and while Nate, the rest of the family and the police are looking for her, many place names

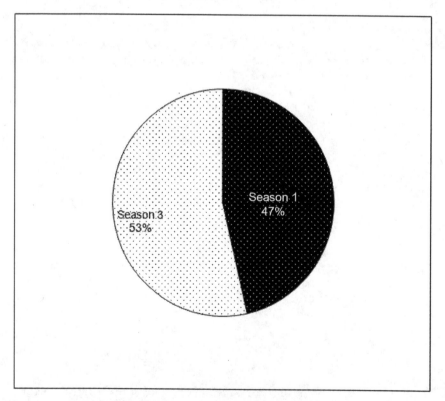

Figure 7.1 Distribution of CSRs in the analysed seasons of *Six Feet Under*

(cities, towns, roads, etc.) are mentioned in their search for her possible whereabouts.

Regardless of the distribution in the two seasons, the data that can be evinced from the number of CSRs is that the density in their occurrence (44 percent) is slightly lower than in *Life on Mars* (45 percent) and much lower than in *Friends* (58.5 percent): that would indicate that this show relied less on CSRs for the creation of its dialogue than the other two shows, especially *Friends*.

Translation Strategies

The following is an analysis of the strategies used by Italian adapters to translate the CSRs contained in *Six Feet Under*. The graph in Figure 7.2 shows an overall breakdown of the 709 instances of translation strategies[5] which have been implemented in the Italian version in relation to CSRs in Series 1 and 3.

The graph confirms the preponderance of the strategies of loan, elimination and official translation, as in the previous case studies. On the other

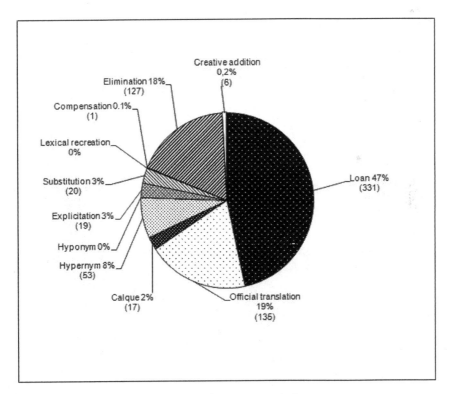

Figure 7.2 Translation strategies used in *Six Feet Under*

hand, it is also evident that the strategy of official translation has been implemented frequently by the adapters of this series, exceeding by one point the percentage of elimination. The rest of the strategies follow more or less the usual trend, but it should be noted that substitution offers the lowest rate of all three series as it has been chosen in only 3 percent of cases (compared to the 8 and 4 percent, respectively, of *Friends* and *Life on Mars*). A first assessment could be that the more creative strategies, including substitution, which require a search for imaginative solutions, have been neglected in favour of easier solutions such as loan, elimination and official translation.

In the case of *Six Feet Under*, however, it is also useful to take a look at the graphs in Figures 7.3 and 7.4 relative to the two seasons which have been analysed as they show a major discrepancy: in the third season, loan doubles its incidence in comparison to the first season, at the expense of most of the other strategies, notably elimination, explicitation and, to a lesser degree, official translation and generalisation. The reason for this difference may be very simple. As already mentioned, in the third season there are several occasions in which characters include SC references in their lines,

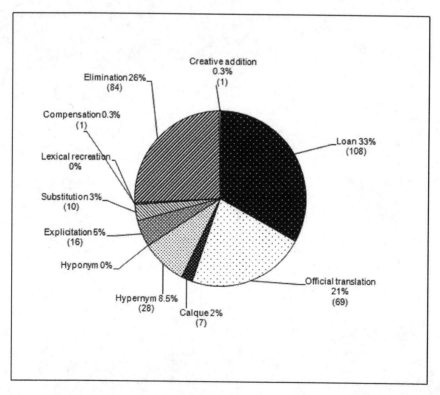

Figure 7.3 Translation strategies used in *Six Feet Under* Season 1

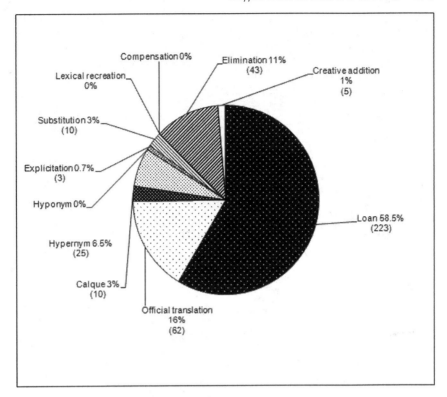

Figure 7.4 Translation strategies used in *Six Feet Under* Season 3

in the form of place names, mostly North American areas and towns, more than large cities. When Lisa, Nate's wife, is reported missing, her family joins the police in trying to find her, studying maps and asking questions which include place names. These names, as we observed in Chapter 4, are customarily transferred as loans unless an official translation exists, which is usually the case for bigger cities and countries.

In the following subsections, the most relevant instances for each category will be analysed. The emphasis, even more than with the other series, is on elimination, which proves also in this case to be the most interesting strategy in that it is the one which best allows the creation of hypotheses and offers insights into the trends and possible motivations of the adapters.

Loan
As it has been already mentioned, this strategy accounts for almost half of the occurrences (47 percent) and has been used by the adapters, in the vast majority of cases, to transfer place names, following a well-established

policy and tradition in Italian translation. In a limited number of instances loan was used for popular proper names, film and song titles, and for brand names of products which are not distributed in Italy (such as medications). The following Example 7.1 is worth commenting on:

EXAMPLE 7.1: SEASON 1 EPISODE 5

CONTEXT: David, a practising Episcopalian, is talking to a friendly priest outside the church where he once used to go with his mother.

ORIGINAL FILM DIALOGUE

FATHER JACK: David, so glad to see you here. It's always nice when someone comes back to the fold.
DAVID: Oh, I've been going to church. I've just been going to a different church.
FATHER JACK: Really? Which one?
DAVID: St. Stephen's.
FATHER JACK: **In the Palisades?**
DAVID: No, St. Stephen's in West Hollywood.

ITALIAN ADAPTATION	BACK-TRANSLATION
PADRE JACK: David, mi fa piacere rivederti. E' bello quando una pecora torna all'ovile.	FATHER JACK: David, I'm pleased to see you again. It's nice when a sheep comes back to the fold.
DAVID: Grazie, ma non è che ho smesso di praticare. Andavo solo in un'altra chiesa.	DAVID: Thanks, but it's not that I stopped practising. I just went to another church.
PADRE JACK: Ah be', in quale?	FATHER JACK: Oh well, which one?
DAVID: A Santo Stefano.	DAVID: **St. Stephen's.**
PADRE JACK: Quella sulla scogliera?	FATHER JACK: **The one on the cliff?**
DAVID: No, Santo Stefano a West Hollywood.	DAVID: No, **St. Stephen's** in West Hollywood.

This is an example of an adaptation which fails to have the same impact on the TA as it has on the SA. West Hollywood is a town near Los Angeles which is well-known, in the USA, for its social justice legislation. It was, among other records, the first city to create same-sex domestic partnership registration and various related benefits for its residents. As a result, according to a 2002 demographic analysis (http://www.weho.org/Modules/ShowDocument.aspx?documentid=623), 41 percent of the city's population is made up of gay or bisexual men. Father Jack's facial reaction to David's words in the scene reveals that he is well aware of the implied meaning of his change of church—a meaning that would not have been perceived by the vast majority of Italians for whom the name of West Hollywood, transferred with a loan, would only evoke cinema-related images. This same CSR appears in one other instance which will be analysed in Example 7.6. In this, as in the following instance, one could argue that the adaptation reveals a lack of awareness of gay-related themes. More broadly speaking, it reveals an ignorance of some aspects of the SC which have not been widely exported.

Official Translation

Official translation has been used in this series slightly more often than in the case studies formerly analysed, exceeding elimination by one point with an occurrence of 19 percent. Although this strategy frequently involves an effort of research by the adapters, in the case of *Six Feet Under* this procedure was implemented, in the vast majority of cases, to translate place names and nationalities (34 percent) and currency, mainly 'dollars' (27 percent). As already stressed, place names and currency terms are customarily and traditionally transferred by either a loan or an official translation, so their incidence does not shed any particular new light on adapters' behaviour. Allusions to works of fiction are the only other relevant category translated by using this strategy (15 percent).

Calque

Calque in *Six Feet Under* has been seldom implemented (2 percent of occurrences, 17 times) and has been used mostly to give unofficial, literal translations of titles and quotations from books, films or songs, such as, for instance, the Italian literal translation of a song by Madonna; the literal translation of a quote from a speech by George Bush; the name of a church (as in Example 7.1); and a quote from a book by Carlos Castaneda.

Hypernym

Generalisation by hypernym has been chosen in 8 percent of cases. Whether to avoid mentioning brand names (e.g., Egg McMuffin translated with *panino* [sandwich]) or using names of famous people or characters (e.g., Umpa Lumpas, from the 1971 film by Mel Stuart, *Willy Wonka and the Chocolate Factory*, translated with *ometti* [little men]), generalisation tends to result in a sort of impoverishment, as the next example more clearly demonstrates:

EXAMPLE 7.2: SEASON 1 EPISODE 1

CONTEXT: Claire has asked her brother David if she really has to be present at the family Christmas dinner as she would really like to be somewhere else.

ORIGINAL FILM DIALOGUE

CLAIRE: There are some really excellent parties I could be going to.
DAVID: Claire, this is one of the few times a year we're all together.
CLAIRE: Alright, alright. **Don't get all Pat Robertson** on me. I'll be there. I just . . . I have to drop some stuff off at a friend's house before I head over. Okay? Bye. *(Hangs up.)* **Fuckin' Boy Scout.**

ITALIAN ADAPTATION	BACK-TRANSLATION
CLAIRE: Mi hanno invitato a un casino di feste da sballo.	CLAIRE: I've been invited to a hell of a lot of stone crazy parties.
DAVID: Claire aspetta, la famiglia ormai si riunisce solo a Natale.	DAVID: Claire, wait, the family now gets together only at Christmas.
CLAIRE: Va bene, va bene, **non farmi la predica** anche tu, ci vengo. Solo, dammi una mezz'ora, devo passare da un amico a prendere un po' di cose. Ciao. **Ma quant'è patetico.**	CLAIRE: Alright, alright, **don't you preach to me** too, I'll come. Only give me half an hour, I have to pass by a friend's to get some things. Bye. **How pathetic he is.**

The specific reference to a preacher, Pat Robertson, who undoubtedly conjures up a web of associations among the SA—both political and religious, as he is a media mogul known for his right-wing connections—is impoverished in the Italian version by the generic reference to preaching. A vivid original reference accompanied by an emphatic swear word ('fuckin' Boy Scout'), which closes Claire's last line, has also been diluted into a generic line of sarcastic depreciation: *ma quant'è patetico* [how pathetic he is].

Explicitation
With 3 percent of the total, the strategy of explicitation proves to be more frequently used in *Six Feet Under* than in any of the former case studies. However, the analysis shows that all of the occurrences are relative to the disambiguation of place names, that is, 'Los Angeles' for 'LA' or 'Las Vegas' for 'Vegas', thus the use of this strategy is not creative but conservative in the sense that it replicates a well-trodden formula customarily implemented by audiovisual translators.

Substitution
Chosen only in 3 percent of cases, this represents the lowest percentage for the strategy of substitution in the whole corpus (8 and 4 percent of cases in *Friends* and *Life on Mars*, respectively). In addition, the substitutions found in *Six Feet Under* are not particularly creative, as in all 20 cases they are used to replace SC references or intercultural references with better-known but not particularly inventive elements: blues composer WC is substituted with classical composer Debussy; *The Munsters* TV series (A. Burns and C. Hayward, 1964–1966) becomes *The Addams Family* series (C. Addams,

1964–1966); and actress Salma Hayek is substituted with singer Britney Spears. Two cases are worth commenting on and are both contained in the following example:

EXAMPLE 7.3: SEASON 1 EPISODE 5

CONTEXT: In this funny episode, Claire decided to steal a foot off one of the bodies his brothers were working on for perfectly logical reasons that she explains here to her mother.

ORIGINAL FILM DIALOGUE

CLAIRE: I don't need help! Why is everyone acting like I'm in the **Trenchcoat Mafia?**
RUTH: You stole a foot! A human foot!
CLAIRE: Okay, you wanna know why? Because some guy **who totally scammed me into having sex with him** because I thought he actually cared about me—he told the entire school that I sucked his toes, and then when I confronted him about it, he showed entirely no remorse, so when I saw Nate drop the foot on the floor, I just grabbed it, just to get back at that asshole, okay? It wasn't premeditated. **I'm not Jeffrey Dahmer. I don't get off on hacked-up body parts.**

ITALIAN ADAPTATION	BACK-TRANSLATION
CLAIRE: Ma non mi serve il tuo aiuto! Vi comportate come se fossi **nel mirino della mafia!**	CLAIRE: But I don't need your help! You're acting as if I was **the mafia's target!**
RUTH: Hai rubato un piede! Il piede di un cadavere!	RUTH: You stole a foot! The foot of a corpse!
CLAIRE: D'accordo, vuoi sapere perché? Perché ho conosciuto un ragazzo, **mi ha quasi convinta a fare sesso con lui**, sembrava che gli interessasse qualcosa di me, poi ha raccontato a tutta la scuola che gli ho succhiato l'alluce e quando gliel'ho rinfacciato non glien'è fregato niente. Poi Nate ha fatto cadere i pezzi di quell'uomo e io ho preso il piede per fargliela pagare a quello stronzo. Non è stato premeditato. **Non sono mica Frankenstein. Non vado a rubare i pezzi dei cadaveri.**	CLAIRE: Alright, do you want to know why? Because I met a boy. **He almost convinced me to have sex with him.** It seemed like he cared for me, then he told the whole school that I sucked his big toe, and when I held it against him, he couldn't care less. Then Nate dropped that man's pieces on the floor, and I took the foot to make that asshole pay for it. It wasn't premeditated. **I'm not Frankenstein. I don't go around stealing corpses' pieces.**

This excerpt is interesting for various reasons. First of all, it contains two CSRs which in the original are both linked to topical subjects of American criminality. The first one refers to the 1999 Columbine High

School massacre. The two young killers who perpetrated the massacre of 13 school students belonged to a group which called themselves 'the Trenchcoat Mafia', but the name has no connection to the actual mafia. The name of this gang is now associated with acts of violence perpetrated by high school kids. Jeffrey Dahmer, better known in Italy as the 'Milwaukee monster' (*il mostro di Milwaukee*), was a serial killer who committed gruesome murders involving rapes, dismemberments, necrophilia and cannibalism. If the first element—which we can define an SC reference—was replaced in Italian by a direct and obvious reference to the real mafia, the second substitution is more interesting. The name of an infamous and only too real criminal (internationally known, but whose name is probably not immediately recognisable for most members of the TA) has been replaced by a literary reference to Frankenstein which dilutes the more gruesome (and sexual) impact of the original dialogue but is not out of place. It is also worth noting in this example a censoring, sanitising approach that is quite common in the first episodes of *Six Feet Under*: in the original text Claire was 'scammed' into having sex with the boy, thus they did have sex, while in Italian she was 'almost' convinced, and hence did not have sex.

Compensation

Although the compensation strategy has been used only once in this series, the dialogue excerpt which contains it is interesting because it involves not only linguistic but also non-verbal features:

EXAMPLE 7.4: SEASON 1 EPISODE 2

CONTEXT: Nate is mocking his brother David, whom he suspects of having had sex the night before.

ORIGINAL FILM DIALOGUE

NATE: *(speaking in a robot voice, similar to HAL in* 2001: A Space Odyssey*)* Morning, Dave. Aren't those the same clothes you had on yesterday?
DAVID: Everything I own looks alike.
NATE: I sense you're not being completely honest with me, Dave.
DAVID: Have you changed any since you were 14?
NATE: *(laughs)* Hey. **I'm all for you getting laid**, believe me.
(...)
NATE (*always keeping the HAL voice*): We are looking quite spiffy in that suit, Dave.
DAVID: That's so clever. **You're talking like the computer in the movie.** Wow, you're funny.

ITALIAN ADAPTATION	BACK-TRANSLATION
NATE *(parla con voce normale)*: Buon giorno, David. Che è successo, hai messo gli stessi vestiti di ieri? DAVID: Sono quelli del lavoro, tutti uguali. NATE: Strano ma sento che mi stai nascondendo qualcosa, David. DAVID: Hai smesso di crescere quando avevi quattordici anni, vero? NATE: **Se c'è una donna faccio il tifo per te.** (. . .) NATE *(parla normalmente)*: Con quel completino sei un vero schianto, David. DAVID: **Grazie mille Mr 2001 Odissea nello strazio.** Non sei divertente.	NATE *(speaks with a normal voice)*: Good morning, David. What happened, are you wearing the same clothes as yesterday? DAVID: They are work clothes; they're all the same. NATE: Funny, but I feel you're hiding something from me, David. DAVID: You stopped growing up when you were 14, right? NATE: **If there's a woman, I'm all for you.** (. . .) NATE *(speaks normally)*: With that little suit you're a real knockout, David. DAVID: **Thank you very much, Mr 2001 A Pain Odyssey.** You're not funny.

The dialogue exchange between Nate and David revolves around Stanley Kubrick's *2001: A Space Odyssey* (1968). The allusion to Kubrick's classic is quite subtle as in the original dialogue the film is only evoked by Nate's voice and by the vague words spoken by David ("you're talking like the computer in the movie"), who incidentally, shares the same name with the main character in Kubrick's film. Although the adapters' choice to eliminate Nate's imitation of Hal's voice seems to be quite arbitrary—it is an unmistakable way of speaking which would have been recognised at least by part of the TA—the connotative loss is balanced by an effective compensation: by manipulating the film title in David's last line—*Grazie mille Mr 2001 Odissea nello strazio* [Thank you very much, Mr 2001 A Pain Odyssey]— the dialogue manages to achieve its goal of conferring sarcastic humour. The strategy that has been adopted is that of compensating the erasure of a paralinguistic feature (the tone of voice) by introducing a verbal play on a CSR. As a result, the nature of the joke changes completely from a joke containing a paralinguistic element to one based on word play with an allusion.[6]

However, the dialogue in this example is also notable for Nate's reaction when he thinks that David is hiding a sexual encounter. His crude, amused remark, 'I'm all for you getting laid', in which no gender is indicated, is adapted into the paternalistic *Se c'è una donna faccio il tifo per te* [If there's a woman, I'm all for you]. Although in this second episode Nate does not yet know that his brother is homosexual, and thus he is probably thinking of a woman, the evident purpose of the adaptation is that of toning down the cruder sexual contents and, when it is the case, sanitising potentially sensitive themes by translating openly homosexual or ambiguous subjects and lexicon into the more accepted language of conventional heterosexuality. One of the means to achieve this end, as some of the following examples will show, is the elimination of CSRs.

Elimination

Elimination accounts for 18 percent of occurrences unevenly distributed between the two seasons: the 26 percent in the first season totals more than double the eliminations contained in the third (11 percent). If the increase of loans in the third season, analysed earlier, partly explains these divergent figures, another explanation may also be attempted: elimination can be an extremely manipulative strategy, and a decreasing number of occurrences in the later season might signify that the adapters found more reasons to introduce greater departures from the original in the first episodes, when a series normally endeavours to find its ideal target audience. By manipulating the text in this way, the adapters try to achieve a more general consensus that may entice a larger audience. The following analysis of some of the cases of elimination of CSRs may support this view.

In the next excerpt, the original dialogue exploits the Hollywood imagery and other visual motifs:

EXAMPLE 7.5: SEASON 1 EPISODE 3

CONTEXT: David and his boyfriend, Keith, are in a shop, choosing a ceiling fan.

ORIGINAL FILM DIALOGUE

DAVID: *(pointing to a ceiling fan)* What about that one?
KEITH: That's a little too **Mayberry** for me. Something simple and clean, like the ones that hang in the deserted truck stop . . . and **that handsome drifter blows into town**.
DAVID: Of course. What about that one?
KEITH: Uh . . . Not bad. **I could see Ava Gardner lying beneath it, plotting to steal Clark Gable away from Grace Kelly.**

ITALIAN ADAPTATION	BACK-TRANSLATION
DAVID: Quello lassù ti piace? KEITH: Un po' troppo **country** per me. Voglio qualcosa di semplice, di lineare, come quelli dei bar che si vedono nei film, quando **il protagonista** fa il suo ingresso in città.	DAVID: Do you like the one up there? KEITH: A bit too **country** for me. I want something simple and clean, like those in the bars you see in films, when **the protagonist** makes his entrance in town.

> DAVID: Capito il concetto. Che te ne pare di quello?
> KEITH: Mm, già meglio. **Buono per stare al fresco a riflettere, aiuterebbe anche te a prendere la decisione giusta.**
>
> DAVID: Got the concept. What about that one?
> KEITH: Mm, better. **Good to be in the cool to reflect; it would help you too to take the right decision.**

This example shows how the Italian translation neglects some of the typical (or stereotypical) features of gayspeak[7] for what seems to be an inappropriate analysis of this particular idiolect. A whole gay imaginary is lost in translation. Not only are all the famous Hollywood names, and John Ford's film *Mogambo* (1953), which is not quoted but evoked, eliminated from the Italian version, but the gay fantasy of the 'handsome drifter' becomes the neutral image of *il protagonista* [the protagonist]. Incidentally, the stylistic mention, in the original text, of 'Mayberry', from the title of an American TV series (*Mayberry R.F.D.*, B. Ross, 1968–1971) set in an idyllic country town, is translated into the less colourful 'country'. The use of 'country' as an adjective, which is of common usage in Italian as a loan word, conveys the sense of 'rustic', which is implied in Mayberry, but not the atmosphere of a bucolic, small town, which is also part of the original sense.

Gayspeak features are also ignored in the translation of the next excerpt:

EXAMPLE 7.6: SEASON 1 EPISODE 8

CONTEXT: David is furious because Federico did a job for another company, although he is a Fishers' employee. Nate is trying to find reasons to excuse him.

ORIGINAL FILM DIALOGUE

NATE: Stop being such a **drama queen**.
DAVID: Stop acting like you're honorary **mayor of West Hollywood** all of a sudden. He lied to our faces.

ITALIAN ADAPTATION
NATE: Non fare il **melodrammatico**.
DAVID: E tu non fare l'**avvocato delle cause perse** per difendere la carogna.

BACK-TRANSLATION
NATE: Don't be so **melodramatic**.
DAVID: And you, don't act like the **lawyer of lost causes** to defend the rascal.

According to Hayes (1976/2006: 71), the richest features of social gayspeak are found in the lexicon, particularly in compound constructions. In this sense, the lexical item 'queen' is possibly the most widely employed stem word for building compounds used for a limitless series of images to describe sexual preferences (i.e., 'size queen'), subculture types ('queen of tarts', a pimp for hustlers), to make fun of a man's hobbies or interests ('poker queen' for someone who likes playing cards) or as an all-purpose term of derogation ('Queen Mary' for someone fat). Arguably, the elimination of the 'queen' compound in this dialogue reveals, even more than the conscious will to replace a gay connotation, the lack of an appropriate term in the TL. The relative poverty of the Italian gay lexicon as compared to the richness of the corresponding English terminology is a fact. The Italian culture has opened up to homosexual themes much more slowly than the Anglo-Saxon world.[8] One of the first consequences of this state of affairs is that the language of homosexuals has long remained in Italy the language of a ghetto, and still today the relatively poor lexicon available is an objective obstacle even for the most unprejudiced translator. Sometimes, a poor translation might not be due necessarily to a tendency to conscious manipulation but simply to the lack of a lexical counterpart.

David's original repartee in the above dialogue mentions the same town of West Hollywood (practically an area of Los Angeles) which appeared in an earlier example. On this occasion, the reference has been eliminated. By mentioning the 'mayor of West Hollywood', an area with a very large gay population, as noted earlier, David is reacting to a series of gay-friendly comments that Nate has been making for the whole episode, undoubtedly to show his brother, whom he has just discovered to be homosexual, his open-mindedness about the subject. Earlier on, Nate had in fact made this comment to David:

EXAMPLE 7.7: SEASON 1 EPISODE 8

CONTEXT: Nate is encouraging David as he realised there's someone who clearly fancies him.

ORIGINAL FILM DIALOGUE

NATE: That kid wants to jump your bones. Oh, come on, David. **I watch *Will and Grace*.** I've got gay-dar.

ITALIAN ADAPTATION	BACK-TRANSLATION
NATE: Lo sconosciuto ti vuole saltare addosso. Andiamo, **sono un uomo di mondo** e ho il gay-radar.	NATE: That someone you don't know wants to jump on you. Come on, **I'm a man of the world,** and I've got gay-radar.

Although the content of the line does not change in its substance, the elimination of the CSR sensibly alters the effective lightness of tone. It is ironic that the sitcom *Will & Grace* (David Kohan, Max Mutchnick 1998–2006,

USA)—a successful, 10-year-long series whose male main character is gay—was in fact never heavily manipulated nor censored in Italy.

Another feature that characterises *Six Feet Under* is its portrayal of intelligent, complex, multifaceted women. If Ruth (the mother) struggles hard, in the course of the five seasons, to come to terms with the conflict between her traditional, potentially conservative views and a more modern, open, liberal outlook that her children and her own innermost personality urge her to embrace, the women of the younger generation, notably Brenda—Nate's girlfriend—and Claire—the Fishers' youngest child—are outspoken, independent, strong personalities whose idiolects are characterised by the use of sophisticated, cultured references and allusions. Brenda, the daughter of two psychoanalysts, is more of an ironic intellectual, while Claire (in her late teens and a blossoming artist) is caustic, surly, and often aggressive. Their lines frequently include SC references specifically linked to a US reality and overt or covert allusions to works of art and literature that in some cases might be unfamiliar even to a portion of the SA. The next excerpt containing a classical cultural reference is a good illustration of this last type of eliminated CSRs:

EXAMPLE 7.8: SEASON 1 EPISODE 10

CONTEXT: Brenda is blaming her mother for her objectionable mothering skills.

ORIGINAL FILM DIALOGUE

BRENDA: It's a wonder I'm even alive, considering the mothering skills you have! **You're like fucking Medea!** You know what the really sick thing is, Mother? You have no idea what you've done to me.

ITALIAN ADAPTATION	BACK-TRANSLATION
BRENDA: Con una madre come te, è un miracolo che sia ancora viva. **Tu pensi solo a ... *(non udibile)***	BRENDA: With a mother like you, it's a miracle I'm still alive. **You only think of ... *(inaudible)***

Brenda makes a citation from classical literature that her mother, a psychoanalyst, can understand immediately. The mythical Jason's wife, who out of revenge against him, kills the children they had together, is for Brenda the perfect definition for the woman who tormented her and her brother during their childhood. In Italian the reference is eliminated, and the too-intellectual line is lost among ambient sounds and overlapping conversations, while the two characters are filmed in a long shot which facilitates the manipulative work of the adapters.

Claire's lines, too, are remarkable for their intelligence and wit, often including popular or more high-end CSRs which, in both cases, contribute in the original text to elevate the tone of the discourse. Unfortunately, the

204 *Coffee Bars in Slumber Rooms*

impact of Claire's dialogues also suffers from repeated eliminations, as in the next excerpt:

EXAMPLE 7.9: SEASON 1 EPISODE 2

CONTEXT: Claire is protesting because she doesn't want to miss a day of school to attend the opening of her father's testament.

ORIGINAL FILM DIALOGUE

CLAIRE: Great, I have to miss another day of school? What am I, like **some poor knocked-up Victorian waif** who has to stay hidden from view?

ITALIAN ADAPTATION	BACK-TRANSLATION
CLAIRE: Cioè, devo perdere un altro giorno di scuola? Si può sapere che male ho fatto per essere **condannata all'ergastolo in questa casa?**	CLAIRE: What, shall I miss another day of school? Could you tell me what I did wrong to be **sentenced to life imprisonment in this house?**

If not an explicit literary quotation, still Claire's words have a Dickensian flavour and are implicitly aimed at an audience which can relate, at least in general terms, to the condition of the poor in Victorian England. This educated allusion would be understood by a selected but not restricted part of the Italian audience, and it is indeed arguable whether a greater number of people would get the joke in the USA. None of these considerations affected the handling of the dialogue. The solution chosen by the adapters in fact eliminates Claire's ironic reference, which associates poor Victorian women who could not get an education to her own situation, that of a girl prevented from going to school by her family. The replacement is a nondescript line referring to a life imprisonment, which is an exaggeration of Claire's condition as she usually enjoys a great amount of freedom in her family.

In the next excerpt, an SC reference in the original lines gives an amusing twist to an otherwise generic comment:

EXAMPLE 7.10: SEASON 1 EPISODE 5

CONTEXT: Claire reproaches her mother for coming into her room without knocking on the door first.

ORIGINAL FILM DIALOGUE

CLAIRE *(talking to the computer while playing a video game)*: Suck on that, you little fuck! *(laughs, then notices RUTH)* Hi, there's this thing called 'knocking'. It's, like, protected in the first amendment.

Coffee Bars in Slumber Rooms 205

ITALIAN ADAPTATION	BACK-TRANSLATION
CLAIRE: Adesso perché non ridi bastardo? Ciao. Di solito quando c'è una porta chiusa si bussa prima di entrare. **IL RESTO DELLA FRASE È ELIMINATO.**	CLAIRE: Now why don't you laugh, you bastard? Hello. Usually when a door is closed, one knocks before coming in. **THE REST OF THE PHRASE IS ELIMINATED.**

In this case, as well as diluting the explicitly obscene language of the opening line, the adapters have taken advantage of the fact that part of the dialogue is recited off screen, thus enjoying the freedom of editing out what they must have perceived as a problematic line because of being very specific to the US legal system—and this, in spite of the fact that many American films have made the word 'amendment' (usually translated into Italian by a calque) familiar to the Italian audiences. Claire uses the reference to the 'first amendment'—which regards, among other things, the freedom of speech and print—not very appropriately to make an ironic remark on her mother's breaking into her room without knocking. Notwithstanding the potential knowledge of the term by the TA, the CSR was eliminated from the Italian adaptation by an editorial cut.

These are just a few examples including CSRs that show how these two characters' idiolects in particular have been dramatically altered in translation and how the elimination of CSRs has played a fundamental part in this rewriting process: being deprived of many of their intellectual and educated remarks, which give substance to their reasonings, the two women often come across as a pair of somewhat annoying rebels without a cause.

Another textual area which counts a considerable number of eliminations is the realm of overt and covert allusions. *Six Feet Under* shares with many other contemporary fiction works the postmodern taste for quoting, elaborating, interweaving, and playing on allusions to other fictional works and characters. Along with the use of a number of loans and official translations, the tendency towards elimination of these types of CSRs is marked. The following example, which involves both a visual and a verbal allusion, is noteworthy:

EXAMPLE 7.11: SEASON 1 EPISODE 8

CONTEXT: In the death prologue of the eighth episode, a woman dies a horrible death while celebrating with her friends.

ORIGINAL FILM DIALOGUE

Chloe stands up and sticks her head out of the sunroof. She rejoices in her newfound freedom.
CHLOE: I'm king of the world! I'm king of the world! I'm king of the world!

> At that moment, the limo passes a low-hanging traffic light on the side of the road, and her face is smashed in. Her friends are splashed with blood and scream in terror. The screen fades to white.
>
> | ITALIAN ADAPTATION | BACK-TRANSLATION |
> |---|---|
> | CHLOE: Sono la padrona del mondo! | CHLOE: I'm the master of the world! |

The description included in the example, which tells of Chloe standing up on the car seat and sticking her head out of the rooftop, is fundamental to understand the visual impact of the scene. However, it is not wholly accurate. It should be added that as well as sticking her head out, Chloe is standing in such a way as to stick half of her body, from the waist up, out of the car: she makes a swaying movement which, aided by the words she utters—the now famous line "I'm king of the world!"—reminds audiences of the iconic scene from *Titanic* (James Cameron 1997) in which Leonardo DiCaprio similarly sways on the ship's prow, his body blown by the wind in an image of joy and freedom. Unfortunately, the association is lost in Italian as Chloe's words do not quote the film's official literal translation: *Sono il re del mondo!*—words which are now embedded in the Italian culture as part of its transnational consciousness. Arguably, the Italian translation would force the viewer to a greater cognitive effort as he or she only has the images to recuperate the original reference. However, in this case the image without the words is not enough to help the audience associate the swaying woman to DiCaprio, thus the CSR can be considered irremediably lost.

Nevertheless, the film *Titanic* seems to be very much part of Italian contemporary culture, so much so that, as well as inspiring a substitution, it offers the inspiration for one of the few additions encountered in the series, as it will be seen in the next section.

Creative Addition

With six occurrences, creative addition accounts for 0.2 percent of the total percentage. Additions in this series appear to be positively integrated in the dialogue, as if the adapters' creativity functioned best when given free rein. It is notable that five of the six added CSRs are allusions to popular films or TV programmes, showing how intertextual allusions are considered an important vehicle to capture the audience's attention when the texts are familiar to the TC. One of the added allusions includes a line in which a boy refers to a mature lady as *signora in giallo* [lady in yellow], the official Italian translation of the title of the popular TV show *Murder, She Wrote* (Peter S. Fischer 1984–1996) with Angela Lansbury as a senior detective. Season 3 Episode 3 contains the same allusion to *Titanic* which disappeared from the episode mentioned in the former section: in a scene of sexual climax,

David does not exclaim in Italian the equivalent of 'Oh my God!', as in the original, but the phrase: *Sono il re del mondo!* [I'm king of the world!], which even without any visual encouragement is recognisable as an explicit quotation from *Titanic*. This phrase is unusual in Italian as an expression of joy and contentment and would not have been used if it did not allude to this film. In another Italian dialogue, David's boyfriend, Keith, feels the need to explicitate that Viggo Mortensen acted in *Il signore degli anelli (The Lord of the Rings (trilogy)*, Peter Jackson 2001, 2002, 2003), a comment, added off screen, which the original Keith did not consider necessary and which can also be considered a form of elaborate explicitation.

The next excerpt, too, contains an amplification of the original allusion by means of a creative addition:

EXAMPLE 7.12: SEASON 3 EPISODE 7

CONTEXT: Nate is always asking his relatives to keep an eye on his daughter for him, but this time Claire reacts with fury.

ORIGINAL FILM DIALOGUE

NATE: So how about it, can you watch Maya for me today? Twenty bucks.
CLAIRE: I can't.
NATE: Well, why not?
CLAIRE: Russell and I are going to the art store.
NATE: Claire?
CLAIRE: Nate? You know **this isn't the matrix. The rest of us who don't have babies, we're real.** Watch my baby; watch my baby. Jesus Christ.

ITALIAN ADAPTATION	BACK-TRANSLATION
NATE: Che fai, me la guardi tu Maya oggi? Venti dollari.	NATE: What, will you watch Maya today? Twenty dollars.
CLAIRE: Ah, non posso.	CLAIRE: Ah, I can't.
NATE: Perché no?	NATE: Why not?
CLAIRE: Nate. **Non siamo dentro Matrix. Quelli che non hanno figli sono persone vere come l'eletto.**	CLAIRE: Nate. **We're not inside Matrix. Those who don't have children are real people, like The One.**
CLAIRE: Guarda mia figlia, guarda mia figlia. E che cazzo.	CLAIRE: Watch my baby; watch my baby. What the fuck.

The Italian adaptation does not limit itself to keep, as a loan, the reference to the popular film *The Matrix* (Larry and Andy Wachowski 1999), whose plot is mostly set in a world which is not real but a sort of computer programme; it also adds a further reference to the same film, which is not present in the ST, by including *l'eletto* [the elected], 'The One' in the original film, who is the real human being chosen to liberate others from the tyranny of machines.

However seldom resorted to, creative addition introduces in the few instances in which it is used an amused element of intertextual pleasure which suitably blends into the context.

Further Reflections on the Nature of the References

In the previous sections, a reflection has been presented on the nature of the references contained in *Six Feet Under* and the strategies implemented by the translators to deal with them. Undoubtedly, understanding the nature of the reference is crucial to gauge the reasons behind the various translational options. Given their importance in the characterisation of the series, the following sections focus on two different cultural and semantic fields which, in addition to the gay subjects and cultured references highlighted in the previous sections, have been severely manipulated in the translation process.

Sociopolitical Issues

Elements pertaining to US culture which have not previously travelled sufficiently, such as the cremation company Poseidon Society or the area of West Hollywood, did not make it to the TT. As already seen in the previous chapters, the category of SC elements is one of the most interesting ones to analyse from a translational perspective as they tend to highlight the subjective nature of CSRs: what belongs to the source culture and what can be considered to be intercultural are very much left to the personal knowledge of the translators and adapters and to their individual evaluations of the TA's degree of permeability and receptivity towards foreign elements.

The transfer becomes more problematic when an SC reference is apparently intercultural because its name may coincide lexically but not semantically with similar concepts in the TL. Typical examples are political concepts or references to institutions or laws, which translators sometimes solve with a calque but which in this series have been mostly eliminated. As in the case of the reference to the 'first amendment' cited in Example 7.10, other references to US political concepts have not come through in the Italian adaptation. The following are two representative examples:

EXAMPLE 7.13: SEASON 1 EPISODE 3

CONTEXT: Nate, who was at first adamant in trying to convince his brother to sell their family business to a bigger company, has now changed his mind and decided that keeping it might be the right thing to do.

ORIGINAL FILM DIALOGUE

DAVID: We could still sell to Kroehner and both manage Fisher & Sons.
NATE: Yeah, but then we're just spokesmodels working to make **fat Republican stockholders** richer. And Kroehner doesn't give a shit about people. We care. We can help them through their grief. That's what we do.

ITALIAN ADAPTATION	BACK-TRANSLATION
DAVID: Ma possiamo andare avanti con la vendita e mantenere solo la gestione. NATE: Sì, però finiremmo col diventare solo delle marionette che servirebbero soltanto a far ingrassare **il ricco**. E alla Kroehner non gliene frega niente delle persone. Strappiamo via la gente dai loro artigli.	DAVID: But we can go along with the selling and just keep managing. NATE: Yes, but we would end up becoming just puppets which would only serve to make the **rich man** fat. And Kroehner couldn't care less about people. Let's tear people away from their claws.

EXAMPLE 7.14: SEASON 1 EPISODE 33

CONTEXT: David—an actively practising religious man—is at a deacon's meeting whose themes are same-sex marriages and parenthood.

ORIGINAL FILM DIALOGUE

WALTER: The Church rejects homosexual practice as incompatible with Scripture.
DAVID: So, because of their random genetics, gay people should be denied any romantic or sexual love?
WALTER: **That is liberal claptrap!** It's not genetics! It can be overcome!

ITALIAN ADAPTATION	BACK-TRANSLATION
WALTER: Ti rammento che la Chiesa definisce la pratica omosessuale come incompatibile con le Scritture. DAVID: Così solo a causa di uno scherzo genetico i gay si dovrebbero privare dell'amore romantico o fisico. WALTER: Ah, **non ti riempire la bocca con tutti questi paroloni**. Non si tratta di genetica. Un istinto, si può vincere.	WALTER: I remind you that the Church defines homosexual practice as incompatible with the Scriptures. DAVID: Then only because of a genetic trick, gay people should deny themselves any romantic or physical love. WALTER: Ah, **don't fill your mouth with all these big words**. It's not a question of genetics. An instinct can be overcome.

In these cases, not only the political references to Republicans and liberals have been eliminated in the Italian version, but the dialogues have also been completely rewritten. The lexical items 'Republican' and 'liberal' are often translated into Italian with what is apparently an official translation: *repubblicani* and *liberali*.[9] In fact, both these words refer to radically different concepts in the two cultures, and this may be the reason why the adapters have decided to solve the possible conundrum by eliminating the references *tout court*.

References to the institutional life of a country may be difficult to transfer into another culture because they simply do not exist in the host community, but they tend to contribute even more than other elements to give substance to the dialogue exchanges and to make them sound natural on the lips of real people. Once again, the strategy of elimination appears to be the most favoured by translators as well as the most revealing, in line with the overarching simplification and banalisation of the dialogue which, in the case of this particular series, is typical of the whole adapted text.

In line with other important issues tackled by this series, the sociopolitical aspects which are so vividly depicted in the original dialogue are translated into generic comments which are simply not as realistic.

Visual and Verbal References to Death

The opening credits and the way in which each episode's opening scene is constructed are meant to attract the audience's attention to the main theme of the programme from the very beginning. A haunting soundtrack reinforces the impact of the montage of images which include: a black bird crossing the blue sky; two people's holding hands suddenly unclasping; the close-up of the naked feet of a corpse with the morgue's habitual toe tag, whilst the rest of the body is covered with a white sheet; a single wheel on a linoleum floor, which the viewers soon discover to belong to a stretcher wheeling off a dead body along a corridor; the head of a dead woman with her eye in extreme close-up being gently made up; someone in a black suit opening the back door of a hearse with a coffin inside; a tombstone; the open hearse with the sun reflected on its window; two framed photographs of people; the claws of a black crow; glimpses of a coffin being carried off in the cemetery; a close shot of a crow's head; and the name of the creator of the series, Alan Ball, inscribed on a tombstone. A fade to white is used to usher in the first scene of every episode, which usually shows new characters dying unforeseen, grotesque, and disturbing deaths described in all their crudity. An inscription with the name and the years of birth and death is then followed by a fade to white. This is the customary prologue to every episode whose plot revolves primarily around the lives of the various members of the Fisher family and, marginally, around the stories of the dead people and their mourning relatives who have taken the decision to resort to the services of the Fishers' funeral home.

This detailed description is meant to highlight how images, before any dialogue is spoken, draw the audience into a world which is quintessentially North American, bound to US culture and to its specific customs. Many members of the Italian audience, watching these opening scenes, may experience mild culture shock. One of the reasons is that, contrary to what might be popular belief—according to which Italian funeral customs are usually depicted in foreign films in their most folkloric, traditional, mainly rural and outdated colours[10]—death in urban Italy is a taboo subject and a taboo word which is not to be openly discussed. In AVT, more specifically, this is also proven by the fact that if a film is not a thriller, the words *morte* [death] and *morto* [dead] in titles tend to be almost always omitted, substituted by distributors with an Italian euphemism or left untranslated in English. The Italian Disney Buena Vista company has it as a mandatory, written rule for adapters, that the words related to death are never to be translated literally but should be translated with euphemistic synonyms like "he or she has gone" or "he or she is no longer here".[11]

The feeling of cultural estrangement on the part of the TA grows after the realisation that not only are these scenes related to death but that some of them refer to a different kind of death. They reveal the striking differences in death-related customs between the SC and the TC. Some of these iconic images are the toe tag and—especially—the corpse being prepared to be made to look as good or even better than it looked when the person was alive. Toe tags are not normally used in Italian morgues, and open-casket vigils in the form of parties that require the corpse to be specially made up are usually reserved in Italy to state or celebrities' funerals, and even then they are extremely rare. It is true that some more traditional, mainly rural and old-fashioned communities still maintain traditions in which death and dead people are more openly displayed, but that is not the case in modern, urban societies in which loved ones, once deceased, are rapidly hidden from view.

Of course, decades of exposure to US films have made the Italian audiences accustomed to all these unfamiliar traditions—including the one of giving chatty parties after the funeral—but the fact remains that an objective resistance has to be overcome when the theme of death, described in its many facets, so openly proclaims to be the main focus of a television series.

In the following example, it is not so much the blatant manipulation of the homosexual content of the original, which I have discussed elsewhere (Ranzato 2012: 378–379), that caught my attention in relation to the present analysis, but the reference to a custom which is truly culture specific:

> EXAMPLE 7.15: SEASON 1 EPISODE 1 (PILOT)
>
> CONTEXT: Ruth is talking about her husband's new purchase to her son David, a homosexual young man who, in this pilot episode, has not yet come out.
>
> ORIGINAL FILM DIALOGUE
>
> RUTH: I think your father is having some sort of midlife crisis.
> DAVID: It would have made so much more sense to invest in re-paneling for the chapel or **adding coffee bars to the slumber rooms.**

RUTH: Well, I'd much rather he buy himself a fancy new hearse than leave me for a younger woman, or a woman my age for that matter, or heaven forbid, a man, like my cousin Hannah's husband did. God sure has dealt that woman some blows in this life.

ITALIAN ADAPTATION	BACK-TRANSLATION
RUTH: Tuo padre ci teneva, si è fatto un regalo per la crisi di mezza età.	RUTH: Your father wanted it very much; he bought himself a present for his midlife crisis.
DAVID: Era meglio investire per ridrappeggiare la cappella o mettere le macchinette del caffè nella camera ardente.	DAVID: It would have been better to invest in re-paneling for the chapel or adding coffee bars to the slumber rooms.
RUTH: È comunque sempre meglio che si sfoghi con un'auto nuova piuttosto che tradendomi con una ragazzina o con una donna della mia età. Gli uomini come il marito di mia cugina Hannah il cielo li dovrebbe castigare. Il Signore ha riservato dure prove a quella povera donna.	RUTH: Anyway it's always better that he satisfies himself with a new car than betray me with a young girl or a woman my age. Heaven should punish men like my cousin Hannah's husband. God has reserved that poor woman some hard trials.

The reference to objects so mundane and recreational as coffee bars, set in a solemn and grave place as a 'slumber room' (the viewing room in a funeral home), cannot be more distant from the TA's mentality. Translated literally into Italian, this line has the potential of stirring surprised reactions from the audience, and it is evidence of how inconsistent the whole dubbing process can be. It is indeed surprising that a translation that proves to be so manipulative only two lines after—suppressing as it does an explicit reference to a man's homosexuality—decides to keep such an exotic element as coffee bars in slumber rooms virtually unaltered by the use of a literal translation.

As can be expected, many dialogue exchanges in *Six Feet Under* include CSRs in relation to death subjects, some of which have already been analysed. When the references are made to very popular elements, they serve the purpose of rendering the image which is evoked more realistic by anchoring it to the everyday world in all its crudity. In the case of more sophisticated allusions, the quote is often used to make the reference sarcastically cultivated. The analysis of the corpus has shown that the reaction of the Italian adapters, with few exceptions, is generally that of manipulating death-related references to make them less unpalatable, as in the following example:

> **EXAMPLE 7.16: SEASON 1 EPISODE 4**
>
> CONTEXT: David and Nate are discussing the possibility that a big chain of funeral homes will swallow up their small family business.
>
> ORIGINAL FILM DIALOGUE
>
> DAVID: They sell cremations. Cheap cremations. Now for a fraction of what we charge, **you can now dump off the relative you never really liked anyway at the Torch Mart across the street.**
>
> | ITALIAN ADAPTATION | BACK-TRANSLATION |
> |---|---|
> | DAVID: Lì faranno solo cremazioni a buon mercato, non più di un decimo della nostra tariffa, credo. Per dirla in due parole è **come se andassi a comprare una cremazione in un supermercato.** | DAVID: They'll be doing only cheap cremations there, not more than a tenth of our fee, I think. To say it in just a few words, **it's as if you went to a supermarket to buy a cremation.** |

David is making a pun on Walmart, the international corporation of department stores which he compares to the big funeral home chain company that intends to buy a building across the street from them to create a crematorium (to which David alludes by using the term 'torch', in the sense of torching corpses). This image can be considered to be far too graphic and crude for a culture, such as the Italian culture, which has a problem in talking freely about death and which—as a Catholic country—looks upon cremation with suspicion. In this example, the key term in the original excerpt, the one which gives the line its sardonic impact, is the phonetic wordplay on the CSR (Walmart/torch mart). Its elimination serves only to soften the image, although the concept remains more or less the same.

The next example contains the allusion to a literary character which is quite familiar to the Anglo-Saxon world:

> **EXAMPLE 7.17: SERIES 1 EPISODE 3**
>
> CONTEXT: Nate has gone to the morgue to recover the body of a dead person.
>
> ORIGINAL FILM DIALOGUE
>
> ATTENDANT: He's like in a lot of pieces.
> NATE: **Humpty Dumpty**, I know.

ITALIAN ADAPTATION	BACK-TRANSLATION
INSERVIENTE: E' come una specie di puzzle.	ATTENDANT: He's like a kind of puzzle.
NATE: Me l'hanno detto che è ridotto male.	NATE: They told me he was a mess.

Humpty Dumpty is a character in an English children's limerick, an egg which at the end of the story breaks into pieces. It also figures famously in Lewis Carroll's *Through the Looking Glass* (1871/2007). People in Italy are not very familiar with Humpty Dumpty as it is a character known mainly to lovers of English literature, so a literal reference in this case would have risked not being understood by most of the audience.[12] Nonetheless, there is an attempt at compensation in the Italian adaptation by the introduction of the substantive 'puzzle' in the attendant's line. By referring to a puzzle, the translation maintains some of its original flavour, although the effect of the English is more grotesque and incisive because Nate associates the image of a dismembered corpse to a lovable character from the world of childhood. Again, the reality of death is transferred to the Italian screen with images of lesser impact.

The same way to describe the bad shape of a corpse by resorting to a CSR is solved in the next excerpt with a substitution:

EXAMPLE 7.18: SEASON 1 EPISODE 8

CONTEXT: The ghost of a dead person on whose corpse the Fishers are working on haunts David and appears to him in unforeseen occasions.

ORIGINAL FILM DIALOGUE

While DAVID works on MARC, MARC's ghost appears behind DAVID. His face is battered and bruised, but he is smiling and jovial.
MARC: Oh, God, I look like something **Chef Boyardee** makes!

ITALIAN ADAPTATION	BACK-TRANSLATION
MARC: Ma tu guarda, non ti sembro una specie di quadro di **Picasso**?	MARC: Just look at me. Don't I look like a sort of **Picasso** painting?

The substitution of an implicit cooking recipe—Boyardee is a popular chef of Italian origin—with an explicit Picasso painting is not out of place as the latter has the power of evoking subjects who have all their features dislocated. Thus the substitution found here is that of an SC reference (Boyardee's recipes are not known outside the USA) with one from a third culture,

Spanish, although admittedly very international. However, once again, by using a CSR in the original which has to do with food and the material aspect of death, the impact on the SA is arguably more disturbing than that made on the TA by conjuring up the image of an abstract, cubist painting.

In addition, the dialogue quoted in Example 7.3 shows—this time through substitution—the way in which the Italian adaptation has dealt with potentially disturbing contents related to the gruesome details of death. On this occasion, the name of the macabre serial killer Jeffrey Dahmer has been replaced by that of the iconic fictional character of Frankenstein, the only instance in which a literary reference is not eliminated but introduced in the adapted text.

These are just a few examples illustrating the strategies used by Italian adapters to present the subject of death in a different light than the usually more graphic descriptions found in the ST, which often resorts to CSRs to produce a more realistic and effective message.

CONCLUSIONS: DISMANTLING THE GAY IMAGINARY

Six Feet Under dealt with sensitive issues in a way which was unprecedented for a television series broadcast in Italy on a public channel. As stated in the introduction of this chapter, this show has been included in the corpus because ideological issues might be expected to come up in the analysis. Subjects related to death and homosexuality, in particular, had never been so openly displayed and delved into on any television show before.[13] It was thus a matter of particular interest for me to try to detect the presence of any possible overt and covert manipulative and censoring practices in the Italian dubbing which might tend to euphemise, dilute or alter homosexual content and change the words of homosexuality in the first place as well as other sensitive issues that have been highlighted in the examples already illustrated. As has been foregrounded, a manipulative policy in the adaptation of this series is indeed a fact, and the analysis has shown how the particular nature of certain CSRs and their handling in translation play a significant part in shaping the form and content of the Italian dialogue.

The adaptation of *Six Feet Under* shows how the two concepts of manipulation and censorship, discussed in Chapter 3, are sometimes separated by a very thin line. It is difficult not to interpret some of the cases illustrated—and many more which have not been included in the present work because they involve linguistic rather than culture specific features—as expressions of a conscious policy suggested or influenced by the patronage that be and aimed at edulcorating and ultimately eliminating sensitive references. The nature of these references is usually embedded in sexuality but also original contents which might disturb viewers because of their striking distance from the TC are the target of this policy, for example those related to death. Only examples in which the translation of CSRs played an important role in shaping and remodelling the form and substance of the Italian dialogue have been included in this chapter, but they are enough to give the measure of the translating policy. Many more instances could be given to illustrate a censoring attitude that is more evident in the first season of the series. As discussed in the case of *Friends*, television series need time to adjust and find their own target audience in the original as well as in their translated reincarnation. This has also been the case with *Six Feet Under*, whose Italian adaptation, with time, partly evolved to reflect more closely the reality of its main themes and its crude and sophisticated language. This adjustment seems to be proven by the radical increase in the usage of the loan strategy in the third season (58.5 percent compared with 33 percent in the first season)[14] and the decrease of eliminations (11 percent in the third season compared with the 26 percent in the first).

Issues related to the demographic of the potential target audience and the time of broadcast seem to be at the heart of some translation strategies. In this sense, pilot episodes and first seasons in general, as well as programmes broadcast in prime time, tend to be more censored than others, probably because they have yet to build an audience and, in the interest of the broadcasters, that audience has to be as large as possible from the very beginning. The much lower percentage in the use of the strategy of elimination in the third series compared to the first one seems to point in this direction: once the prospective target audience has been established, there is space for more latitude, which in the cases analysed means the freedom to be more literal and closer to the original than constrained by the assumed norms of the TL and TC.

Nonetheless, in the whole of its five seasons, the Italian rewriting never fails to convey the feeling that the purpose of the Italian adapters has been to produce a more reassuring programme, one that would lose its more sophisticated features and would dilute the more 'dangerous' contents. The result is that of a series rewritten with the intention to be made more palatable to the TA than it was to the original audience, which entails sacrificing some of the most intelligent dialogue exchanges by means of eliminating crucial cultural references. Overall, this is a rather sad outcome for one of the most acclaimed examples of auteur television.

It is my contention that one of the most telling areas that displays the Italian adapters' attitude towards this series is their bold, censoring handling of contents and words related to homosexuality. It is much more than just a matter of sanitisation: it is the purposeful dismantling of a network of associations which in the original text overtly relate to a gay imaginary. In the worst cases, homosexuality is not even acknowledged, and it is translated into a heterosexual and normalising lexicon through substitutions and eliminations.

The original *Six Feet Under* is notable for its clarity of intent. The series is clearly aimed at cultivated, liberal-minded viewers and does not make compromises to attract a more general audience. It does not pretend to be what it cannot be, that is, a mainstream product. The authors of the Italian version seemed to have been unsure of what was the best course of action to take, and although the series slowly tried to adjust to its intended TA by keeping more literal to the original, there is ample evidence that the translators did their best not to miss any opportunity to appeal to a more general, broader public.

NOTES

1. Ball had already won an Academy Award for the screenplay of the 1999 acclaimed film by Sam Mendes, *American Beauty*.
2. HBO, a US pay TV channel, is known for programming and producing pioneering fiction series—including *Sex and The City* (Darren Star 1998–2004), *The Sopranos* (David Chase, 1999–2007), *The Wire* (David Simon 2002–2008), *In Treatment* (developed by Rodrigo Garcia, 2008–2010); *True Detective* (Nic Pizzolatto, 2014–in production)—as well as influential drama films and miniseries—such as *Angels in America* (Mike Nichols 2003). It is considered one of the main sites for what has come to be known as quality TV, and its productions are regarded as having a distinctive, cutting-edge style (Feuer 2007; McCabe and Akass 2007; Edgerton and Jones 2009; Leverette et al. 2008).
3. All the publicity created for *Six Feet Under* (trailers, adverts, etc.) shows the emphasis placed on the creative genius behind the show, Alan Ball.
4. This series has been analysed for its contents and language specifically related to homosexuality in Ranzato (2012, 2015) and for its handling of allusions in Ranzato (2014). It has also been explored by Bucaria (2006) for the translation into Italian of its humorous features.
5. As it has already been noted, the total number of strategies varies from the number of CSRs because some strategies involve the introduction of new elements not present in the original text.
6. I am following Martínez Sierra's (2008: 153) classification of jokes. Zabalbeascoa (2005: 187), on whose own classification Martínez Sierra based his study, included these jokes in the larger category of *chistes dependientes de la lengua* (jokes depending on language).
7. Gayspeak is a word coined by Hayes (1976/2006: 64) who argues that homosexuals are America's largest subculture and that they have their own way of speaking of which he identifies a number of linguistic features. One of them is the development of an important cluster of images from stage and film: "Famous Hollywood stars of the thirties and forties figure importantly, especially if the roles they play are campy or treat of tragic love". For an analysis of gayspeak and gay subjects in AVT, see Ranzato (2012).
8. The words 'gay', 'transgender', 'coming out' and 'drag queen', are now words recognisable by most Italian people, but they are just about the only words of homosexual jargon to have entered mainstream language. In the case of the English language, as early as 1941, Legman (1941/2006: 19) included 146 terms in his American glossary which contained "only words and phrases current in American slang, argot, and colloquial speech since the First World War, and particularly during the period between 1930 and 1940". According to the author, the glossary was far from exhaustive, though it was part of a longer list of 329 terms—the selection being words which were used exclusively by homosexuals. A great number of these words are now part of standard English or are slang words used also by the general public. The Italian

lexicon of homosexuality lacks the inventiveness of English, shies away from neologisms and prefers to resort to borrowing.
9. If the term 'Republican' is generally identified with conservative politics and 'liberal' with more progressive positions in US culture, very different, sometimes opposite, associations are triggered by the words *'repubblicano'* and *'liberale'* in Italy due to historical reasons which cannot be explored here.
10. Incidentally, Nate himself describes with approval one of these Italian mourning traditions when, in the pilot episode, he recalls a scene he witnessed on a little volcanic island off the coast of Sicily.
11. Dubbing adapter Serena Paccagnella kindly forwarded an internal sheet of "compliance guidelines" from Disney, which asks dubbing adapters to avoid: "any type of four-letter words; expressions like *figo/fico* [cool; but the obscene, original meaning of the slang word is linked to female genitals] and derivatives; *casino/i* [mess; but literally 'whore-house'] and derivatives; swearing and cursing; insults or unrespectful expressions; jokes on priests, on the Church, and exclamations like *Oh Dio* [Oh God], *Oh Madonna!* etc.; insults or offensive words like *scemo* [stupid], *cretino* [moron], *deficiente* [half-wit], *handicappato* [handicapped] (. . . always remember that even if they are common expressions, Disney is extremely careful not to hurt the sensibilities of those people who might be suffering from those particular conditions: for example, in the case of the word *handicappato*, someone who really has a handicap, etc . . .); careful with the use of racist terms; never refer to well-known brands: Coca-cola, McDonald's, Sony, Fiorucci, Playstation, cigarette brands, building companies, clothing brands etc. (covert publicity); avoid the word *morto/a* [dead]" ("Disney compliance guidelines", my translation). The same avoidance of sensitive terms, including death-related words, is true not only for Disney but also for other types of cartoons (Parini 2012: 325–337).
12. However, times change, and the fact that this character featured prominently in the Dreamworks animation film *Puss in Boots (Il gatto con gli stivali*, Chris Miller 2011) may probably have an impact on people's awareness of this character.
13. The more specifically gay series *Queer as Folk* (Russell T. Davies 1999–2000, UK) was cancelled after much controversy, before ever being aired, by the public channel La7, considered one of the most progressive in Italy. It was later broadcast in 2002, in the late evening/night, by the pay TV channel Gay TV. Its slightly more sanitised American version (Ron Cowen and Daniel Lipman 2000–2005) was broadcast in 2006–2007 by the pay TV channel Jimmy.
14. See section on Translation Strategies, however, for a diegetic reason which can partly explain this data.

REFERENCES

Akass, Kim and Janet McCabe (eds.). 2005. *Six Feet Under TV To Die For*. London: I.B. Tauris & Co.

"Ascolti: Bonolis il più visto in prima serata". 2004. http://www.pubblicitaitalia.it/archivio?id=114895, last accessed 29 March 2015.

Bettridge, Daniel. 2009. "Best US television shows". *Times Online*: https://acs.thetimes.co.uk/?gotoUrl=http%3A%2F%2Fwww.thetimes.co.uk%2Ftto%2Farts%2Ftvradio%2F%3Ftoken%3Dnull%26offset%3D72%26page%3D7, requires login.

Bucarla, Chiara. "The perception of humour in dubbing vs subtitling: The case of Six Feet Under", *ESP Across Cultures* 2 (2006): 34–46.

Carroll, Lewis. 1871/2007. *Through the Looking Glass*. London: Penguin.

Carter, Bill. 2002. "Big networks show respect to 'Sopranos'". *The New York Times*: www.nytimes.com/2002/05/13/business/big-networks-show-respect-to-sopranos.html?pagewanted=all&src=pm, last accessed 29 March 2015.

Carter, Bill. 2004. "HBO, looking at 'Deadwood,' sees cavalry riding to rescue". *The New York Times*: www.nytimes.com/2004/06/16/arts/hbo-looking-at-deadwood-sees-cavalry-riding-to-rescue.html, last accessed 29 March 2015.

Cericola, Rachel. 2005. "Happy endings: the 6 best TV finales". TV Fodder: www.tvfodder.com/archives/2005/08/happy_endings.shtml, last accessed 29 March 2015.

Edgerton, Gary R. and Jeffrey P. Jones (eds.). 2009. *The Essential HBO Reader*. Lexington: The University Press of Kentucky.

Feuer, Jane. 2007. "HBO and the concept of quality TV", in Janet McCabe and Kim Akass (eds.) *Quality TV. Contemporary American Television and Beyond*. London: I.B. Tauris, 145–157.

Fitzgerald, Toni. 2003. "See 'Anna Nicole' dive without a net". *Media Life*: www.medialifemagazine.com:8080/news2003//mar03/mar10/3_wed/news4wednesday.html, last accessed 29 March 2015.

Hayes, Joseph J. 1976/2006. "Gayspeak", in Deborah Cameron and Don Kulick (eds.) *The Language and Sexuality Reader*. London: Routledge, 68–77.

Legman, Gershon. 1941/2006. "The language of homosexuality: an American glossary", in Deborah Cameron and Don Kulick (eds.) *The Language and Sexuality Reader*. London: Routledge, 19–32.

Leverette, Mark, Brian L. Ott and Cara Louise Buckley. 2008. *It's not TV. Watching HBO in the Post-Television Era*. New York: Routledge.

Martínez Sierra, Juan José. 2008. *Humor y traducción. Los Simpson cruzan la frontera*. Castelló de la Plana: Universitat Jaume I.

McCabe, Janet and Kim Akass (eds.). 2007. *Quality TV. Contemporary American Television and Beyond*. London: I.B. Tauris.

Parini, Ilaria. 2012. "Censorship of *Anime* in Italian distribution", in Jorge Díaz Cintas (ed.) *The Manipulation of Audiovisual Translation*, *Meta* special issue, 57(2): 325–337.

Pasha, Shaheen. 2005. "Showtime: trying to sing 'Soprano'". *CNNMoney*: http://money.cnn.com/2005/08/26/news/fortune500/hbo_showtime/, last accessed 29 March 2015.

Poniewozik, James. 2007. "All-time 100 TV shows". *Time Entertainment*: http://entertainment.time.com/2007/09/06/the-100-best-tv-shows-of-all-time/slide/six-feet-under/#six-feet-under, last accessed 29 March 2015.

Ranzato, Irene. 2012. "Gayspeak and gay subjects in audiovisual translation: strategies in Italian dubbing", in Jorge Díaz Cintas (ed.) *The Manipulation of Audiovisual Translation*, *Meta* special issue, 57(2): 369–384.

Ranzato, Irene. 2014. "'You're talking like the computer in the movie': Allusions in Audiovisual Translation". *Parole Rubate/Purloined Letters* 9: 81–107.

Ranzato, Irene. 2015. "'God Forbid, a Man!': Homosexuality in a Case of Quality TV", in Antonio Bibbò, Stefano Ercolino and Mirko Lino (eds.) *Censura e autocensura*, *Between*, V.9, http://www.betweenjournal.it/

"'Six Feet Under' Finale Draws Viewers". 2005. www.upi.com/Entertainment_News/2005/08/23/Six-Feet-Under-finale-draws-viewers/UPI-28161124842695/, last accessed 29 March 2015.

Wilson, Stacey. 2009. "Top 10 TV series finales: *The Sopranos*, *Friends*, *Cheers*". Film.com/tv: www.film.com/tv/top-10-tv-series-finales-the-sopranos-friends-cheers, last accessed 29 March 2015.

Zabalbeascoa, Patrick. 2005. "Humour and translation—an interdiscipline". *Humour—International Journal of Humour Research*, 18(2): 185–207.

Filmography

2001: A Space Odyssey (2001: Odissea nello spazio), Stanley Kubrick, 1968, UK/USA.
The Addams Family (La famiglia Addams), Charles Addams, 1964–1966, USA.
American Beauty, Sam Mendes, 1999, USA.
Angels in America, Mike Nichols, 2003, USA.
Friends, Marta Kauffman and David Crane, 1994–2004, USA.
In Treatment, developed by Rodrigo Garcia, 2008–2010.
Life on Mars, Matthew Graham, Tony Jordan and Ashley Pharoah, 2006–2007, UK.
The Lord of the Rings (trilogy) (Il signore degli anelli), Peter Jackson, 2001, 2002, 2003, New Zealand/USA.
The Matrix (Matrix), Larry and Andy Wachowski, 1999, USA.
Mayberry R.F.D., Bob Ross, 1968–1971, USA.
Mogambo, John Ford, 1953, USA.
Murder, She Wrote (La signora in giallo), Peter S. Fischer, 1984–1996, USA.
The Munsters (I mostri), Allan Burns and Chris Hayward, 1964–1966, USA.
Puss in Boots (Il gatto con gli stivali), Chris Miller, 2011, USA.
Queer as Folk, Russell T. Davies, 1999–2000, UK.
Queer as Folk, Ron Cowen, Daniel Lipman, 2000–2005, USA.
Sex and The City, Darren Star, 1998–2004, USA.
Six Feet Under, Alan Ball, 2001–2005, USA.
The Sopranos (I Soprano), David Chase, 1999–2007, USA.
Titanic, James Cameron, 1997, USA.
True Detective, Nic Pizzolatto, 2014-in production. USA.
Will & Grace, David Kohan and Max Mutchnick, 1998–2006, USA.
Willy Wonka and the Chocolate Factory (Willy Wonka e la fabbrica di cioccolato), Mel Stuart, 1971, USA.
The Wire, David Simon, 2002–2008, USA.

8 Conclusions

COMPARATIVE EVALUATIONS

This chapter offers a synthesis of the most relevant conclusions reached in the individual case studies and a comparative overview of the three series for what concerns both the translation strategies and the different categories the CSRs fall into. It also highlights the most relevant aspects of the corpus and points to the ways the latter can be further used for research.

At this stage, it is useful to remember that one of the implications of Toury's target-oriented approach is that the socio-historical context in which the translation process takes place becomes fundamental in understanding the behaviour of translators and their norm-oriented choices. The high percentage in the use of some manipulative strategies, notably elimination, used on a regular basis in the three series, seems to indicate the presence of a translational behaviour, in contemporary Italian television, that has its roots in the history of dubbing in Italy. In other words, translators for television in this country seem to often follow the manipulative, and sometimes censoring, pattern which has constrained AVT since the beginning of the dubbing industry.

The ultimate aim, in gathering the data, was to analyse any possible regularities in the strategies implemented to translate CSRs, paying close attention to the translation of sensitive content and of challenging linguistic features because of their possible ideological and sociolinguistic implications. All of these features have been analysed in depth in the various chapters devoted to the case studies. In this conclusive chapter, some comparisons will be drawn between the data relative to the individual series, highlighting some of the most striking regularities but also irregularities in behaviour. The latter are mainly, although not only, linked to the different textual genres of the material included in the corpus, and an evaluation is made of the possible causes for these irregularities.

Regularities in the Types of CSRs

Cultural specificity is a relative term that can be arguably best assessed in situations where two (or more) cultures meet each other. Cultures are

222 Conclusions

not a stable and clear-cut set of practices, but rather they are continuously altering and subject to change. This relativity is reflected in the taxonomy proposed in this research to classify CSRs in a way that can at least partly account for their dynamism in terms of geographic and temporal collocation. Figure 8.1 takes a comparative look at the distribution of CSRs throughout the three series.[1]

Reflecting on the nature of CSRs is particularly useful in the analysis of translation strategies. In this sense, the data included in this graph helps elicit the types of CSRs which were chosen by the authors in their construction of the dialogues and, ultimately, of the characters of the respective series.

The only uniform trend that can be evinced in the graph is the steady use of intercultural references, that is, CSRs originally belonging to the SC that have developed into elements which have been absorbed by the Italian TC in various degrees: they have been used by a percentage of 21 percent (*Friends*), 22 percent (*Life on Mars*) and 23 percent (*Six Feet Under*). All the other categories show various discrepancies.

References to the source culture are markedly more frequent in *Six Feet Under* (44 percent, compared to 34 and 33 percent in *Friends* and *Life on Mars*, respectively), but there is a diegetic reason for this, particularly linked to the use of place names in one of the seasons of *Six Feet Under*, as illustrated in Chapter 7.

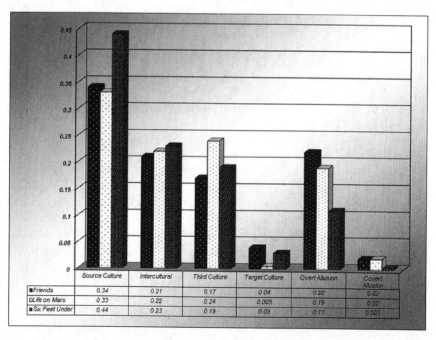

Figure 8.1 Distribution per category through the three series

The data relative to references to a third culture and to the target culture (Italy) are more revealing from an analytical perspective. The highest percentage of third culture CSRs is found in the British *Life on Mars*, due to the frequent references to US culture (55 percent of its third culture references are referred to US elements), a culture to which the British are obviously closely connected. Data prove the US culture to be particularly pervasive in terms of images and associations evoked in this British text. On the contrary, and as it could be expected, the two US series refer to the British culture much less frequently. This is one of the reasons why the figures relative to this category, which includes references to any third culture, are much lower. A total of 17 percent of CSRs in *Friends* refer to a third culture, including, among the most represented, the Chinese, French, Mexican, Russian, and also British ones. The latter, however, despite a strong diegetic British theme developed in some of the episodes, represent only 26 percent of third culture references in *Friends*. A percentage of 19 percent of CSRs in *Six Feet Under* makes reference to a third culture, with no special focus on any of the cultures represented (which include Mexican, Chinese, British, and many others in lower figures). All in all, cultural references of US origin are not only dominant in US productions but also in audiovisual programmes produced in other countries. This situation may be proof of the unbalance in the reciprocal and respective influence of these two cultures—US and British—which share a common language and history, and points to an interesting avenue for further research.

In addition, the wider variety of cultures included in the third culture category in the two US series—from references to Latin American, European, Asian and African countries and nationalities—gives substance to the image of the melting pot which is often associated with this nation. The fact that the British series is set in a historical period which was less open to international influences should not be overlooked. Nevertheless, with Britain's own imperialist colonial past, a more heterogeneous figure in the third culture category could have been expected from this British show which, on the contrary, presents a rather uniform majority of occurrences related to the USA.

Reading these data in close association with the information relative to references to the TC renders it possible to define even more clearly how the British series has a more national colouring. The information relative to the use of TC references, in this case Italian, shows a major discrepancy across series: *Life on Mars* includes only 0.5 percent of occurrences of CSRs connected to Italy, in comparison to the 4 percent (*Friends*) and 3 percent (*Six Feet Under*) of the two US series. This can be easily explained given the important presence of Italians and Italian culture in the USA, particularly since the arrival of the early immigrants in the 19th century, and again it can be argued that it is a testimony to the more varied makeup of the US population and culture in comparison to the more isolated British culture. The argument that this is a fictional image portrayed by audiovisual texts and not the social reality—as, in fact, the British population can be considered just as varied a melting pot as the USA is—is certainly an important matter which, however, cannot be explored here. What is of interest is that these data seem to testify to a greater openness of the US shows towards other cultures, which can be a reason for their greater exportability in comparison to British shows—an exportability which is confirmed by general observations on the production and broadcast of fiction shows: as it has been mentioned in the course of this book, successful British shows are often remade into US versions and localised by translating British cultural references and linguistic features into American ones.[2] On the other hand, US television programmes are exported abroad, including the UK, in their own original, exportable US versions without any need of localisation.

As a conclusive remark on the image of a heterogeneous cultural mix which the data relative to the US series convey, it can be stated that these shows reveal a marketing strategy which is steadily detectable in film and television productions: giving a systematic representation of the various cultures and nationalities which have been absorbed in various degrees by the North American culture is also a way of attracting a wider audience. The role of these strategic marketing considerations together with the aim of striving for a more ethical and inclusive way of representing cultures on screen have the result of US productions offering a portrayal of their varied population composition with a certain degree of systematicity. This, however, is a strategy that British programmes do not seem to have any visible interest in pursuing.

Finally, data relative to the presence of allusions also show a discrepancy between US and UK series, which can be used to highlight the different methods of dialogue construction implemented in the three series. In this respect, the authors of *Six Feet Under* have made much less use of allusions (only 11.3 percent between overt and covert ones) in the creation of their dialogues in clear contradistinction to the use made by the authors of both *Friends* (a total of 24 percent) and *Life on Mars* (21 percent). This means that the former series relies much more than the latter on what in these pages have been termed 'real-world references' and less on intertextual references. Indeed, the authors of *Six Feet Under* seem to be more concerned with giving a crude depiction of reality than with playing postmodernly with allusions to other fictional texts, a creative device that the authors of the other two shows have evidently relished using.

Regularities in Translation Strategies

Textual-linguistic norms, included by Toury (1995: 59) in operational norms, have an impact on the material chosen to replace the original text, thus on the strategies chosen to translate the texts, which in turn are revelatory of certain norm-governed behaviour. Toury's (ibid.) further subdivision into textual-linguistic norms which apply to translation in general and those which apply to particular types of translation only has been taken into account by considering a set of translation strategies, as a taxonomy for analysis, which can be applied specifically to the analysis of AVT material and to dubbed texts in particular (Chapter 4).

As the following comparative Figure 8.2 demonstrates, the three TV series under scrutiny show common patterns in the implementation of some translation strategies.

A quite uniform pattern can be detected especially in the use of the strategy of elimination (*Friends*: 19 percent; *Life on Mars*: 18 percent; *Six Feet Under*: 18 percent). Additionally, the strategies of loan and official translation have been implemented in high percentages which are not very distant to each other: *Friends* shows a percentage of 46 percent; *Life on Mars*, 52 percent; *Six Feet Under*, 47 percent in the use of loans, and they respectively show percentages of 15, 17 and 19 percent in the use of official translation. However, in these cases, there is a peak in the use of loans in *Life on Mars* and a lesser impact of the strategy of official translation in *Friends*.

The elimination of CSRs, chosen in between 18 and 19 percent of the cases, implies a considerable departure from the original text since this strategy

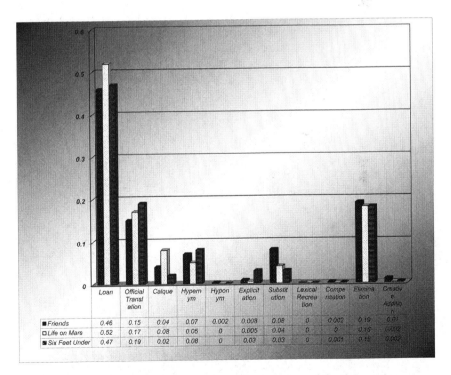

Figure 8.2 Translation strategies: comparative overview of the three series

involves the elimination of a CSR which is not replaced by any other. As has often been stressed (see, e.g., Chapters 5 and 6), eliminations tend to lead to the greatest departures from the ST, and the original dialogue exchanges are adapted in such a way that they usually transform substantially the meaning of the sentences.

Reading the graphs from another perspective, it can also be confirmed that the strategies which have been defined as 'non-creative' in these pages, that is, the less creative strategies of loan and elimination, are always and insistently the ones most preferred by the adapters. Elimination should not be considered a non-creative strategy per se, as the eliminated CSR could theoretically be replaced by imaginative adaptations, but the fact remains that this strategy has been consistently used in a non-creative way in the whole corpus as the examples cited and the many others in the corpus plainly show.

On the other hand, official translation, which often involves an effort of research to find the established equivalent of a given element, is also very frequently used by adapters, but in this corpus, it has been implemented in the great majority of cases to translate CSRs of everyday use, that is, in the case of currencies, place names, measures and terms which do not usually require any in-depth research.

Lexical recreation is absent from all the series, and the use of hyponyms and compensation is only very occasional. More inspired, although potentially and effectively more manipulative, strategies such as substitution and creative addition have been used with less uniformity. In this case, there is a maximum of 8 percent substitutions and 1 percent additions in *Friends*, which proves to be the series with a more varied landscape in terms of strategy implementation.

DIFFERENCES AMONG THE THREE SERIES AND CONCLUSIVE REMARKS

In the study of the three parts of the corpus, each part has shown the presence of different aspects which, while showing an internal regularity within a series, cannot be detected in any relevant way in the other cases. Some of them, as has been seen in the former sections, are linked to the various translation strategies being implemented, whereas some others are more due to the different nature of CSRs. If analysed in combination, these two parameters can offer a multifaceted cultural and linguistic reading of these audio-visual texts. In addition, the analysis of the data can provide further insights into the distinctive features of each series, which in turn, may point to new avenues of research.

If one reads the data in terms of genre, for example, the authors of the sitcom *Friends* have resorted to CSRs in the construction of dialogues and characters much more frequently (58.5 percent) than the authors of the detective series *Life on Mars* (45 percent) and the drama *Six Feet Under* (43.4 percent). This data may contribute to give evidence of the important role played by the use of CSRs in the sitcom genre and highlight the need for further research that would focus on genre as a determining factor. In other words, studying the incidence of CSRs within a particular genre, and not across different genres as in this book, may reveal tendencies in the translators' behaviour that are strictly connected to the type of audiovisual text they are translating, which could be termed 'genre-related norms'. This kind of genre-related research could be, in my opinion, one of the fruitful ways film (and television) studies could be usefully incorporated in AVT in the spirit of Chaume's (2004) suggestions.

Another different feature detected in the series is related to editorial choices. *Life on Mars* is a clear example where the role of Toury's preliminary norms can be evidenced. These norms, as explained in Chapter 2, influence behaviour before the start of the actual translation process, such as the selection of the texts to be translated into the TL and their textual integrity. Preliminary norms may account for the regular pattern of editorial cuts in the montage of this series, which has been fully analysed in Chapter 6. This analysis has shown a consistent policy, on the part of the adapting team, meant to edit out the most problematic parts of every episode, including scenes containing a high number of CSRs. This has been recognised as an extreme strategy whose aim is that of smoothing out culture bumps and which has resulted in an impoverishment of the text in the Italian version, which in turn lacks the cultural and linguistic markedness of the original. Preliminary norms, as acted out on this series, have shown how manipulative translational behaviour is at the root of many decisions. Editorial cuts can also be detected in *Friends*, but their role in the linguistic adaptation process is negligible, and the final message does not seem to be compromised.

However, *Friends* is different from the other two shows in the sense that, the same as it happens with most sitcoms, it makes use of laugh tracks, a non-diegetic element. The editorial choice to mute or substitute the original laughs present in the show has been carried out consistently throughout the whole series. In this case study, too, the role of preliminary norms which govern editorial choices before and beside the actual translation process can also be clearly detected. And in this case too, the manipulation of this particular feature has had the result of depriving the audiovisual text of some original cultural characteristics (see Chapter 5).

In summary, data show that different preliminary norms can be detected in two of the three programmes of the corpus, which in both cases reveal a manipulative policy on the part of the adapting team. It is rather surprising that the editing out has taken place with the least 'problematic' series as *Six Feet Under*, which for its themes was potentially more vulnerable, has been treated differently, and no cuts have been detected. The original time of broadcast, late in the evening, and the makeup of the expected audience, less mainstream in comparison to the ones the other series were aimed at, may have played a role in these preliminary decisions.

Finally, as already pointed out, it was my hypothesis that some television programmes would potentially raise more ideological issues than others. *Six Feet Under*, a series in which so many socially significant subjects are openly dealt with, has shown some regularities of behaviour, especially in the elimination of sensitive issues, which call for an ideological reading of the whole adapted text. This same series has made it possible to highlight how ideological issues may blend with linguistic and sociocultural ones in such a way that it is impossible to draw a clear boundary between them. As has been discussed in Chapter 7, the absence of a rich gayspeak lexicon in the Italian language makes it hard to determine whether some translation choices could be clearly ascribed to ideological censorship or rather to a lack of lexical equivalent or closely connected terms in the TL. This is arguably a Sapir-Whorfian matter, in the sense that language may influence the behaviour of individuals in society rather than the other way around,[3] and an aspect that *Six Feet Under*, more than the other two series, has made evident. In other words, is it the lack of an appropriate lexicon which makes translators more manipulative and censoring than they would be, given the possibility? And although the fact that an area of a lexicon is underdeveloped is itself quite revealing, to follow the Sapir-Whorf line of reasoning is only apparently taking the matter to extremes: linguistic debates on the possible social benefits of a politically correct choice of words, for example, are one of the contemporary applications of the Sapir-Whorfian theory (Mesthrie *et al*. 2005: 8).

In Tourian terms, this is an area in which the search for matricial norms, which govern, among other things, "the very *existence* of target-language material as a substitute for the corresponding source-language material" (Toury 1995: 58), becomes inexorable and has the potential of yielding fruitful results. In this sense, it would be very interesting to carry out a diachronic analysis of how certain terms and references that are named in the SL and that do not seem to have an equivalent in the TL may eventually make it into the other language and culture (see, e.g., the discussion on 'Thanksgiving', Chapter 5).

The search for matricial norms, however, can also safely be conducted when analysing not only linguistic material but also sociocultural behaviour. Under this prism, not only *Six Feet Under* but also *Life on Mars*—in which many cultural elements related to the police force, for example, or to British legislation cannot be associated to similar images in the TC—can be heralded as a clear illustration of how the lack of certain elements or concepts (legislative, historical, social, etc.) in the TC can limit the repertoire of possibilities available to the translators.

Nevertheless, the translation of *Six Feet Under* in particular has shown how the concepts, discussed in Chapter 3, of technical and ideological manipulation (Díaz Cintas 2012: 284–285), and of manipulation and censorship, are sometimes separated by a very thin line. As has been pointed out in the conclusions of that case study, it is difficult not to judge the handling of some of its content as expressions of a conscious policy aimed at edulcorating and ultimately eliminating sensitive references, producing an overall more reassuring programme that has the potential of appealing to a broader audience and thus generating greater income.

The initial assumption that triggered this research was that, in line with Toury's recommendations, a descriptive analysis should be carried out on the basis of a large and varied corpus if meaningful results were to be unravelled. In spite of the different televisual genres under analysis, some important regularities of translational behaviour have been detected. At the same time, the fundamental differences among the series—in terms of genre, period of production and, most importantly, different professionals involved in the translating and adapting process—have required a partly different approach to each case study to account for dissimilarities of behaviour, which sometimes stemmed from different premises. It is my contention that the richness of information gathered on many aspects of the translating process may open up new avenues of research which will help define the role of cultural references in audiovisual texts from different angles and perspectives.

NOTES

1. The overarching and possibly overlapping categories of non-verbal references and asynchronous references, as well as the practically uncountable intertextual macroallusions, are not included in the graph. Non-verbal elements have been included in the overall count, but as this book is mainly focused on translation strategies, visual and paralinguistic elements have been considered in the analysis only when they are relevant in the dialogue exchanges. Asynchronous references on the other hand are characterised by their extreme relativity: virtually any reference can be asynchronous, especially in period shows and costume films, depending on the translator's or researcher's temporal viewpoint.
2. Some US remakes of British shows are the already mentioned *Life on Mars* (T. Jordan and A. Pharoah, 2008–2009) (Chapter 6) and *Queer as Folk* (R. Cowen and D. Lipman, 2000–2005) (Chapter 7). Other examples include *Prime Suspect* (Lynda La Plante 1991–1996, 2003–2006, UK; 2011–2012, USA), *The Office* (Ricky Gervais and Stephen Merchant 2001–2003, UK; developed by Greg Daniels 2005–2013, USA), *Skins* (Jamie Brittain and Bryan Elsley 2007–2013, UK; 2011, USA), *House of Cards* (Andrew Davies and Michael Dobbs 1990, UK; Beau Willimon 2013–in production, USA), to cite some of the best known.
3. As is well-known, what has come to be known has the Sapir-Whorf hypothesis has never been formulated by the two scholars, Edward Sapir and Benjamin Lee Whorf, as such, but rather evinced from some of their individual writings (see Sapir 1949/1985; Whorf 1956). Nevertheless, the influence of 'their' hypothesis has been enormous and can be summarised in the enunciation that the structure of a language affects the speakers' cognitive processes, that is, the ways in which they conceptualise the world.

REFERENCES

Chaume, Frederic. 2004. "Film studies and translation studies: two disciplines at stake in audiovisual translation". *Meta* 49(1): 12–24.

Díaz Cintas, Jorge. 2012. "Clearing the smoke to see the screen: ideological manipulation in audiovisual translation", in Jorge Díaz Cintas (ed.) *The Manipulation of Audiovisual Translation, Meta* special issue, 57(2): 279–293.

Mesthrie, Rajend, Joan Swann, Andrea Deumert and William L. Leap. 2005. *Introducing Sociolinguistics*. Edinburgh: Edinburgh University Press.

Sapir, Edward. 1949/1985. *Selected Writings in Language, Culture, and Personality.* Berkeley: University of California Press.

Toury, Gideon. 1995. *Descriptive Translation Studies and Beyond*. Amsterdam: John Benjamins.

Whorf, Benjamin Lee. 1956. *Language, Thought and Reality: Selected Writings.* Cambridge, MA: MIT Press.

Filmography

Friends, Marta Kauffman and David Crane, 1994–2004, USA.
House of Cards, Andrew Davies and Michael Dobbs, 1990, UK.
House of Cards, Beau Willimon, 2013-in production, USA.
Life on Mars, Matthew Graham, Tony Jordan and Ashley Pharoah, 2006–2007, UK.
Life on Mars, Matthew Graham, Tony Jordan and Ashley Pharoah, 2008–2009, USA.
The Office, Ricky Gervais and Stephen Merchant, 2001–2003, UK.
The Office, developed by Greg Daniels, 2005–2013, USA.
Prime Suspect, Lynda La Plante, 1991–1996, 2003–2006, UK.
Prime Suspect, Lynda La Plante, 2011–2012, USA.
Queer as Folk, Ron Cowen, Daniel Lipman, 2000–2005, USA.
Six Feet Under, Alan Ball, 2001–2005, USA.
Skins, Jamie Brittain and Bryan Elsley, 2007–2013, UK.
Skins, Jamie Brittain and Bryan Elsley, 2011, USA.

Appendix
Sample Pages From the Corpus

FRIENDS

The One Where It All Began (Pilot)
Matrimonio mancato (Missed wedding)

Season 1 Episode 1 (Pilot)

1/1

ORIGINAL FILM DIALOGUE 03.37–03.48

MONICA: *(pointing at Rachel)* De-caff. *(To all)* Okay, everybody, this is Rachel, another **Lincoln High** survivor. (To Rachel) This is everybody. This is Chandler, and Phoebe, and Joey, and—you remember my brother Ross?

ITALIAN ADAPTATION	BACK-TRANSLATION
MONICA: Decaffeinato. Bene, ragazzi, questa è Rachel, è un'altra superstite del **liceo Lincoln**. Siamo tutti qui: lui è Chandler, lei è Phoebe, poi c'è Joey e... ricordi mio fratello Ross?	MONICA: Decaffeinated. Well, guys, this is Rachel, another **Lincoln high school** survivor. We're all here: he is Chandler, she is Phoebe, then there's Joey and... you remember my brother Ross?

1/2

ORIGINAL FILM DIALOGUE 04.11–04.28

RACHEL: ... I was looking at this gravy boat, this really gorgeous **Limoges gravy boat**, when all of a sudden (to the waitress that brought her coffee) Sweet'n'Lo? I realized that I was more turned on by the gravy boat than by Barry! And then I got really freaked out, and that's when it hit me: how much Barry looks like **Mr. Potato Head**.

232 Appendix

ITALIAN ADAPTATION	BACK-TRANSLATION
RACHEL: ... e stavo guardando una salsiera bellissima. Una **salsiera d'argento** veramente meravigliosa. Quando a un tratto—c'è lo **zucchero?**—mi sono resa conto che ero più eccitata dalla salsiera d'argento che da Barry! E allora mi sono davvero spaventata, e mi sono anche accorta di come Barry somigli a **E.T.**	RACHEL: ... I was looking at this beautiful gravy boat, this really gorgeous **silver** gravy boat, when all of a sudden—is there any **sugar?**—I realized that I was more turned on by the gravy boat than by Barry! And then I got really freaked out, and I realized how much Barry looks like **E.T.**

1/3

ORIGINAL FILM DIALOGUE 06.43–06.54

PHOEBE *(sings)*: **Raindrops on roses and rabbits and kittens, bluebells and sleigh bells and something with mittens** ...

ITALIAN ADAPTATION	BACK-TRANSLATION
PHOEBE: ... Can caminin can caminin spazzacamin Can caminin can caminin spazzacamin felice e gioioso problema non ha Can caminin can caminin spazzacamin ...	PHEOBE: *sings the Italian version of the "chimney boy" song of Mary Poppins.*

1/4

ORIGINAL FILM DIALOGUE 08.22–08.42

ROSS: So Rachel, what're you, uh ... what're you up to tonight?
RACHEL: Well, I was kinda supposed to be headed for **Aruba** on my honeymoon, so nothing!
ROSS: Right, you're not even getting your honeymoon, God. No, no, although, **Aruba**, this time of year ... talk about your—(thinks) big lizards ...

ITALIAN ADAPTATION	BACK-TRANSLATION
ROSS: Allora che programmi avevi questa sera?	ROSS: So Rachel, what programmes did you have tonight?
RACHEL: Be', ecco, avrei dovuto essere diretta ad **Aruba** per la mia luna di miele ... e perciò niente!	RACHEL: Well, right, I should have been headed for **Aruba** for my honeymoon ... and so nothing!

ROSS: E' vero, non hai fatto neanche la tua luna di miele... no, no, anzi ad **Aruba** in questo periodo dell'anno ci sono dei bei, dei lucertoloni...

ROSS: It's true, you haven't even done your honeymoon... No, no, actually in **Aruba**, this time of year there are some beautiful, some lizards...

1/5

ORIGINAL FILM DIALOGUE 11.10–11.21

JOEY: There's lots of flavors out there. There's **Rocky Road**, and **Cookie Dough**, and Bing! Cherry vanilla. You could get 'em with jimmies, or nuts, or whipped cream!

ITALIAN ADAPTATION

JOEY: Ci sono un sacco di gusti da scegliere. C'è il gusto **Rocky**, il **gusto gianduia** e bingo, ciliegia vanigliata. Li puoi mangiare con le cialde, o con le noci o con la panna montata.

BACK-TRANSLATION

JOEY: There's lots of flavors to choose from. There's **Rocky** flavor, **gianduia** *(nut chocolate)* flavor, and bingo, vanilla cherry. You can eat them with wafers or nuts or whipped cream.

1/6

ORIGINAL FILM DIALOGUE 11.47–11.49

MONICA: What, you wanna spell it out with **noodles?**

ITALIAN ADAPTATION

MONICA: Vuoi scriverlo con le **fettuccine?**

BACK-TRANSLATION

MONICA: Do you want to write it with **fettuccine?**

1/7

ORIGINAL FILM DIALOGUE 12.54–13.04

[Scene: Monica's Apartment, Rachel is watching *Joanie Loves Chachi*.]
JOANIE: I, **Joanie**, take you **Charles** as my lawful husband.
PRIEST ON TV: We are gathered here today to join **Joanie Louise Cunningham** and **Charles, Chachi-Chachi-Chachi, Arcola** in the bounds of holy matrimony.

ITALIAN ADAPTATION	BACK-TRANSLATION
JOANIE: Io, Joanie, prendo te, Charles, come legittimo sposo. SACERDOTE IN TV: Tu prendi Joanie, Charles, come tua legittima sposa ...	JOANIE: I, Joanie, take you Charles as my lawful husband. PRIEST ON TV: You take Joanie, Charles, as your lawful wife ...

1/8

ORIGINAL FILM DIALOGUE 12.55–12.59

RACHEL: Oh, yeah, but Joanne loved Chachi! That's the difference!

ITALIAN ADAPTATION	BACK-TRANSLATION
RACHEL: Oh, sì ... ma Joanie era innamorato di Charles. E' tutta qui la differenza!	RACHEL: ... but Joanne was in love with Charles! That was all the difference!

1/9

ORIGINAL FILM DIALOGUE 13.06–13.10

ROSS: Do you know how long it's been since I've grabbed a spoon? Do the words 'Billy, don't be a hero' mean anything to you?

ITALIAN ADAPTATION	BACK-TRANSLATION
ROSS: Lo sapete da quanto tempo è che non prendo un cucchiaino? Da quando si diceva 'fate l'amore, non fate la guerra'.	ROSS: Do you know how long it's been since I've taken a teaspoon? Since the time people said 'make love, not war'.

1/10

ORIGINAL FILM DIALOGUE 13.49–13.55

JOEY: Listen, while you're on a roll, if you feel like you gotta make like a Western omelet or something ...

ITALIAN ADAPTATION	BACK-TRANSLATION
JOEY: E visto che ci sei, se ti va di fare anche una frittatina o qualcosa del genere.	JOEY: Listen, while you're at it, if you feel like making a little omelet too or something like that.

1/11

ORIGINAL FILM DIALOGUE 15.04–15.16

JOEY: Yeah, I'm an actor.
RACHEL: Wow! Would I have seen you in anything?
JOEY: I doubt it. Mostly regional work.
MONICA: Oh wait, wait, unless you happened to catch **the Reruns' production of Pinocchio**.
CHANDLER: 'Look, **Geppetto**, I'm a real live boy.'

ITALIAN ADAPTATION	BACK-TRANSLATION
JOEY: Io faccio l'attore.	JOEY: I'm an actor.
RACHEL: Ehi, forse ti avrò visto in qualcosa.	RACHEL: Hey, maybe I've seen you in something.
JOEY: Ah, non penso, soprattutto emittenti locali.	JOEY: Ah, I don't think so, mostly local broadcasters.
MONICA: Aspetta, a meno che tu non abbia visto **una seconda visione** del film **Pinocchio**.	MONICA: Wait, unless you've seen **a rerun of the film Pinocchio**.
CHANDLER: "Guarda **Geppetto** sono un bambino in carne e ossa".	CHANDLER: "Look, **Geppetto**, I'm a child in flesh and bones".

1/12

ORIGINAL FILM DIALOGUE 17.38–17.44

CHANDLER: And yet you're surprisingly upbeat.
RACHEL: You would be too if you found **John and David boots** on sale, 50 percent off!

ITALIAN ADAPTATION	BACK-TRANSLATION
CHANDLER: Eppure sei incredibilmente gasata.	CHANDLER: And yet you're incredibly upbeat.
RACHEL: Be', lo saresti anche tu se avessi trovato **questi stivali** al saldo del 50%!	RACHEL: Well, you would be too if you had found **these boots** on sale, 50 percent off!

1/13

ORIGINAL FILM DIALOGUE 21.42–21-44

CHANDLER: Kids, new dream . . . I'm in **Las Vegas**. I'm **Liza Minnelli** . . .

ITALIAN ADAPTATION	BACK-TRANSLATION
CHANDLER: Ragazzi, un altro sogno, mi trovo a **Las Vegas**, io sono **Liza Minnelli** . . .	CHANDLER: Guys, another dream: I'm in **Las Vegas**; I'm **Liza Minnelli**.

SUMMARY

Season 1 Episode 1 (Pilot)

Strategies
- 13 Loan
- 1 Official tr.
- 3 Hypernym
- 4 Substitution
- 4 Elimination

Nature of cultural references

SOURCE CULTURE
Rocky Road
Cookie Dough
Western omelet
John and David boots
Aruba (2)
Las Vegas

INTERCULTURAL
Sweet'n'Lo
Liza Minnelli

THIRD CULTURE
Limoges
Noodles

OVERT ALLUSION
Raindrops on roses and rabbits and kittens, bluebells and sleigh bells and something with mittens . . .
Billy, don't be a hero
Mr. Potato Head
Joanie (3)
Charles (3)
Pinocchio
Geppetto

Total references 22

Name Index

Accolla, Tonino 46
Addams, Charles 196, 220
Adolfi, John 35, 52
Agost Canós, Rosa 56, 100
Akass, Kim 2, 6, 8, 10, 187, 217–19
Alighieri, Dante 69
Allen, Woody (Allan Stewart Konigsberg) 26, 27, 93, 103, 143, 148, 150, 186
Allodoli Ettore 41, 50
Álvarez, Román 25, 26, 101
Aniston, Jennifer 107
Appelbaum, Josh 184
Argento, Dario 64
Ashford, Michelle 151, 186
Austen, Jane 72, 75, 100

Baccolini, Raffaella 2, 8, 25, 27, 51
Bagatella, Tiziana 153
Baker, Mona 15, 18, 25–7
Ball, Alan 6, 9, 11, 17, 27, 103, 187, 210, 217, 220, 230
Ballester Casado, Ana 25, 81, 94, 100
Banfi, Emanuele 2, 8
Baños Piñero, Rocío 105, 147
Bardot, Brigitte 177–8
Baron Cohen, Sacha 7–8
Barrymore, John 35
Bassnett, Susan 20, 25, 100
Baum, L. Frank 163, 185
Bava, Mario 184, 186
Beaudine, William 8, 11
Ben-Porat, Ziva 70, 100
Berk, Michael 133, 149
Berry, Chuck (Charles) 161, 185
Bettridge, Daniel 187, 218
Bianconi, Giovanni 8, 11
Biarese, Cesare 46, 50
Billiani, Francesca 25

Bird, Maria 158, 186
Bolan, Marc (Mark Feld) 170
Bollettieri Bosinelli, Rosa Maria 2, 8–9, 25, 27, 51
Bompiani, Valentino 30
Bonann, Gregory J. 133, 149
Bowie, David (David Robert Jones) 64, 100, 152, 159, 185
Branagh, Kenneth 46
Brazil, Mark 151, 186
Brennan, Ian 184, 186
Briareo, Gustavo 42, 50
Brinkley, Christie (Christie Hudson) 125
Brittain, Jamie 94, 103, 229–30
Brown, Lesley 28, 50
Brunamonti, Luigi 106
Brunetta Gian Piero 10, 31, 38–40, 50
Bruti, Silvia 2, 9, 49–50
Bucaria, Chiara 217–18
Buckley, Cara Louise 9–10, 219
Buffagni, Claudia 47, 50
Bugarski, Ranko 59, 100
Bugner, Joe (József Kreul) 178
Bullock, Sandra 90–91
Buonomo, Leonardo 6, 9
Burns Allan 196, 220
Bury, Rhiannon 6, 9
Bush, George 195
Buttafava, Giovanni 49–50

Calzada Pérez, Maria 51–2
Cameron, David 97
Cameron, James 206, 220
Camilleri Andrea 8, 11
Carrey, Jim 46
Carroll, Lewis (Charles Lutwidge Dodgson) 214, 218
Carter, Bill 188, 219

Name Index

Cary, Edmond 43, 50
Casini, Gherardo 30
Castaneda, Carlos 195
Castellano, Alberto 25, 50–51
Cericola, Rachel 187, 219
Charlton, Bobby (Robert) 169–70
Chase, David (Davide DeCesare) 187, 217, 220
Chaume Varela, Frederic 24, 26, 44–5, 50, 59, 100, 105, 115, 147, 230
Chesterman, Andrew 24, 26–7, 77, 100
Chiaro, Delia 58, 62, 100, 114, 147
Chion, Michel 115–16, 147
Chomsky, Noam 15
Cicognani, Bruno 41, 50
Clair, René (René Chomette) 35, 52
Clark, Anthony 162, 185
Clark, Barbara 114, 147
Clay, Cassius 178
Clinton, Bill (William) 84, 125
Clooney, George 25, 27
Cohen, Larry (Lawrence) 184, 186
Columbus, Chris 149
Cooper, Gary (Frank James) 36, 172
Coppola, Francis Ford 42, 52
Cousteau, Jacques 61
Cowen, Ron 218, 220, 229–30
Crane, David 5, 11, 14, 27, 103, 105, 149, 186, 220, 230
Cresti, Emanuela 2, 9
Crowe, Russell 125
Cuddon, J. A. 55–6, 100
Curtiz, Michael (Mihály Kertész) 162, 186

D'Agostino, Patrizia 42, 50, 52
D'Amico, Masolino 49–50
Damigelli, Antonella 189
Danan, Martine 3, 9, 37, 50
Daniels, Greg 229–30
Darbelnet, Jean 75–7, 80, 84, 92, 103, 125, 148
Davies, Andrew 229–30
Davies, Russell T. 218, 220
Davis, Geena (Virginia) 137–8
Debenedetti, Giacomo 42, 50
Debussy, Claude 196
Delabastita, Dirk 43, 50, 114, 147
De Mauro, Tullio 2, 9, 39–40, 51
Dhamer, Jeffrey 197–8, 215
Díaz Cintas, Jorge xiv, 2–3, 9, 24–6, 28, 36, 45, 51, 57, 60, 73, 82–9, 91–3, 95, 100–1, 135, 147, 228, 230

DiCaprio, Leonardo 206
Dickens, Charles 72, 101
Di Fortunato, Eleonora 10, 25–7, 47, 50–52
Di Stefano, Sergio 106
Dobbs, Michael 229–30
Doorslaer, Luc van 9, 102
Dors, Diana (Diana Fluck) 180

Eastwood, Clint 61, 103
Eco, Umberto 8–9
Edgerton, Gary R. 2, 6, 9, 151, 185–6, 217, 219
Ejkhenbaum, Boris 18
Ekland, Britt (Britt-Marie Eklund) 91–2
Elsley, Bryan 94, 103, 229–30
Eugeni, Anna Teresa 106
Even-Zohar, Itamar 4, 9, 12, 17–20, 26

Fahy, Thomas 6, 9
Falchuk, Brad 184, 186
Fawcett, Peter 21, 26, 29, 51, 67, 101
Fellini, Federico 49, 96
Ferrándiz, Ignacio 184
Ferzetti, Fabio 7–9
Feuer, Jane 217, 219
Finkel, A. M. 53, 101
Fischer, Peter S. 206, 220
Fitzgerald, Toni 188, 219
Fleming, Victor 64, 103, 163–4, 185–6
Florin, Sider 53, 103
Ford, John (John Martin Feeney) 201, 220
Formentelli, Maicol 2, 185
Forster, E. M. 69, 101
Foucault, Michel 21, 26
Foy, Ciaran 184, 186
Franco Aixelá, Javier 53–4, 81, 101
Freddi, Luigi 34, 36, 40, 48, 51
Freddi, Maria 9–10, 146–8

Galli, Augusto 43
Galli, Rosina 43
Gambier, Yves 9, 56, 101–102
Garcia, Rodrigo 217, 220
Garibaldi, Giuseppe 184
Garinei, Pietro 134
Garland, Judy 164
Garzelli, Beatrice 47, 50
Gauguin, Paul 150
Gavioli, Laura 8, 25, 27, 51
Genette, Gérard 70, 100–1
Gentile, Giovanni 35, 49
Gervais, Ricky 229–30

Ghia, Elisa 2, 10, 185
Gili, Jean 33–6, 51
Giolitti, Giovanni 31–2, 48, 52
Giovannini, Sandro 134
Giraldi, Massimo 25–6
Goris, Olivier 25–6, 44, 51
Gottlieb, Henrik 80–1, 96, 101
Graham, Matthew 5, 11, 16, 27, 103, 151–2, 184, 186, 220, 230
Gutiérrez Lanza, Camino 16, 26

Hanks, Tom (Thomas) 45
Hanna, William 113, 149
Hardy, Oliver 42, 49, 174
Harvey, Monica 164, 185
Hayek, Salma 197
Hayes 201, 217, 219
Hays, William H. 34, 37, 48
Hayward, Chris 196, 220
Heiss, Christine 2, 9
Hermans, Theo 20, 24–6, 78, 101
Hillis Miller, Joseph 18, 26
Hitler, Adolf 36–7
Holmwood, Leigh 153, 185
Holz-Mänttäri, Justa 15, 26
Homer 22, 141, 147
Hönig, Hans 15, 26
Howard, Ron (Ronald) 146, 149
Hutcheon, Linda 77, 100–1

Intoppa, Luca 189
Irwin, William 56, 70–1, 101
Ivir, Vladimir 77–8, 87, 101
Ivory, James 69, 103

Jackson, Peter 207, 220
Jakobson, Roman 18
Jancovich, Mark 2, 9
Jauss, Hans Robert 29, 51
Johnson, Anthony L. 55, 101
Jones, Jeffrey P. 2, 6, 9, 217, 219
Joyce, James 31, 51
Jordan, Tony 5, 11, 16, 27, 103, 151–2, 184, 186, 220, 229–30

Karamitroglou, Fotios 25–6
Kaskenviita, Rauni 70, 101
Katan, David 29, 51, 80, 101
Kauffman, Marta 5, 11, 14, 26, 103, 105, 149, 186, 220, 230
Kidron, Beeban 72, 103
King, Martin Luther Jr. 110, 148
Kleiser, Randal 62, 103
Klum, Heidi 125

Kohan, David 202, 220
Kosunen, Riina 56, 101
Kubrick, Stanley 74, 92–3, 103, 169, 186, 199, 220
Kurosawa, Akira 42, 52
Kussmaul, Paul 15, 26
Kwiecinski, Piotr 59, 101

Lambert, Mary 184, 186
Lancia, Enrico 25–6
Lansbury, Angela 206
La Plante, Lynda 229–30
Laura, Ernesto G. 31–2, 51
Laureati, Donatella 106
Laurel, Stan (Arthur Stanley Jefferson) 42, 49, 174
Lawrence, D. H. (David Herbert) 30, 51
Lee, Francis 170
Leemets, Helle 54, 101
Lefevere, André 4, 9, 12, 18, 20–2, 25–6, 95, 100–1
Legman, Gershon 217, 219
Leibovitz, Annie (Anna-Lou) 123–5
Lennon, John 160, 185
Leppihalme, Ritva 3, 9, 55–6, 70, 78–9, 81–2, 85, 101–2
LeRoy, Mervyn 184, 186
Leverette, Mark 2, 10, 217, 219
Lingstrom, Freda 158, 186
Lionello, Oreste 25, 27, 49, 51
Lipman, Daniel 218, 220, 229–30
López Rodríguez 81, 102
Lubitsch, Ernst 43, 52
Lucas, George 169, 186
Lyons, James 2, 9

McCabe, Janet 2, 6, 8, 10, 187, 217–19
McCartney, Paul 148, 185
Mack Smith, Denis 35, 51
Madonna (Madonna L. V. Ciccone) 65, 195
Maguire, Sharon 72, 103
Mailhac, Jean-Pierre 54, 59, 80, 102
Maraschio, Nicoletta 2, 10–11
Mariano, Paul 25, 27
Marie, Michel 51
Marinetti, Filippo Tommaso 30
Martí Ferriol, José 25, 27
Martin, Ian Kennedy 71, 103, 162, 186
Martínez Sierra, Juan José 217, 219
Massidda, Serenella 2, 10
Mattson, Jenny 146, 148
Mayo, Archie 36, 52

Name Index

Melelli, Fabio 25–6
Mendes, Sam 81, 103, 217, 220
Mengaldo, Pier Vincenzo 2, 10
Merchant, Steven 229–30
Mereu, Carla 50–1
Mesthrie, Rajend 228, 230
Meyer, Herman 55, 102
Milestone, Lewis 174, 186
Miller, Arthur 129, 148
Miller, Chris 218, 220
Montini, Franco 8, 10
Morgan, Abi 151, 186
Mortensen, Viggo 207
Munday, Jeremy 23–4, 27
Muñoz Sánchez, Pablo 2, 9
Murphy, Eddie 46
Murphy, Ryan 184, 186
Mussolini, Benito 3, 31, 33, 35–8, 48, 52, 144–5
Mutchnick, Max 202, 220

Nedergaard-Larsen, Birgit 80, 82, 102
Nelson, Robin 2, 10, 153, 185
Nemec, André 184
Newman, Sydney 174, 186
Newmark, Peter 59–60, 78, 85, 94, 102
Nichols, Mike 217, 220
Nida, Eugène 59, 87, 102
Nixon, Agnes 129, 149
Nord, Christiane 23–5, 27

Obama, Barack 57, 102
Ott, Brian L. 10, 219
Ottoni, Filippo 44, 51

Paccagnella, Serena 218
Pacino, Al (Alfredo) 46, 52
Palencia Villa, Rosa María 49, 51
Pannofino, Francesco 45
Paolinelli, Mario 10, 25–7, 47, 50–2
Parini, Ilaria 218–19
Parker, Trey 72, 103
Parrot, James 49, 52
Pasha, Shaheen 188, 219
Pasolini, Pier Paolo 2, 10
Pavarotti, Luciano 64
Pavesi, Maria 2, 9–10, 20, 27, 44–6, 51, 146–8, 185
Pavolini, Alessandro 30
Pedersen, Jan 3, 10, 57, 60–2, 65, 67, 77, 81–2, 85, 94–6, 102, 105, 125, 148, 167, 185
Perego, Elisa 45–6, 51, 87, 102

Pérez-González, Luis 10, 27
Pérez López de Heredia, María 47, 52
Petrarca, Francesco 87–8
Petrunti, Silvia 6, 10
Pharoah, Ashley 5, 11, 16, 27, 103, 151–2, 184, 186, 220, 229–30
Picasso, Pablo 70, 214
Pio XI (Achille Ambrogio Damiano Ratti) 31, 52
Pizzolatto, Nic 217, 220
Pizzuto, Antonio 31, 51
Polo, Marco 36, 52
Polverelli, Gaetano 37, 49
Poniewozik, James 187, 219
Ponzio, Antonello 153
Postgate, Oliver 180, 186
Powell, Enoch 179
Pucci, Joseph Michael 70, 102
Pym, Anthony 58, 65, 102

Quaglio, Paulo 105, 148
Quargnolo, Mario 34–5, 49, 52

Raffaelli, Sergio 2, 10, 32, 40–2, 52
Ramière, Nathalie 57–9, 96, 102
Rantanen, Aulis 60, 102
Ranzato, Irene 25, 27, 139, 146, 148, 184–5, 211, 217, 219
Ravano, Anna 164, 185
Reitherman, Wolfgang 49, 52
Remael, Aline 45, 51, 57, 60, 73, 82–9, 91–3, 95, 100, 135, 147
Renzi, Matteo 97
Reo, Don 134, 149
Ricci, Steven 37–8, 52
Richardson, Kay 151–3, 184, 186
Richart Marset, Mabel 50, 52
Richmond, Fiona 177–8
Riefenstahl, Leni 37
Roberts, Chris 105, 113, 148
Robertson, Pat 195–6
Roeg, Nicolas 85, 103
Romero Fresco, Pablo 105, 148
Rosenberg, Scott 184
Ross, Bob 201, 220
Rossi, Fabio 2, 10–11
Rossini, Gioachino 62
Rourke, Mickey 46
Ruben, Joseph 184, 186
Ruffin, Valentina 42, 50, 52
Rundle, Christopher 30, 50, 52
Ruokonen, Minna 56, 102

Sagal, Robert 175, 186
Santamaria Guinot, Laura 57, 82, 102
Sapir, Edward 59, 103, 228–30
Saussure, Ferdinand de 15
Savinio, Alberto 42, 52
Schäffner, Christina 23, 27, 29, 52
Schwartz, Douglas 133, 149
Setti, Raffaella 2, 11
Seuss, Dr. (Seuss Geisel, Theodor) 146, 148–9
Shakespeare, William 57, 71, 88, 103, 148
Shuttleworth, Mark 18, 27
Simon, David 217, 220
Snell-Hornby, Mary 15, 27
Sobrero, Alberto A. 2, 8
Sollima, Stefano 8, 11
Southey, Robert 113, 148
Spadaro, Rosario 1, 8, 11
Spohr, Susan J. 114, 147
Steele, Danielle 140, 146
Sternberg, Josef von 35, 52
Stewart, James 43
Stone, Matt 72, 103
Straniero-Sergio, Francesco 29, 51
Streisand, Barbra 125
Stuart, Mel 195, 220
Suchet, Myriam 47, 52

Tagliamonte, Sali A. 105, 113, 148
Taivalkoski-Shilov, Kristiina 47, 52
Talbot 28, 30–1, 37–8, 41, 52
Tarantino, Quentin 8, 11
Temperini, Fabrizio 189
Tertullian (Quintus Septimius Florens Tertullianus) 48, 52
Thatcher, Margaret 173
Thompson, Robert J. 153, 184, 186
Tolstoy, Lev 70, 103
Tomaszczyk, Jerzy 53, 103
Toulouse-Lautrec, Henri de 150

Toury, Gideon 4, 11–17, 19, 23–4, 27, 221, 224, 227–30
Tranfaglia, Nicola 37, 52
Troisi, Massimo 63
Turner, Bonnie 151, 186
Turner, Terry 151, 186
Tynjanov, Jurij 18

Väisänen, Susanne 56, 101
Valentino, Rodolfo (Rodolfo Guglielmi di Valentina D'Antonguella) 34
Van Wert, William 49, 52
Venuti, Lawrence 27, 103, 148
Vermeer, Hans J. 12, 23–4, 27
Vidor, King 35, 52
Vittorini, Elio 30
Vidal, Carmen-África 25–6, 101
Vinay, Jean-Paul 75–7, 80, 84, 92, 103, 125, 148
Vlahov, Sergej 53, 103

Wachowski, Andy 207, 220
Wachowski, Larry (Lana) 207, 220
Walker, Robert G. 8, 11
Weiner, Matthew 150, 186
Weir, Peter 136, 149
Whedon, Joss 91, 103
Whitehouse, Mary 161
Whitman-Linsen, Candace 44, 52
Whorf, Benjamin Lee 228–30
Wilder, Billy (Samuel) 77, 103
Williamson, Kevin 91, 103
Willimon, Beau 229–30
Wilson, Stacey 187, 219
Wonder, Stevie (Stevland Hardaway Morris) 124, 148

Yacowar, Maurice 151, 186

Zabalbeascoa, Patrick 73, 103, 217, 219
Zanotti, Serenella 2, 9, 47, 50
Zemeckis, Robert 45, 52

General Index

adaptation(s) 2, 17, 20–1, 28, 45–6, 72, 76–7, 79, 81, 85, 92, 100n, 104–5, 111, 117, 130, 133, 138–9, 142, 145, 160, 170, 177, 180, 182, 189, 194–5, 200, 205, 207–8, 214–16, 226–7
adapter(s) 4, 7, 17, 20, 25n, 29, 44–8, 50n, 73, 88, 93–8 passim, 106, 117–119, 123, 125, 130–2, 135–6, 138–9, 141–2, 144, 153, 157–8, 165, 171–4, 179, 181–2, 191–3, 195, 199–200, 203–18 passim, 226
The Addams Family (La famiglia Addams) 196
addition, creative addition 35, 77–80, 82–4, 87–8, 93, 95–6, 119, 139–41, 146n, 171, 181, 206–8, 226
The Adventures of Rin Tin Tin (Le avventure di Rin Tin Tin) 8n
The Adventures of Marco Polo (Uno scozzese alla corte del Gran Khan) 36
All My Children (La valle dei pini) 129
allusion(s) 53–7 passim, 60, 64, 70–2, 74, 78–9, 86, 93, 110, 117, 123, 134, 136, 138–40, 143, 155, 157–60, 162, 165, 169–70, 177–9, 181, 195, 199, 203–7, 212–3, 217n, 224, 236; macroallusion(s) 64, 72, 85, 147n, 162–3, 165, 229n
American Beauty 81, 217n
Angels in America 217n
The Aristocats (Gli aristogatti) 49n
Ashes to Ashes 151–2, 155

asynchronous references 64, 72, 74–5, 100n, 143, 147n, 151, 155, 165, 169, 174, 176–7, 180, 229n
The Avengers (Agente speciale) 174

The Bad Seed (Il giglio nero) 184n
Baywatch 133
Being George Clooney 25n
Der blaue Engel (The Blue Angel / L'angelo azzurro) 35
Blossom (Blossom—Le avventure di una teenager) 134
Borat: Cultural Learnings of America for Make Benefit Glorious Nation of Kazakhstan (Borat) 7–8n
The Bridges of Madison County (I ponti di Madison County) 61
Bridget Jones's Diary (Il diario di Bridget Jones) 72
Bridget Jones: The Edge of Reason (Che pasticcio, Bridget Jones!) 72
Buffy the Vampire Slayer (Buffy l'ammazzavampiri) 90–1

calque, literal translation 2, 20, 50n, 76–9, 81–3, 85–6, 109, 119, 129–30, 169, 171, 174–5, 195, 205–6, 208, 211–12
Catholic Church, Catholics 31, 33, 213
censorship 3–4, 21, 25n, 28–50, 144, 198, 203, 215–16, 221, 228–9
La chica de ayer 184n
Citadel (Rapporto confidenziale) 184n
Clangers 180
Il commissario Montalbano 8n

General Index

compensation 74, 78, 83–4, 93, 111, 119, 135, 146n, 171, 182, 198–9, 214, 226
concretisation, hyponym 84, 89, 119, 131, 171, 182, 226
creative addition *see* addition
cuts *see* editing

Dawson's Creek 90–1
death (subject and words) 187, 189, 190, 205, 210–15, 218n
descriptive translation studies xiv, 4, 6, 12, 16, 22–5, 229
Desperate Housewives 94
diachronic analysis 4, 14, 98, 104, 127, 129, 182, 228
dialect(s) 7, 35, 39–43, 57
Django Unchained 8n
Doctor Kildare (Il dottor Kildare) 174–5
Dodge City (Gli avventurieri) 160–2
Don't Look Now (A Venezia . . . un dicembre rosso shocking) 85
Dr. Seuss' How the Grinch Stole Christmas (Il Grinch) 146n

editing, editorial choices, cuts 3, 16–17, 48, 58, 72, 165, 168, 171, 181, 205, 227
elimination, omission 22, 62, 72, 77–84, 91, 93–5, 97, 113–14, 119, 125–7, 129, 130, 134–7, 139, 141–3, 145, 146n, 157, 161–4, 168, 171, 177–83, 191–3, 195, 199–205, 208–11, 213, 215–16, 221, 225–6, 228–9, 236
explicitation 77, 79–84, 87–8, 95, 112, 119, 123, 131–3, 141, 171, 177, 192, 196

fansubbing 2, 8n
Fascism, Fascist(s) 3, 30–42, 48–49n, 144
The Flintstones (Gli Antenati/I Flintstones) 113
Flower Pot Men 158
Forrest Gump 45
Friends xiii, 4–6, 14, 23, 61, 67, 71, 84, 86, 88–9, 98, 104–147 *passim*, 154, 171, 178, 182, 184, 191–2, 196, 216, 222–7, 231–6

gayspeak, gay themes 17, 21, 138, 164, 189, 194–5, 201–3, 208–9, 215–18, 228
generalisation, hypernym 77–9, 81–2, 84, 87–9, 119, 130–2, 136, 146n, 162, 168, 171, 175, 177, 192, 195, 236
genre xiii, xiv, 3–4, 6, 21–2, 99, 104, 114, 116, 150–1, 167, 182, 184, 221, 226–7, 229
Ghost (Ghost—Fantasma) 125
Glee 184n
The Godfather (Il padrino) 42, 49n
Gomorra—La serie 8n
Gone With the Wind (Via col vento) 185n
The Good Son (L'innocenza del diavolo) 184
Grease 62

Halleluja! (Alleluja) 35
Hays code 34, 37, 49n
horizon of expectation(s) 22, 28–9
The Hour 151, 155
House of Cards (UK) 229n
House of Cards (USA) 229n
hypernym *see* generalisation
hyponym *see* concretisation

ideology, ideological xiv, 6, 20–9 *passim*, 35–6, 39, 48, 98, 144–5, 189, 215, 221, 228
intercultural references 64, 66–7, 123–4, 139, 142–3, 155, 158, 162, 172, 184n, 196, 208, 222, 236
intertextual, intertextuality, intertextual references 23, 55–8, 64–5, 70–2, 93, 100n, 147n, 159, 162–3, 165, 206, 208, 224, 229n
intertitles 32, 34–5, 40, 49n
In Treatment 217n
isochrony 44, 62, 88, 91, 131, 177, 182
Istituto Luce 33–4, 38, 48n
It's Alive (Baby Killer) 184n

Kill, Baby . . . Kill! 184n
Kumonosu-jo (Throne of Blood / Il trono di sangue) 43

laugh track 114–16, 146n, 227
lexical recreation 83–4, 92, 119, 142, 171, 182, 226

Life on Mars (UK) xiii, 5–6, 16, 22–3, 71–3, 75, 85, 90–1, 97, 150–85 *passim*, 191–2, 196, 222–9 *passim*
Life on Mars (USA) 151–2, 229n
lip-synch, synchronisation 2, 14, 43–4, 49n, 62, 90–1, 93–4, 127, 129, 131, 133, 135, 177–9, 182
literal translation *see* calque
loan 2, 82–5, 91, 98, 118–19, 123–7, 136–7, 141–3, 145, 157–8, 162, 164, 171–3, 177, 182–4, 191–5, 200–1, 205, 207, 216, 225–6, 236
Looking for Richard (Riccardo III—Un uomo, un re) 46
The Lord of the Rings (trilogy) *(Il signore degli anelli)* 207

macroallusion *see* allusion
Mad Men 150–1, 155, 184n
Manhattan Murder Mystery (Misterioso omicidio a Manhattan) 93
manipulation 3–4, 20, 22, 24, 25n, 28–9, 35, 48, 62, 74, 95, 108, 116, 123, 136, 138, 141–2, 146n, 173, 181, 183–4, 199–200, 202–3, 208, 211–13, 215, 221, 226–8
Masters of Sex 151
The Matrix (Matrix) 207
Mayberry R.F.D. 200–1
Midnight in Paris 150
Ministero dei beni e delle attività culturali e del turismo 7n, 21, 47, 50n
Mogambo 201
monocultural references 61, 65, 57, 117, 146n, 167
Mrs. Doubtfire (Mrs. Doubtfire— Mammo per sempre) 125
The Munsters (I mostri) 196
Murder, She Wrote (La signora in giallo) 206
The Mutiny on the Bounty (Gli ammutinati del Bounty) 174

non-verbal 43, 58, 73, 114–15, 198; non-verbal references 64, 72–4, 98, 143, 147n, 156, 229n
norms 3–4, 6, 12–17, 23–5, 29, 216, 221, 224–5, 227–8

official translation, 70–1, 79, 83–6, 98, 111, 119, 123, 125, 127–9, 132, 137, 141, 157, 169, 171, 174–5, 183–4, 191–3, 195, 205–7, 225–6, 236
The Office 229n
omission *see* elimination

Pardon Us (Muraglie) 49
patronage 13, 20–2, 29, 117, 215
Pet Sematary (Cimitero vivente) 184n
polysystem 17–20, 99n
Prime Suspect 229n
Puss in Boots (Il gatto con gli stivali) 218n

quality TV, quality programmes 2–3, 8n, 152–3, 181, 184n, 217n
Queer as Folk 218n, 229n

real-world references 64–5, 70, 100n, 159, 224
Romanzo criminale 8n
A Room with a View (Camera con vista) 69

Sex and The City 217n
The Shining 92, 125, 169
The Shop Around the Corner (Scrivimi fermo posta) 43
The Show of Shows (La rivista delle nazioni) 35
Six Feet Under xiii, 4, 6, 17, 22, 73, 87–8, 90, 95, 187–218 *passim*, 222–8 *passim*
Skins 94–5, 229n
skopos 23, 25n, 62
Some Like It Hot (A qualcuno piace caldo) 77
The Sopranos (I Soprano) 187, 217n
sound, soundtrack 2, 20, 34–5, 39, 40, 43, 61, 69, 74, 96, 114–16, 127, 140, 156, 159, 161–2, 165, 170, 203, 210
source culture (SC) references 64–8, 117, 123, 139, 155, 165, 177–8, 184n, 193, 196, 198, 203–4, 208, 214
Sous les toits de Paris (Under the Roofs of Paris / Sotto i tetti di Parigi) 35
South Park 72
Star Wars (Guerre stellari) 169

subtitling, subtitles xiii, 1–2, 7–8n, 18, 24–5n, 37, 43, 45, 57–8, 60–2, 70, 73, 77, 80–3, 89, 94–6, 99, 105, 135, 146, 159, 162, 184n
substitution 43, 68–9, 74, 77–8, 81–5, 89–92, 95, 97, 109, 114–16, 119, 125, 127, 129, 133–5, 137, 145, 157, 171, 177–8, 192, 196–8, 206, 211, 214–16, 226–7, 236
The Sweeney 71, 162–3, 165

target culture (TC) references 64, 68, 70, 96, 123, 172, 184n, 223
That 70s Show 151
third culture references 63–70 *passim*, 123, 127, 133, 143, 155, 172, 177–8, 214, 223, 236

Titanic 112, 206–7
transcultural references 61–7 *passim*, 146n
True Detective 217n
2001: A Space Odyssey (2001: Odissea nello spazio) 73–4, 93, 198–9

Ufficio di revisione cinematografica 21, 32

Will & Grace 202
Willy Wonka and the Chocolate Factory (Willy Wonka e la fabbrica di cioccolato) 195
The Wire 217n
Witness (Il testimone) 136
The Wizard of Oz (Il mago di Oz) 64, 85, 163–5